Assessing Foreign Language Proficiency of Undergraduates

Richard V. Teschner
Editor

American Association of University Supervisors, Coordinators, and Directors of Foreign Language Programs (AAUSC)

Issues in Language Program Direction
A Series of Annual Volumes

Series Editor
Sally Sieloff Magnan, University of Wisconsin-Madison

Managing Editor
Charles J. James, University of Wisconsin-Madison

Assessing Foreign Language Proficiency of Undergraduates

Richard V. Teschner
Editor

Heinle & Heinle Publishers
Boston, Massachusetts 02116, U.S.A.

Manufactured in the United States of America.

Heinle & Heinle Publishers is a division of Wadsworth, Inc.

ISBN 08384-39152

10 9 8 7 6 5 4 3 2 1

Contents

Acknowledgments

It is with genuine appreciation that we – the volume editor, the series editor, and the managing editor – extend sincere thanks in the name of the membership of the AAUSC to Heinle & Heinle Publishers, and in particular to publisher Stan Galek, whose continued support has turned this series into a tradition. We also thank Elizabeth Holthaus, India Koopman, and Roberta Winston for their careful attention to detail in guiding the manuscript through production. It continues to be a pleasure to work with a firm that is devoted to innovation and quality in foreign language education, one product of which is the present volume.

To those members of the editorial board who provided us with perspicacious critiques of the manuscripts on very short notice, we extend our sincerest appreciation. Without their assistance, this volume would not have seen fruition.

In closing, the volume editor wishes to express his personal thanks to José L. Bártoli, of New York City, for a lifetime of friendship, challenge, and support.

Richard V. Teschner
Sally Sieloff Magnan
Charles J. James

Introduction

Assessing Foreign Language Proficiency of Undergraduates – the second in the annual series Issues in Language Program Direction sponsored by the AAUSC and published by Heinle & Heinle – is a collection of 12 papers diverse in theme but unified in purpose: to add to the already-substantive body of literature written on proficiency since the swift ascent of this term to the status of professional household word 10 years ago, and to expand the rather sparse body of literature relating proficiency as a concept to North American lower-division undergraduate language programs. Taking as axiomatic the notion that proficiency in 1991 encompasses a considerably broader spectrum of interests and concerns than it did in the early 1980s, when the proficiency movement often appeared to focus solely on speaking in general and the oral interview in particular, the present volume sets forth vantage points that range from the broadest of overviews to the most concentrated of empirical investigations. Proficiency in the 1990s is no longer seen as a "unifying principle" that presumes we are fairly certain about just how a second/foreign language (FL) is learned and, in consequence, precisely how one should be tested. Rather, and perhaps paradoxically, we have come to view "proficiency" more as it was conceptualized initially: as an essentially flexible way of evaluating how well someone speaks, comprehends, writes, reads, and functions in another language and culture.

Given this focus, it is not surprising that the specifics of testing are the prime concern of most of the papers presented here: listening tests; reading tests; picture-description tests; departmental exit exams; placement tests and systems; self-assessment tests; prefabricated publisher-provided testing programs that accompany textbooks; process-centered tests; and others.

Readers seeking more global assessments of FL testing, however, are invited to begin their involvement with this volume by turning first to the four selections that deal primarily with testing as a general topic. Nuessel's "Foreign Language Testing Today: Issues in Language Program Direction," for example, is a comprehensive treatment of language testing's major topics, including, among others, what it means to test, what terms testers employ, what types of tests are used (or are usable), how teaching methods dovetail with tests, and what role technology can play in language testing. Nuessel regrets the disparities that exist between our tests (which often date back to other times) and the increasing sophistication of our teaching materials.

A historical perspective on FL testing and an experience-driven critique of certain aspects of the proficiency movement is provided by Hagiwara ("Assessing the Problems of Assessment"), who urges that any proficiency guidelines remain just that – guidelines (not standards) – and recommends an agenda for university FL program directors that would include investigations and projects ranging from the macro (the extent to which proficiency-based techniques are used nationally) to the micro (the establishment of proficiency guidelines for special purposes). Hagiwara also urges us not to overlook our classrooms' native speakers and the often-unique problems their performance can present.

In "Testing in Foreign Language Programs and Testing Programs in Foreign Language Departments: Reflections and Recommendations," Bernhardt and Deville effectively remind us that any testing program that is not characterized by honesty (assessment according to the objectives of the language program) and integrity (whereby tests are valid assessments of what they purport to measure) creates trials to be survived, not evaluation experiences to promote learning. Along the way the authors set forth the characteristics of good tests, the testing of each of the four skills as a special problem, and the specific implications for FL program directors of what is called "seriousness of purpose."

Hammerly ("Two Philosophies of Language Program and Language Testing Design") offers a serious, broad-based challenge to much of what is currently viewed as axiomatic in the FL teaching profession. Using empirical data from Canadian research conducted by himself and others, Hammerly argues that holistic FL teaching approaches (global, top-down, "natural") are inherently inferior to linear methods ("cumulative mastery," bottom-up). Suggestions for testing in a cumulative mastery program follow, with examples from Spanish.

Of the eight contributions to this volume that are more topically focused, two deal with issues of placement, though from very different perspectives – and this despite the fact that the respective authors teach sister languages at the same institution. Wherritt, Druva-Rousch, and

Moore ("The Development of a Foreign Language Placement System at the University of Iowa") thoroughly describe both the Foreign Language Assessment Project (FLAP), which centers on a 50-minute, machine-gradable test in each of the three major languages, and the Foreign Language Incentive Program (FLIP), which employs a series of carrots-and-sticks designed to encourage high school FL mastery and discourage false beginning. Heilenman's focus, on "Self-Assessment and Placement: A Review of the Issues," examines the surprisingly voluminous literature on this topic to conclude that self-assessment, though time-consuming when developing the instrument, is feasible, valid, and beneficial to students because it helps them learn how to learn and prompts them to become successful monitors and evaluators of their own progress.

Exit requirements constitute the core of Fleak's "Using an Exit Requirement to Assess the Global Performance of Undergraduate Foreign Language Students" at the University of South Carolina. In this local adaptation of certain aspects of the Oral Proficiency Interview, students are tested on all four skills by an economical yet thorough format. If passed, the exit exam exempts students from the university's language requirement; the same exit exam constitutes the "final" in the last course in the required FL sequence.

While there is nothing new – at least in such fields as mathematics and science – to the concept of process-oriented testing (whereby students receive partial credit for accomplishing steps toward the learning goal), the concept is new to FL teaching but can be implemented without difficulty, as Magnan explains in "Just Do It: Directing TAs toward Task-based and Process-oriented Testing." Magnan points out that the unconventional imperative that begins her title has a dual meaning: on the one hand it encourages us to get students doing things through the target language by using it in class for natural communicative purposes, and on the other hand it exhorts us as program directors to begin a serious search for innovative techniques of communicative language testing.

By no means all supervisors have the time, however, to initiate such a search, let alone carry it out from process to product. It is for them – as they turn to commercially prepared materials – that Walz has written "A Survey and Analysis of Tests Accompanying Elementary French Textbooks," the first thorough discussion on this topic to appear in print. Walz concludes that eight of the twelve best-selling texts he analyzes include a salutary mix of achievement and proficiency-oriented tasks that go a long way toward making textbook goals more commensurate with tests.

Each of the remaining three articles – Lee's, Bacon's, and Ballman's – focuses on a separate testing modality. Lee's "On the Dual

Nature of the Second Language Reading Proficiency of Beginning Language Learners" defines reading, examines stages of reading development as established by antecedent research in often-conflicting categorizations, and sets forth types of performance that characterize readers at various stages. He suggests four ways language teachers can gain an indication of beginning-level reading proficiency. Bacon's "Assessing Foreign Language Listening: Processes, Strategies, and Comprehension" examines reasons for listening, identifies various stages of comprehension, discusses factors that may impede comprehension, looks at learners' comprehension strategies, offers listening activities to encourage awareness and to practice listening techniques, and finally suggests how to assess comprehension. In Ballman's "The Oral Task of Picture Description: Similarities and Differences in Native and Nonnative Speakers of Spanish," we learn what appears to have been a secret until now: what happens when educated native speakers are asked to perform apparently simple tasks, such as describing a brief series of cartoonlike drawings in a sequence.

In keeping with the intent of the AAUSC Issues in Language Program Direction series, *Assessing Foreign Language Proficiency of Undergraduates* has sought to present papers that, while focusing on a variety of topics, address a common problem in language program direction: how to assess, effectively and efficiently, the diverse aspects of an FL program while confronted more frequently than not by situational constraints that can be imposing. One hopes that this goal has been accomplished here.

Richard V. Teschner
Volume Editor
University of Texas – El Paso

Foreign Language Testing Today: Issues in Language Program Direction

Frank Nuessel
University of Louisville

Demonstrable proficiency in a second language is becoming increasingly important for our undergraduate curricula because of our profession's worthwhile desire to continue to improve the quality of instruction and, more important, its results. Besides this internally generated mandate for pedagogical effectiveness, there are external forces at work on the postsecondary academic scene – namely, the move to assess the "value-added" effect of undergraduate education. The "assessment" movement that had its genesis in the 1980s was the topic of a special issue (September-October 1990) of the quarterly publication *Change (The Magazine of Higher Learning)*. Likewise, in its "Special Edition: Proceedings of the 1989 Priorities Conference," *Foreign Language Annals* devoted an entire issue (October 1990, vol. 23, no. 5) to professional concerns. The first "priority" was testing, which featured a position paper by Henning (1990) and three reactions (Shohamy, 1990; Stansfield, 1990; and Lange, 1990).

The proficiency movement in second language instruction meshes nicely with the national movement to evaluate performance on completion of a prescribed curriculum. As a result, second language educators are in a position to synchronize the two trends to enhance the quality of undergraduate instruction. Additional demands for proficiency in a second language become increasingly important in a global economy, given that internationalization is essential to rapidly transforming societies. In this environment, it is incumbent on the profession to develop a curriculum to promote this proficiency. One aspect of such a curriculum is the need to produce an acceptable means of clearly defining what we mean by "proficiency" so that we can certify with some degree of assurance and integrity that our students possess widely recognized and measurable linguistic skill levels (see Omaggio, 1986). Nevertheless, it must be kept in mind that a high level of oral proficiency is not possible after the completion of a prescribed sequence of second language classes by secondary school or beginning-intermediate university students. Additional course work will be necessary to achieve even a proficiency level of ILR 2 (see Lantolf & Frawley, 1985, p. 337).

In this essay, certain theoretical concepts of testing will be set forth in nontechnical language. Moreover, specific and practical techniques for language-specific testing will also be indicated. The term *proficiency,* it should be noted, has come to refer to oral-aural proficiency, in part because of the not-insignificant influence of the present format of the ACTFL-ETS (American Council on the Teaching of Foreign Languages/Educational Testing Service) proficiency test. Consequently, this paper will deal largely with this aspect of the proficiency movement. Despite the widespread acceptance of the term *proficiency* to designate oral-aural proficiency, however, this notion also encompasses reading and writing (Omaggio, 1985, 1986). In addition to these behavioral abilities, cultural understanding is also involved – that is, an appreciation of cultural differences and a recognition and avoidance of cultural stereotypes (Kramsch, 1987).

The purpose of this essay is five-fold: (1) to discuss basic concepts and terminology related to proficiency, testing, and test typologies; (2) to examine types of assessment instruments; (3) to discuss the relationship of teaching method to assessment; (4) to allude to the potential role of technology; and (5) to suggest ways in which tests can be made proficiency-oriented.

Proficiency

Prior to any discussion of the main topic of this essay, certain basic questions require an answer. The first is, What is proficiency? The response to this question is neither simple nor uncontroversial. Much confusion has surrounded the notion of proficiency in language as this concept relates to its meaning and the interpretation of the widely promulgated ACTFL "provisional" guidelines (*ACTFL Provisional Proficiency Guidelines*, 1984). In 1986, the ACTFL provisional proficiency guidelines were modified and reflect changes in terminology in response to earlier critiques (e.g., Lantolf & Frawley, 1985; Savignon, 1985). These emendations are reproduced in Omaggio (1986, pp. 433-43).

Omaggio (1986, pp. 1-40; see also Liskin-Gasparro, 1984) devotes the entire first chapter of her book on proficiency-oriented instruction to questions related to the history and definition of this concept. Levy and Omaggio (1985, p. 9) provide a useful definition of proficiency:

> *Proficiency* is a construct that enables us to define competence in a language in terms of (1) the *functions* one can carry out in the second language; (2) the *contexts* in which the language user can operate comfortably and adequately; and (3) the *accuracy* with which those various functions are carried out in a given context.

Levy and Omaggio (1985, p. 9) further clarify that proficiency does not refer to an instructional methodology, a set of goals, or a prioritized enumeration for teaching the four skills plus cultural understanding. Rather, this term refers to the ability to function effectively in a second language and the divergent cultures often encompassed within a given nation – for example, Spain with its Spanish-speaking Basques, Catalans, and Gallicians or Mexico with its sometimes-bilingual Spanish-speaking indigenous populations.

Proficiency encompasses the "receptive skills" (listening, comprehension, and reading), and the "productive skills" (speaking and writing), as well as "cultural understanding," though it must be noted that, thus far, most attention has been dedicated to listening and speaking. Because "proficiency" has often come to designate oral proficiency in casual and professional circles, the notion of proficiency in terms of the so-called four skills and culture deserves reaffirmation. Omaggio's (1986) useful volume on proficiency-based instruction provides an overall blueprint. It should be noted that the *ACTFL Proficiency Guidelines* are not without their detractors. Lantolf and Frawley (1985), for example, cite Savignon (1985), who warns against the dangers of facile or impetuous acceptance of the ACTFL provisional proficiency guidelines without adequate research into some of their basic tenets. One problem related to the ACTFL-ETS guidelines is the original use of the phrase "*the* native speaker," although this notion, as it is widely understood, is at best faulty and perhaps even completely erroneous (cf. Paikeday, 1985; Ballmer, 1981). Another problem cited is the determination of classroom hours needed to achieve a given level of proficiency. Far more classroom hours (480 = at least eight 4-credit-hour semesters) seem to be necessary to achieve a level of IRS 2/ACTFL

Advanced than would be available in the traditional college baccalaure-
ate program (Lantolf & Frawley, 1985, p. 337; Omaggio, 1986, p. 21).
Characteristic of the proficiency movement is the extensive use of
"authentic" materials (maps, train and plane schedules, menus, etc.)
along with problem-solving activities, games and so forth (see Krashen
& Terrell, 1983, pp. 95-128; Omaggio, 1986, passim). The rationale for
these materials, aside from their intrinsic interest for student and
teacher alike, is to simulate authentic linguistic situations that the student is likely to encounter in a country where the target language is
actually used. A focus on this type of discourse-level activity, as opposed
to the mechanical and sentence-level semantic exercises so characteristic of earlier approaches to second language instruction, is seen to
facilitate the acquisition of functional proficiency skills.

Tests and Testing

Testing is a subject that can require much technical and statistical
knowledge (see Arkin & Colton, 1970; Crocker, 1969; Franzblau, 1958;
Hatch & Farhady, 1982; Henning, 1987; Oller, 1979). The purpose of
this essay, however, is to minimize the use of professional jargon and
numerical abstraction. Rather, a practical approach to recommendations for proficiency testing will be employed. The interested reader
may wish to consult Clark (1989) and Clifford (1989) for useful
overviews on the subject of second language testing.

Titone and Danesi (1985, p. 154) pose the important and basic
question, What is a test? Their response is helpful to an understanding
of this fundamental query:

> A test can be defined as a method of measuring an individual's ability,
> skill, or knowledge in some area. A test can be either formal or in-
> formal. The former involves some form of quantification . . . whereas
> the latter is qualitative assessment of observed behavior. . . . To a stu-
> dent a test usually constitutes a learning or achievement goal; to a
> teacher it can become a valuable empirical indicator of teaching
> effectiveness.

Of critical importance to the worth of any test are its *reliability* and its
validity. The former term, according to Titone and Danesi (1985, p.
154), refers to the "consistency or accuracy with which a test measures
whatever it is supposed to measure." The latter, however, means "the
extent to which a test measures what it is intended or expected to measure" (Titone & Danesi, 1985, p. 155). Both of these notions receive
elaborated discussion in Henning (1987, pp. 73-106), Hughes (1989,
pp. 22-43), and Underhill (1987, pp. 104-8).

Test Typology

Theorists (Clark, 1972; Harris, 1969, p. 3; Henning, 1987, pp. 4-9; Hughes, 1989, pp. 9-21; Titone & Danesi, 1985, pp. 155-61; Valette, 1988, pp. 5-6) discuss, among other things, the types of tests that are available for use in the classroom according to format and function. In this section, we will briefly examine these classificatory schemata.

Test format is one way of categorizing tests. The standardized, or mass-produced, test is commonly called an objective test. We are familiar with this format in the Scholastic Aptitude Test and the Graduate Record Examination, to name but two well-known examples. In general, as Oller (1979, p. 233; see also Hughes, 1989, pp. 59-62) notes, the preparation of multiple-choice tests (the form par excellence of objective tests) "is sufficiently challenging and technically difficult to make them impracticable for most classroom needs."

The subjective test, or teacher-prepared examination, may include multiple-choice questions but lacks the massive testing of such items to verify their reliability and validity. Normally, such tests are prepared a short time before the testing date and little time is available to test the tests themselves. The current generation of second language textbooks frequently consists of multielement "packages" with as many as 12 possible components (textbook, instructor's annotated edition, teacher's guide, workbook, audiotape program, test bank, tape script and answer key, reader, Computer Assisted Language Learning [CALL] program, video program, video guide, and teacher's kit with its transparencies, slides, and realia; see Ariew, 1987, p. 42). One of the peripherals is often a "test bank" of made-to-order examinations. Frequently, these testing kits are quite similar to the subjective tests created by the second language teacher, albeit sometimes lacking the creativity and individualization the teacher can offer, and oftentimes without proficiency-oriented testing techniques (Omaggio, 1986, pp. 309-56; see also Walz, 1991, this volume).

Tests may be additionally categorized as to their purpose. In general, there are four basic classes: achievement, aptitude, diagnostic, and proficiency (Henning, 1987, pp. 4-8; Hughes, 1989, pp. 9-21; Titone & Danesi, 1985, pp. 155-58). The *achievement* test is designed to measure what a student has learned from a prescribed curriculum. The progress-achievement test evaluates "chunks" of the classroom experience, while the final-achievement test determines the effect of the entire curriculum. In this sense, the former shapes and the latter sums up the entire curricular experience. *Aptitude* tests, however, are predictive, because this form of assessment seeks to measure the suitability of the test taker for the subject being tested. *Diagnostic* tests evaluate the student's strengths and weaknesses. Finally, *proficiency* tests measure a student's command of prior learning in a subject without reference to the content of a given curriculum.

Yet another way of grouping tests is in terms of *discrete point* versus *integrative* testing. The former refers to the testing of a particular element. In the case of a language, this might be phonemic discrimination, word formation, the lexicon, and so forth. The latter, on the other hand, tests the ability to use different language skills in context simultaneously.

Finally, we may speak of *norm-referenced* and *criterion-referenced* testing. Norm-referenced testing means that we measure a student's performance relative to that of others who are taking the same test. Criterion-referenced testing signifies the student's performance in terms of an objective standard of attainment. The latter test format is the type employed in proficiency examinations.

It is likely that most second language teachers rely on virtually all types of formats and functions for their evaluation procedures in the course of their professional careers. What is important here is to determine how to test for proficiency both effectively and efficiently. For one thing, the approaches to testing employed should reflect the types of language acquisition activities carried out in the classroom prior to testing. This aspect of evaluation will now be addressed.

Testing, Methodology, and the Curriculum

Testing is an vital component of the second language curriculum because these instruments are designed to assess what students have learned and, collaterally, how well teachers have taught, both progressively and conclusively. In this regard, one of the goals of the *ACTFL Proficiency Guidelines* is to establish a set of standards that is widely recognized as representing basic levels of proficiency.

There is an ever-present danger, however, that teachers will "teach to the test" to ensure that their instructional input is validated. Likewise, students will study only those elements of the class work which are likely to appear on the test in order to secure good grades. While this type of arrangement is disdained by second language professionals, it is difficult to deny that such practices exist in many institutions. This use of testing is, after all, a means to an end. Hughes (1989, p. 1) has labeled the effect of testing on teaching and learning "backwash," which may be either negative or positive. It is clearly desirable that any use of testing be pedagogically beneficial rather than detrimental.

In this vein, Valette (1989, p. 262), addressing herself to language instruction at the secondary level, observes that "we should not forget the real importance of tests . . . lies not in their reliability and validity but in their ability to influence instruction." Along these same lines, Byrnes (1989, p. 266) states that "the concept of assessment in terms of functional use seems finally to have encouraged the profession to tackle one of its perennial problems, namely finding in the *product* of instruction, as ascertained through testing, important clues for organizing and, ultimately, improving the *process* of instruction." Thus, testing may be viewed as a sort of diagnostic for the whole curriculum that may lead to a radical restructuring of second language syllabi and teacher training programs alike.

In her useful treatise, Larsen-Freeman (1986) outlines the principles and techniques of eight methodologies used in part or in full by second language teachers (Grammar-Translation, Direct Method, Audio-Lingual Method, Silent Way, Suggestopedia, Community Language Learning, Total Physical Response, and Communicative Approach). To these, one might add Di Pietro's (1987) Strategic Interaction method. Each of these methodologies has a set of guiding principles and associated techniques to facilitate classroom activities that reinforce the essential principles of the approach. Along these same lines, Krashen and Terrell (1983, p. 166) observe that to achieve relevance in testing it is necessary "to co-ordinate what is tested directly with the goals of the course." If those goals are proficiency in one or all of the linguistic skills, then the methods and concomitant techniques will have to be coordinated accordingly.

Evaluative procedures and the means devised by the instructor in a second language course to implement these processes will derive from the way in which the class is conducted. In this view of testing, the method drives the form of the evaluation. To exemplify this point, one may compare two methods discussed by Larsen-Freeman (1986), Grammar-Translation and the Communicative Approach. These two methodologies are antithetical in their principles and techniques. Consequently, the tests employed in such contrary methods would be very different in format and structure, since activities and exercises carried out in the classroom would ideally be reflected in the testing program. When this is not the case, the result is a negative "backwash" in Hughes' (1989) sense and a likely infelicitous outcome for student and teacher alike.

Testing and Technology

Today, the most widely recognized technological device is the computer and the software programs designed to propel it. Indeed, computers offer the promise of reducing time spent on repetitive learning tasks (Nuessel, 1989). Nevertheless, in his discussion of Stevens et al. (1986, pp. xi-xv), Smith (1987, p. 2) observes that in those instances in which CALL is unsuccessful, at least three factors are involved: "(1) substandard exemplars, (2) insufficient teacher training, and (3) conflicting ideologies."

Computer hardware and software, as well as other forms of technology, also produce certain limitations, for example, unavoidable and at-times-rapid obsolescence, expensive development costs, standardization problems, and high equipment costs. Pusack and Otto (1990) address the issue of proficiency-assessment and instructional technologies by proposing to the profession a number of rational recommendations. Among the most significant of these are the revamping of the curriculum, collateral research and development programs, and revision of teacher training programs. Garrett (1990) argues that an essential component of utilizing existing and emerging technologies is a research element that enables the profession to integrate such developments with the instructional part in meaningful and worthwhile ways.

The current decade will continue to see technological innovations that are likely to surprise us all. Applications of new and existent technology to proficiency-based curricula should form a part of our teacher training and faculty development programs if they are not already in place. Many of these innovations will be compatible with proficiency goals and adaptable to them.

Proficiency Testing and the Undergraduate Curriculum

Who will ultimately receive the protracted and costly proficiency testing required to certify that a student has achieved a given level of achievement in a language – all undergraduates enrolled in a language course? language minors? language majors? It should be obvious that the expense of proper training, time, and other logistical factors will ultimately determine that only a small number of language students will receive a full-length Oral Proficiency Interview (OPI). It is, of course, both logical and desirable that all *language majors* take an OPI, whereas most – a far more numerous and patently less focused population – will not. If we are to introduce proficiency as a meaningful objective in the language curriculum, it will be necessary to take that fact into account. Reification is not facilitation. Thus, many secondary and post-secondary schools have added the word *proficiency-oriented* to their curricula, despite the fact that they are not (Omaggio, 1984).

This essay does not wish to suggest that the ACTFL-ETS OPI is the sole means of evaluating proficiency. Alternatives to this assessment instrument are currently being explored (e.g., the Center for Applied Linguistics' Simulated Oral Proficiency Interview). Likewise, nothing prevents qualified professionals from designing equally reliable and valid measures of proficiency that are less costly, yet theoretically and methodologically defensible. (See Valdman, 1987, 1988, for further discussion.)

To provide an achievable goal for the large numbers of students who populate our elementary, intermediate, and advanced classes, instructors need to create a language curriculum with proficiency-oriented activities (Omaggio, 1986, pp. 407-32) and develop testing procedures (Omaggio, 1986, pp. 309-56) that reflect the types of activities to be encountered in a true proficiency test of the type alluded to above. Underhill (1987), mindful of the increased emphasis on testing of oral proficiency, developed a manual designed to facilitate this process. Pragmatic in its approach, Underhill's text seeks to provide a balanced initiative in the testing of students' oral abilities. Time, resources, efficiency, and a worthwhile testing procedure are among his prime concerns. In this pragmatic vein, the rest of this discussion will be devoted to concrete suggestions for developing proficiency-oriented evaluation in our undergraduate curriculum.

Preparation for Testing

In the best of all possible worlds, proficiency testing would be carried out only in an environment in which all of the teaching staff engaged in the instruction of multiple-section courses at the postsecondary level would receive training in proficiency testing. This group would include permanent faculty, teaching assistants, and part-time lecturers (see Muyskens, 1984). Such an approach, of course, would require time, resources, universal cooperation, and much goodwill. In the absence of this idealized situation, at least one or more members of the permanent teaching staff should receive training in proficiency testing and make a commitment to training others in the group in the appropriate methods. In those departments with coordinated language programs, the appropriate person would be the language-specific coordinator.

What follow are a few suggestions for establishing a necessary foundation to facilitate a practical, proficiency-oriented evaluation program:

1) Involve the affected faculty and staff members in the decision-making process. Failure to do so may result in active or passive sabotage of worthwhile curricular innovations.

2) Select a textbook that is harmonious with proficiency-based activities (see Nuessel, 1990). This is a crucial, though often-overlooked, step in sound curricular development. Ideally, the activities in the textbook should reflect the kinds of assessment strategies to be found in formative and summative evaluation instruments.

3) Train evaluators in teaching procedures designed to impart proficiency. This step may entail the use of some faculty development resources for training in proficiency interviews through workshops sponsored by appropriate organizations, such as ACTFL. Once properly trained in the appropriate methods, these individuals can serve as departmental resource persons.

4) Establish clearly defined proficiency goals (see Omaggio, 1985, 1986). Typically, these include statements such as those exemplified by Medley (1985, pp. 27-32; see also Omaggio, 1986, pp. 408-10, and Steiner, 1975). Such goal statements would have the following format:

    After two semesters of a given language, students will be able to
    a) ask questions about how to get to a particular place (museum, bank, train station) in a city where the target language is used;
    b) talk about their lives and life stories; and
    c) relate incidents that took place in the past.

5) Prepare an analytic rating instrument with sufficient gradation to separate levels of achievement (Hughes, 1989, pp. 110-14; Madsden, 1983, pp. 120-22, 168-74; Omaggio, 1986, pp. 346-52; Underhill, 1987, pp. 98-103).

The contents of the rating form would ideally include the following elements: accuracy in the use of vocabulary; range of lexical control; ability to employ grammatical structures (questions, requests, statements) correctly and in appropriate contexts; aptitude in understanding and responding satisfactorily to questions and comments from an interlocutor; capability in producing comprehensible pronunciation and intonation; and cultural knowledge designed to avoid stereotypical views and facilitate the appreciation and recognition of particular cultural values. Each of these subdivisions would then receive a numerical value. Omaggio's (1986, pp. 346-47) rating schema is a particularly manageable example for proficiency-based curricula.

Techniques for Proficiency Testing

Testing techniques is the primary subject of at least two books (Madsden, 1983; Underhill, 1987) and of portions of other important texts (Clark, 1972; Harris, 1969; Hughes, 1989; Lado, 1964; Omaggio, 1986; Valette, 1988). One of them (Hughes, 1989, p. 59) states that testing techniques "are means of eliciting behavior from candidates which will tell us about their language abilities." In this section, some practical suggestions will be made for proficiency testing in post-secondary schools that offer multiple sections, especially of elementary- and intermediate-level language classes.

Hughes (1989, p. 8) correctly observes that "all tests cost time and money – to prepare, administer, score, and interpret. Time and money are in limited supply, and so there is often likely to be a conflict between what appears to be a perfect testing solution in a particular situation and considerations of *practicality*." Thus, time and effort dedicated to test construction and its concomitant tasks ought to be worthwhile and advantageous to all concerned. Clearly, such factors as the achievement of positive "backwash" and curricular enhancement and improvement are sought-after objectives in the testing procedure.

The following list of suggestions for effective testing is practical, hence designed to help the instructor harmonize theory and practice to achieve meaningful evaluation for both student and teacher. In very general terms, language class activities and exercises should involve the four skills of understanding, speaking, reading, and writing, plus cultural comprehension.

Oral Proficiency

In the 1980s, professional activity, language association meetings, and general discussion all centered on the proficiency principle. The most widely recognized feature of this trend is the ACTFL OPI, with its focus on speaking and only indirectly on comprehension. The first part of this section will deal with this component. In general, an oral interview procedure should be developed and refined prior to actual implementation. In the case of multisection language courses, this facet may be achieved through an initiation course for teaching assistants, a faculty development program for full-time faculty, in-service workshops for secondary teachers, or a teacher training program for neophyte instructors (see Muyskens, 1984). Such procedures should be pretested where feasible and modified if necessary.

As previously noted, the oral interview ought to reflect activities that occur in the classroom. This task familiarity helps to reduce student anxiety and thus allows the language learner to perform to the best of his or her abilities. The following general recommendations describe a procedure for developing a program for oral proficiency testing. Moreover, specific elements of such a proficiency examination are offered. Since these suggestions are subject to empirical verification, modifications may be necessary.

1) Schedule an appropriate time and place for the oral proficiency component of the class. Practice mock proficiency interviews in the classroom with volunteers prior to the real assessment so as to alleviate undue fear. This allows students to achieve at their highest levels.

2) Include (if possible) two evaluators in the process, to ensure that assessments are accurate and fair. Each rater should score the interviewee separately, with subsequent comparison of notes and a final, coordinated evaluation.

3) Discuss the results of the evaluation with the student to point out strengths and weaknesses. Schedule at least two such oral assessments to detect progress over time. The first evaluation should be formative in its intent.

4) Develop an array of personalized questions that draw initially from the grammar and vocabulary of the course textbook. Place each question on a separate note card to facilitate variation. Group the questions by level of difficulty. Begin with easy questions (What's your name?, Where do you live?, etc.) to establish a good rapport and to alleviate stress. Introduce more challenging questions subsequently. Such questions might provide a stimulus for an authentic language situation, as in demonstrating the ability to compliment, persuade, warn, or even insult someone and to recognize these same speech acts in the discourse of another speaker.

5) Develop an inventory of carefully chosen realia (advertisements, cartoons, menus, maps). Ask graded questions concerning these materials (What product is this? Why do you use it? Who is the person in the picture? Can you describe the sequence of events in this cartoon?; see Mollica, 1988).

6) Introduce auditory stimuli as a means of promoting imaginative usage of the target language. Mollica (1988) espouses the use of recorded sounds as an effective means of soliciting worthwhile linguistic responses from students. In this procedure, Mollica advocates the use of a single auditory cue (typing sound) as an occasion to ask questions about the person who is performing this task (Can you describe the person? Where does he or she work? At what salary? etc.).

7) Provide sufficient time to ensure that enough data have been elicited to assess fairly the student's abilities. Limit the proficiency interview, however, to a fixed time frame. Don't schedule the interviews all on one day! Consistency and quality demand that this type of endeavor be carried out deliberately.

8) Elicit sustained speech from the student. Provide the student with a set of options to discuss. One procedure is to place a brief scenario (Di Pietro, 1987) on a note card and ask the student to respond as if he or she were in this situation – for example, losing one's money or passport in another country, or wanting to go to a particular place.

9) Prompt the student to ask questions. Create a number of scenarios on note cards that describe particular, albeit familiar situations in which the student will have to seek information – for instance, meeting a new person in class, or getting directions to the main shopping district.

Writing Proficiency

Writing for proficiency is an active skill that requires adequate preparation in order to achieve a felicitous outcome for student and instructor alike. Following are techniques to facilitate a positive result:

1) Guide the student in the writing assignment. Provide a theme based on topics and grammar in the textbook, and include a sequenced set of suggestions for the student to incorporate in the development of an essay. Provide related vocabulary. Allow the student to express his or her feelings or views on the topic. An example of this sort of exercise might be the following:

Describe what you did this morning: When did you wake up? When did you get up? What did you eat? When did you leave your residence? How did you get to the university? What classes did you study for? And so on. (If the goal of the exercise is to communicate this information, the teacher may elect to provide a few items of key vocabulary.)

Prepare an inventory of such writing assignments for future use.

2) Provide photocopies of uncaptioned pictures, cartoons, or action sequences. Request that students write a description of these visual materials.

3) Combine reading and writing proficiency by including in the test a passage that reflects the content and vocabulary of the current lesson. Evaluate comprehension through well-thought-out true-false questions. Prepare content questions. Include personalized questions to elicit the student's reactions (What would he or she do in

this circumstance? Does he or she like or dislike something in the reading selection?).

Reading Proficiency

The student should be expected to demonstrate the ability to read and decipher a variety of documents, such as train schedules, menus, applications, banking materials, newspaper articles, and simple literature. This important skill can be assessed in a variety of traditional ways, among them translation, reading aloud, true-false questions, multiple-choice questions, question-answer, and cloze (see Larson & Jones, 1984, pp. 127-30).

1) Provide exemplars of the documents noted in the preceding paragraph and create a variety of exercise types (carefully constructed true-false statements, content questions, or personalized questions). The instructor may even wish to include multiple-choice questions, though a caveat must be offered since, as Oller (1979, p. 223; see also Owen, 1985) notes, this technique is "intrinsically inimical to the interests of instruction."

2) Produce a document in which students must identify pronominal antecedents. Omaggio (1986, pp. 321-23) exemplifies this reading comprehension strategy by asking students to circle pronouns and draw a line to the corresponding antecedents. Other related exercises might deal with agreement phenomena (subject-verb, noun-adjective).

Cultural Outcomes

What does it mean to be culturally aware? For Hirsch (1987), it means that a student knows a certain number of discrete and enumerated facts about this and other societies. While many have argued that Hirsch's approach is culturally biased, he nonetheless insists that students who follow his suggestions will at least know something.

For some professionals, cultural understanding refers primarily to knowledge of literature and the fine arts, what some would label "civilization." For others, this same designation means the ability to function effectively in such daily activities as shopping, using public transportation, and knowing how to compliment or even insult someone when necessary.

There are many ways to define culture. Seelye (1974, p. 23) and Brooks (1968) have provided useful definitions (see also Omaggio,

1986, pp. 357-406). Brooks (1968, p. 210) specifies five distinct areas of this notion: biological growth, personal refinement, literature and fine arts, patterns for living, and the sum total of a way of life. In fact, an entire book (Kroeber & Kluckhohn, 1960) treats the multiplicity of definitions. Allen (1985) has provided us with some worthwhile suggestions on how to integrate and assess this aspect of the second language curriculum.

Techniques for assessing cultural understanding within the framework of the ACTFL-ETS guidelines require a measure of creativity in order to achieve reliability and validity. Prior to developing assessment materials for cultural comprehension, the reader would be well advised to consult Kramsch's (1987) insightful discussion of the complexities surrounding the accurate and fair depiction of another culture. The following exemplary suggestions provide an example of this facet of the second language curriculum with several applicable evaluation strategies. The format of these exercises can be utilized with other cultural spheres (family unit, social sphere, political systems and institutions, environment, religion, art, and the humanities; see Omaggio, 1986, p. 368).

Advertisements derived from well-known newspapers published in countries where the target idiom is the official language present an opportunity to employ authentic materials as well as an instrument to assess cultural knowledge. Mollica (1978) has demonstrated how announcements for films can be exploited for their linguistic and cultural content. After an appropriate discussion of these materials in the classroom, the second language instructor may utilize the cultural information conveyed as the basis for various evaluative activities.

1) Ask students to match a list of film directors (column A) with the films they have directed (column B).

2) Reproduce an actual film advertisement. Pose a series of oral or written questions that focus on aspects of the target culture (What elements of the film does the advertisement highlight? Why? How does this item compare with the film announcements in your local newspaper?).

3) Compare and contrast cultural differences between the United States and the target culture (Omaggio, 1986, p. 387). Provide a series of written statements related to behavior associated with attending a film in that country and in the United States. Direct the student to place a check mark in one of two columns labeled "United States" or "target country" (e.g., Italy, Spain).

Concluding Remarks

Assessment of student performance in the second language curriculum constitutes an essential component of instruction. There are numerous kinds and purposes of second language testing. Recognition of the essential differences determines who, what, when, where, how, and why we test (see Clark, 1989). Although testing may be used to form and summarize student performance, assessment also determines the content of the curriculum and patterns of instruction in subtle ways. While testing is sometimes a stepchild to other facets of the curriculum, its neglect or improper usage can certainly have a deleterious effect (negative backwash) on our instruction. A more deliberate and reflective approach to assessment, however, will improve and enhance second language education (*positive* backwash).

Since the 1980s, much attention has been paid to the promotion of proficiency in the second language curriculum because of the *ACTFL Proficiency Guidelines*. Although many secondary and postsecondary foreign language programs are nominally designated "proficiency-oriented," this appellation is sometimes more fictional than factual. This essay has attempted to synthesize a number of important aspects of testing. First, an attempt has been made to review and define a number of basic concepts, such as proficiency, tests, and testing. Next, typologies of testing instruments and the possible positive or negative impact of these assessment tools on the curriculum were examined. Third, the current and potential role of emerging technologies on language evaluation was considered. Fourth, general preparatory recommendations for developing and integrating proficiency-oriented language testing with the curriculum were offered. Finally, a set of practical suggestions for proficiency testing in the four skills (speaking, understanding, reading, writing) and cultural comprehension ensued.

A significant part of the time we devote to our instructional commitments pertains to the creation, preparation, and evaluation of assessment materials. Despite this frequent and recurrent aspect of our professional lives, it is rare to hear a discussion of the topic of testing among our colleagues (and, some might argue, any topic related to instructional concerns). In the past decade, our profession has undergone fundamental shifts in the way we teach a second language. This transformation is reflected in many of our basic and intermediate textbooks and their associated materials.

Now, as this essay has sought to demonstrate, far more emphasis is being placed on proficiency, or the demonstration of actual ability to use the target language in its various manifestations (speaking, comprehension, writing, reading), and on the culture within which the language operates. Nevertheless, it is dismaying to encounter the disparity that exists between the type of assessment tools that many of us continue to employ and the methods, techniques, and pedagogical materials currently available to us.

In part, this problem reflects the obligation that we as teachers have to continue renewing and updating ourselves on such matters through professional literature, meetings, and workshops. Moreover, as instructors of future teachers we have a responsibility to make certain that our graduating seniors and our graduate students learn how to utilize current and emerging methodologies and to evaluate accurately and properly the skills we claim to impart with appropriate and effective assessment techniques. Failure to prepare the next generation of teachers to assess the skills they are supposed to be teaching will perpetuate existing curricular problems. The present volume is a step in the right direction.

Works Cited

ACTFL. *ACTFL Provisional Proficiency Guidelines*. *Foreign Language Annals* 17 (1984): 453-59.

_____. *ACTFL Proficiency Guidelines*. Yonkers, NY: ACTFL Materials Center, 1986.

Allen, Wendy W. "Toward Cultural Proficiency." *Proficiency, Curriculum, Articulation: The Ties That Bind*. Ed. Alice C. Omaggio. Middlebury, VT: Northeast Conference on the Teaching of Foreign Languages, 1985: 137-64.

Ariew, Robert. "Integrating Video and CALL into the Curriculum: The Role of the ACTFL Guidelines." *Modern Media in Foreign Language Education: Theory and Implementation*. Ed. William Flint Smith. Lincolnwood, IL: National Textbook Company, 1987: 41-66.

Arkin, A. & R. R. Colton. *Statistical methods*. 2d ed. New York: Barnes & Noble, 1970.

Ballmer, T. "A Typology of Native Speakers." *A Festschrift for Native Speaker*. Ed. F. Coulmas. The Hague: Mouton, 1981: 51-67.

Breen, Michael. "The Evaluation Cycle for Language Learning Tasks." *The Second Language Curriculum*. Ed. Robert Keith Johnson. Cambridge: Cambridge University Press, 1989: 187-206.

Brooks, Nelson D. "Teaching Culture in the Foreign Language Classroom." *Foreign Language Annals* 1 (1968): 204-17.

Byrnes, Heidi. "Who Is in Charge of the Learner-Curriculum-Testing Connection?" *Georgetown University Round Table on Languages and Linguistics*. Ed. J. E. Alatis. Washington, DC: Georgetown University Press, 1989: 265-75.

Clark, John L. D. *Foreign Language Testing: Theory and Practice*. Philadelphia: Center for Curriculum Development, 1972.

_____. "Multipurpose Language Tests: Is a Conceptual and Operational Synthesis Possible?" *Georgetown University Round Table on Languages and Linguistics*. Ed. J. E. Alatis. Washington, DC: Georgetown University Press, 1989: 206-15.

Clifford, Ray T. "Technological, Methodological, and Assessment Challenges: Can the Foreign Language Teacher Survive? *Georgetown University Round Table on Languages and Linguistics*. Ed. J. E. Alatis. Washington, DC: Georgetown University Press, 1989: 198-205.

Crocker, A. C. *Statistics for the Teacher*. Hammondsworth: Penguin, 1969.

Di Pietro, Robert J. *Strategic Interaction: Learning Language through Scenarios*. Cambridge: Cambridge University Press, 1987.

Franzblau, A. N. *A Primer of Statistics for Non-statisticians*. New York: Harcourt, Brace & World, 1958.

Garrett, Nina. "Reaction: Applying Instructional Technologies." *Foreign Language Annals* 23 (1990): 427-29.

Harris, David. *Testing English as a Second Language*. New York: McGraw-Hill, 1969.

Hatch, Evelyn & Hossein Farhady. *Research Design and Statistics for Applied Linguistics*. Rowley, MA: Newbury House Publishers, 1982.

Henning, Grant. *A Guide to Language Testing: Development, Evaluation, Research*. New York: Newbury House Publishers, 1987.

_____. "Priority: Testing Priority Issues in the Assessment of Communicative Language Abilities." *Foreign Language Annals* 23 (1990): 379-84.

Hirsch, E. D., Jr. *Cultural Literacy: What Every American Needs to Know*. New York: Vintage Books, 1987.

Hughes, Arthur. *Testing for Language Teachers*. Cambridge: Cambridge University Press, 1989.

Kramsch, Claire J. "Foreign Language Textbooks' Construction of Foreign Reality." *Canadian Modern Language Review* 44 (1987): 95-119.

Krashen, Stephen D. & Tracy D. Terrell. *The Natural Approach: Language Acquisition in the Classroom*. Hayward, CA: Alemany Press, 1983.

Kroeber, Alfred E. & Clyde Kluckhohn. *Culture: A Critical Review of Concepts and Definitions*. New York: Vintage Books, 1960.

Lado, Robert. *Language Testing: The Construction and Use of Foreign Language Tests*. New York: McGraw-Hill, 1964.

Lange, Dale L. "Reaction: Priority Issues in the Assessment of Communicative Language Abilities." *Foreign Language Annals* 23 (1990): 403-7.

Lantolf, James P. & William Frawley. "Oral Proficiency Testing: A Critical Analysis." *Modern Language Journal* 69 (1985): 337-45.

Larsen-Freeman, Diane. *Techniques and Principles in Language Teaching*. New York: Oxford University Press, 1986.

Larson, Jerry W. "Reaction: Applying Instructional Technologies." *Foreign Language Annals* 23 (1990): 419-20.

_____ & Randall L. Jones. "Proficiency Testing for the Other Language Modalities." *Teaching for Proficiency, the Organizing Principle*. Ed. T. V. Higgs. Lincolnwood, IL: National Textbook Company, 1984: 113-38.

Levy, Stephen L. & Alice C. Omaggio. "Introduction." *Proficiency, Curriculum, Articulation: The Ties That Bind*. Ed. A. C. Omaggio. Middlebury, VT: Northeast Conference on the Teaching of Foreign Languages, 1985: 9-11.

Liskin-Gasparro, Judith E. "The ACTFL Proficiency Guidelines. A Historical Perspective." *Teaching for Proficiency, the Organizing Principle*. Ed. T. V. Higgs. Lincolnwood, IL: National Textbook Company, 1984: 11-42.

Madsden, Harold S. *Techniques in Testing*. New York: Oxford University Press, 1983.

Medley, Frank W., Jr. "Designing the Proficiency-based Curriculum." *Proficiency, Curriculum, Articulation: The Ties That Bind*. Ed. A. C. Omaggio. Middlebury, VT: Northeast Conference on the Teaching of Foreign Languages, 1985: 13-40.

Mollica, Anthony. "The Film Advertisement: A Source for Language Activities." *Canadian Modern Language Review* 34 (1978): 221-43.

_____. "Verbal Dueling in the Classroom: Audio and Visual Stimuli for Creative Communicative Activities." *Language Teaching and Learning: Canada and Italy*. Ed. Valeria Sestieri Lee. Ottawa: Canadian Mediterranean Institute, 1988: 101-22.

Muyskens, Judith A. 1984. "Preservice and Inservice Teacher Training: Focus on Proficiency." *Teaching for Proficiency, the Organizing Principle*. Ed. T. V. Higgs. Lincolnwood, IL: National Textbook Company, 1984: 179-200.

Nuessel, Frank. "The Role of CALL in Second-Language Education." *Language Teaching Strategies* 4 (1989): 3-12.

_____. "Guidelines for the Objective Evaluation of Pedagogical Texts. *Language Teaching Strategies* 5 (in press).

Oller, John W., Jr. *Language Tests at School: A Pragmatic Approach*. London: Longman Group Limited, 1979.

Omaggio, Alice C. "The Proficiency-oriented Classroom." *Teaching for Proficiency, the Organizing Principle*. Ed. T. V. Higgs. Lincolnwood, IL: National Textbook Company, 1984: 43-84.

_____. *Teaching Language in Context: Proficiency-oriented Instruction*. Boston: Heinle & Heinle Publishers, 1986.

_____ (Ed.). *Proficiency, Curriculum, Articulation: The Ties That Bind*. Middlebury, VT: Northeast Conference on the Teaching of Foreign Languages, 1985.

Owen, David. *None of the Above: Behind the Myth of Scholastic Aptitude*. Boston: Houghton Mifflin Company, 1985.

Paikeday, Thomas. *The Native Speaker Is Dead!* North Belamore, NY: Paikeday Publishing, 1985.

Pusack, James P. & Sue K. Otto. "Priority: Instruction. Applying Instructional Technologies." *Foreign Language Annals* 23 (1990): 409-17.

Savignon, Sandra J. "Evaluation of Communicative Competence: The ACTFL Proficiency Guidelines." *Modern Language Journal* 69 (1985): 129-34.

Seelye, H. Ned. *Teaching Culture: Strategies for Foreign Language Educators*. Skokie, IL: National Textbook Company. 1974.

Shohamy, Elana. "Reaction: Language Testing Priorities – A Different Prospective." *Foreign Language Annals* 23 (1990): 385-94.

Smith, William Flint. "Modern Media in Foreign Language Education: A Synopsis." *Modern Media in Foreign Language Education: Theory and Implementation*. Ed. Wm. Flint Smith. Lincolnwood, IL: National Textbook Company, 1987: 1-12.

Stansfield, Charles W. "Reaction: Some Foreign Language Test Development Priorities for the Last Decade of the Twentieth Century." *Foreign Language Annals* 23 (1990): 395-401.

Steiner, Florence. *Performing with Objectives*. Rowley, MA: Newbury House Publishers, 1975.

Stevens, Vance, Roland Sussex & Walter V. Toman. *A Bibliography of Computer-aided Language Learning*. New York: AMS Press, 1986.

Stevick, Earl. *Teaching Language: A Way and Ways*. Rowley, MA: Newbury House Publishers, 1980.

Stone, LeeAnn. "Reaction: Applying Instrumental Technologies." *Foreign Language Annals* 23 (1990): 421-22.

Titone, Renzo & Marcel Danesi. *Applied Psycholinguistics: An Introduction to the Psychology of Language Learning and Teaching*. Toronto: University of Toronto Press, 1985.

Underhill, Nic. *Testing Spoken Language: A Handbook of Oral Testing Techniques*. Cambridge: Cambridge University Press, 1987.

Valdman, Albert (Ed.). *Proceedings of the Symposium on the Evaluation of Foreign Language Proficiency*. Bloomington, IN: Committee for Research and Development in Language Instruction, 1987.

_____. "The Assessment of Foreign Language Oral Proficiency." Special issue of *Studies in Second Language Acquistion* 10, no. 2 (1988): 121-261.

Valette, Rebecca M. *Modern Language Testing*. 2d ed. New York: Harcourt, Brace & Jovanovich, 1988.

_____. "Language Testing in the Secondary Schools: Past Experience and New Directions." *Georgetown University Round Table on Languages and Linguistics* Ed. J. E. Alatis. Washington, DC: Georgetown University Press, 1989: 255-65.

Walz, Joel. 1991. "A Survey and Analysis of Tests Accompanying Elementary French Textbooks." This volume.

Assessing the Problems of Assessment

M. Peter Hagiwara
University of Michigan

More than any other academic discipline, foreign language instruction has seen the rise and fall of approaches and methodologies. As the director of a large, college-level French program and the instructor of a course in applied linguistics and methodology for graduate teaching assistants and undergraduate majors in the teacher certification program, I have monitored such trends and kept students informed about them for more than three decades.

I was initiated into language teaching in the late 1950s when, with the passage of the National Defense Education Act, the traditional grammar-translation approach was beginning to be supplanted by audiolingualism (AL) and propagated through the teacher retraining programs of the NDEA institutes. In the mid-1960s, programmed instruction – in some ways a forerunner of the early computer-assisted instruction (CAI) – also became popular. The rigid pattern practice drills and dialogue memorization of AL were subsequently replaced by audio-visual methods, leading in some cases to the revival of a more "humanistic" direct method and a reexamination of the tenets of AL instruction; in turn, suggestions for other approaches took their inspiration from the cognitive code theory of learning.

It was in the 1970s that the learner started to become the focus of pedagogy, with the resulting curricular goals of individualized instruction, teacher/student accountability, and communicative competence.

The end of the decade witnessed a proliferation of experimental and even controversial methods: the "Dartmouth" method, counseling-learning, suggestopedia, total physical response, the confluent approach, the silent way, and others. Some of these were fads, but others have endured and will continue to play a role in language instruction.[1]

The proficiency movement of the 1980s was reminiscent of the AL movement of 30 years before in that it spread across the nation with fervor and zeal through articles, books, workshops, and textbooks that were oriented toward its tenets. It was officially endorsed by the American Council on the Teaching of Foreign Languages (ACTFL), which created its well-known proficiency guidelines (PGs) in an attempt to counter what many perceived was a widespread national inability to speak foreign languages (President's Commission, 1979).

The PGs imply a methodology that is not as inflexible as AL and offer concrete performance objectives for teachers as well as learners. The PGs seek to influence instructional strategies, materials, testing, and teacher training, as attested by the publication of the ACTFL Foreign Language Education Series.[2] In reality, though, how widespread is proficiency-based instruction? Some statewide adoptions seem to be in the making. Yet to my knowledge, based on many visits to high schools and colleges, most language professionals have done little except use materials labeled "proficiency-oriented," even though most teachers have heard of the *ACTFL Proficiency Guidelines* and some claim to have incorporated them into their curriculum.

In this paper, two of the problem areas in implementing the PGs will be discussed: (1) the instructional materials and (2) teacher training for French in terms of oral proficiency. Subsequently, the practicability of the PGs themselves will be analyzed.

Problems with the Instructional Materials

Assuming for the moment that the goals of the PGs (with their underlying supposition that acquisition of communicative competence progresses in a spiral or linear fashion) are to be incorporated into foreign language instruction, it is a relatively simple task to construct a curriculum encompassing several articulated courses at both the college and the secondary school levels by consulting the ACTFL Foreign Language Education Series. It is difficult, however, for a teacher or even a group of teachers to assemble proficiency-oriented materials and develop coherent instructional procedures. The most logical course of action would be to select suitable textbooks – presuming that these exist – that, with their ancillary materials to promote authenticity, best fulfill the objectives.

The proficiency-oriented books often show charts indicating how their contents correspond to the PGs but seldom offer radically new approaches to the drills. As Omaggio (1984, p. 67) admits, many of the classroom drills predate the PGs and had been available "in the literature of the past decade." On the other hand, "authenticity" has been one of the key words in language instruction since the onset of the proficiency movement, as it is reflected in the extensive use of realia and video in some texts.

Grammar Explanations

Since the days of AL, language courses have stressed oral communication as an important objective. The Oral Proficiency Interview (OPI) initially considered function, content, and accuracy to be the major criteria, though grammatical accuracy was later de-emphasized. Nevertheless, it is in precisely this area that the proficiency-oriented textbooks do not reflect the PGs.

The lively disputes in the late 1970s about how much to teach or indeed, whether one is trying to teach too much have until recently gone largely unnoticed by textbook authors. Although most proficiency-oriented textbooks have now adopted a "cognitive code" approach, they still tend to teach *all* verb tenses (including the so-called literary tenses). Undefined grammatical jargon abounds, often requiring reexplanation by the teacher. Some texts continue to present several items all at once just because they are grammatically or lexically related: numbers from 1 to 1 million, reflexive/passive/reciprocal use of the pronominal verbs, all interrogative pronouns, all possessive adjectives, all relative pronouns, and so on. This trend remains prevalent in most of the condensed, or "essentials," textbooks that are beginning to emerge.

Worse still, despite emphasis on oral communication, many texts continue to present language based on its written form. Some seem to consider pronunciation a reflection of orthography, and, as Hagiwara (1980) and Walz (1986) have indicated, the wealth of linguistic data available about spoken language is ignored. Some examples: word boundaries of written language disappear in spoken language; the written form contains many redundancies (e.g., the plural markers in *LeS filmS que j'ai vuS étaiENT intéressantS)*; words like *le* or *te* are often pronounced /l/ or /t/, whether they are spelled *le/te* or *l'/t'*; written French has only three possessive adjective forms for the first, second, or third person singular, whereas spoken French has five owing to liaison; adjective morphology becomes simpler in spoken French if the feminine is taken as the base; most masculine singular prenominal adjectives are pronounced like the feminine form owing to compulsory liaison; the formation of the future and the conditional is simpler in oral French if the stem is derived from the first person singular of the present indicative (with the insertion of the transitional /d/ when the stem ends in a nasal vowel, as in *je viens* > *je viendrai*) instead of the infinitive. If, as has been claimed, the AL method was plagued by an excess of linguists all wanting to have their say, there are too few linguists today who are interested in advising the authors of proficiency-oriented textbooks.

Authenticity and Language Levels

All spoken languages have subcodes, often referred to as registers or levels, ranging from the most formal to the most casual, each level having its own lexical, grammatical, and behavioral components. Native speakers manipulate several, depending on the circumstances in which communication is to be made. In a beginning French class, subcode manipulation begins on the first day with the distinction between *tu* and *vous*, or *Bonjour* and *Salut* in greeting someone, and the complexity increases as students gain more knowledge of the language. Yet many texts are ambivalent about what kind of language to teach, and the issues of levels and their underlying sociolinguistic structures are rarely discussed beyond the first lesson. As a result, while students are informed early that handshaking is very common as part of greeting in French or that the frequency of occurrence of *Monsieur* or *Madame* is much higher than that of the English "equivalent" *sir* or *ma'am*, such features are hardly practiced in class, and some undergraduate majors greet their much older professors with *Salut!*[3]

In colloquial French, the negative particle *ne* is virtually never used, *est-ce que . . . ?* and inversion are rare, subject pronouns exhibit many morphophonemic alternations, and, as discussed by Barnes (1990), Calvé (1985), and Hagiwara (1985), dislocation and certain types of stylistic inversion are quite common for thematic or rhythmic reasons. Moreover, liquid consonants drop out, so that *votre* is pronounced as *vot'*, *il y a* as *y a*, *ils sont* as *i sont*, and the like, and vowel reductions occur as in *v'zêtes*, *p't-être*, and *déj'ner*. The number of liaisons made and the "mute" *e*'s retained also reflect speech levels. Virtually none of the textbooks mention such phenomena or the fact that there is a widening gap between the formal or polite level and colloquial speech.[4] There are no texts that "dare" to omit *ne*, and there are some that teach all interrogative structures (including the strictly intonational and *n'est-ce pas?*) in one grammar segment, attaching equal importance to all of them. As for dislocation, the only type usually presented concerns subject pronouns (*Moi aussi, Toi, tu vas rentrer*), and all other cases involving direct objects and prepositional phrases are omitted. Moreover, in the name of authenticity some texts present an inordinate amount of vocabulary. There is also an unnecessary amount of English used in directions for exercises or activities, despite the claim that students can guess or should learn to guess the meaning of new French words from the context.

Lack of Proficiency-based Testing and Curricular Continuity

Textbooks nowadays come with a variety of ancillary materials, including a test bank. It only takes a cursory examination to discover that the majority of test banks are grammar- and vocabulary-based, hardly reflecting PGs, and some give only vague suggestions about how communicative proficiency may be measured. (Cf. Walz, 1991, this volume.)

While the PGs have been criticized for depicting language development linearly, they at least imply some kind of curricular articulation and offer an opportunity for textbook authors to interpret the guidelines in terms of pedagogical sequencing from first-year to advanced classes. Yet since most publishers concentrate on beginning-level texts (where the market is), there are few second-year college or levels 3-4 high school texts that continue on in the same format as the first-year books. It is also the case that a successful first-year text has rarely been followed by an equally successful continuation. Further, the materials for the intermediate and advanced levels in a large school program are often selected by a different supervisor from that of the elementary courses, thereby making coherent articulation (and progress in proficiency) even more problematic.

The result of all this is that French as presented by textbooks and practiced in class is a strange mixture of colloquial, formal, and what Valdman (1988) calls "pedagogical" language, usually ignoring sociolinguistic and cultural authenticity. Thus, students pretend to communicate in imaginary "survival" situations that, as Hefferman (1986) declares, are far narrower in range than normal real-life conversations, even though a study by Magnan (1986, pp. 432-33) indicates that at the end of one year of college French, 80% achieve an Intermediate-Low rating on the ACTFL scale. Valdman also claims that students can shift successfully from a simpler to a more complex form (e.g., from questions by intonation alone to inversion) and suggests that one form may be used in speech, another in reading, and yet another in writing. Such claims, however, not only remain largely unsubstantiated but also ignore the fact that the "simpler" forms represent another speech level, with its own phonological and morphosyntactic structures.

In sum, truly proficiency-based texts do not exist. Were one written, it would address various learning models and organize its materials according to the situations and needs outlined by the PGs and according to the notional-functional concepts advocated by Guntermann and Phillips (1982). It would provide numerous minidialogues with sufficient cultural contents that lead to longer discourses based on pragmatics. As for grammar, it would be subordinated to communication, as a kind of framework (with clear references to spoken language) when needs arise, and would stress discourse cohesion rather than accuracy of single sentences. Such a radical approach might not meet with commercial success, since for many teachers grammar constitutes an easily quantifiable entity. Thus, the argument for curricula that include grammar–opposed by Balcom (1985) and advocated by Hammond (1988)–is likely to continue. The role played by textbooks in language programs is enormous. Curricular designs, instructional approaches, and contents are largely determined by what is available in published form. As Lange (1990, p. 78) so aptly puts it, "We have handed the design of elementary, secondary, and college curricula to commercial interests."

Problems with Teacher Preparation

Faced with a diversity of instructional strategies and materials, many secondary school foreign language teachers feel ill-equipped to analyze them critically and to adopt what is most suitable for their students. These teachers often remain pedagogically isolated as the only people who teach a subject that is not understood by most of their colleagues, and tend to continue teaching the way they were taught in colleges and universities without keeping abreast of various trends in the profession.[5] Teacher training should not end when the degree is awarded and the state certificate tendered. Teacher education is a continuing process; this fact should be stressed from the outset, and institutions awarding teaching certificates need to be more active in providing in-service activities.[6]

Academic Work

Teacher training poses serious problems at all levels. At universities, the majority of graduate departments place emphasis on literature and only a small number grant a master's degree in teaching, let alone a doctorate in foreign language education. Teaching assistants, most of whom are students in literature, may or may not have genuine interest in the elementary and intermediate language courses they are hired to teach. Moreover, staffing of these courses is generally done as economically as possible, with few teaching qualifications demanded of the teaching assistants, and the faculty member in charge of running the elementary language program often is not trained or even interested in language acquisition methodologies. (See Teschner, 1987, for proof of this situation.) While most departments nowadays appear to give their graduate students some kind of training, consisting of a "methods" course and/or weekly meetings to discuss teaching and testing procedures,[7] it is unreasonable to expect graduate assistants to become competent proficiency-oriented instructors. They may learn some of the techniques by osmosis if the language program adopts the PGs in one form or another. On the whole, however, although most graduate assistants enjoy the teaching experience, the pressure of their own course work is so great that they have no time to investigate the theory and practice of PG-oriented instruction.

At the secondary school level, the majority of teacher preparation programs fall within the "conventional model," consisting of three main components: (1) the study of the language, literature, and civilization of the target language; (2) courses in general education; and (3) a language teaching methods course followed by student teaching. This model represents the most workable solution within the present academic structure, given adequately close liaison among the components. The problem lies not in this schematization but in the *contents* of the course work. Requirements for teacher certification vary widely, but one common pattern appears to be the heavy proportion of coursework in literature and just a single course on culture and civilization. This state of affairs reflects a presumed preeminence of belletristic research and, as mentioned by Grittner (1981, p. 73), Hammerly (1982, p. 142), and Lange (1986, p. 29), the regnant attitude in most language departments, in which cultural knowledge, language teaching, and language pedagogy are viewed as low-prestige affairs.

Few would dispute that all undergraduate language majors ought to study literature as one of their humanistic goals. One reason many prospective teachers may well aspire to teach the aesthetic appreciation of the target language literature is to prepare their students for a program like the Advanced Placement Test. Yet few departments offer a course in the *teaching* of literature,[8] and the fact remains that the majority of secondary school teachers are engaged in the instruction of levels 1 and 2,[9] where language and culture constitute the most important elements.

Training in Teaching

All prospective secondary school language teachers receive some training in methodologies before certification. But in many cases this training consists of a single course, designed to dispense information on lesson planning, on the principle of teaching in a speaking-listening-oriented approach, and on testing (some education departments offer a single methods course for all students in humanities).[10] The problem with this kind of course organization, composed of generalities and tips for teaching, is that it serves only as an *introduction* to the field. Future teachers need to see a clear relationship between theory and practice, the rationale of particular procedures recommended, and the pros and cons of certain approaches in order to evaluate methodologies and materials in an informed manner.

Even if a methods course has the luxury of being geared to a single second language, it has to deal with a myriad of classroom-related matters; therefore, discussion of the theories of language acquisition and of the PGs and how to implement them cannot be the sole focus. A look at well-researched books on methodology that have a coherent synthesis and a balanced approach to language teaching, such as Rivers (1981) and Hammerly (1982), along with proficiency-oriented anthologies like those by Higgs (1984), James (1985), and Byrnes and Canale (1986), will more than prove the point that there indeed exists an enormous body of theoretical and practical knowledge that prospective teachers must assimilate. What is needed is a two-semester sequence in methods as proposed by Lange (1983), so that all the basic elements of language instruction can be covered in more than just a cursory manner.

Moreover, several new technologies have been introduced in the past decade, including CAI and interactive video programs. The importance of CAI can be attested by the number of presentations at national professional conferences as well as at regional and local workshops, and by the fact that an increasing number of articles and reviews of CAI programs have been appearing in professional journals since the mid-1980s. It is necessary for prospective teachers to become familiar with the principles of CAI (and other technological developments) and have hands-on experience with some of the software. This aspect includes acquiring knowledge of an authoring system to produce exercises and tests as well as learning to evaluate the effectiveness of a given software program on the basis of the PGs.

Language Proficiency

Becoming proficient in the second language is unquestionably *the* most critical skill that foreign language teachers must master since it is at the very heart of what they will be doing in the classroom. In language classrooms, teachers provide models and initiate conversation practice, encouraging maximum use of the second language in as many interactive situations as possible. If their proficiency is lacking, it not only limits what they can do but also makes them less able to design communicative types of activities. Teacher preparation should, therefore, aim for as high a level of competence as possible.

The proficiency level expected for teaching a second language is in all likelihood beyond what can be attained through a normal, on-campus college curriculum. It is not surprising that undergraduate majors show a relatively low achievement level in the mastery of the language. Even at the height of AL instruction with its heavy emphasis on spoken language, Carroll (1967, p. 134) found that "the median graduate with a foreign language major can speak and comprehend the language only at about an FSI speaking rating of '2+,' that is, somewhere between a "limited working proficiency" and a "minimum professional proficiency."[11] Many college instructors admit that they have encountered students whose command of the language was so deficient that they really ought not to go into teaching.

It is thus clear that a period of study (ideally an entire academic year) in one of the countries of the target language improves students' proficiency and also enhances their cultural knowledge, both of which are crucial in the classroom.[12] Brickell and Paul (1982, pp. 174-75) report that teachers ranked as the most important contributions to their preparation (1) studying in a foreign country, (2) student teaching, and (3) language courses, especially in listening and speaking. Student teaching was rated 8 on a scale of 1 (low) to 10, and was perceived as second only to study abroad. Yet for various reasons, including financial ones, we are far from making study abroad mandatory for all prospective teachers.

The departments in charge of teacher education need to establish a general proficiency standard and test students through an appropriate method.[13] (The OPI is only one of several possibilities, and it is far from perfect, as will be shown in the next section of this paper.) All prospective teachers need to become familiar with various proficiency tests, and future teachers who are undergraduates should be tested by the end of the third year so that they can improve their rating during their last year in college. Ideally, of course, the test should be administered again before graduation, and those who score low should not be granted a teaching certificate. Adoption of proficiency tests will also necessitate one or more fourth-year language courses in conversation, writing, and grammar review. Moreover, as part of continuing teacher development, graduate-level language courses need to be offered so as to provide useful remedial work for those graduate students who need it.

Problems with the Guidelines and the Oral Proficiency Interviews

The Notion of Proficiency Guidelines

So far I have talked about the proficiency movement in exclusively positive terms and have examined two problems areas in light of it. A "movement" that emphasizes oral proficiency is a natural and logical consequence of the AL method, with its focus on spoken language, and of the methods that succeeded it in the 1970s, based as they were on communicative competence, functional-notional syllabi, contextualization of exercises, less grammar for grammar's sake, and a higher tolerance of learner errors. Language students have always shown an interest in the spoken skill, though they mistakenly believe they can acquire it in a rather short time.[14] In a manner similar to the reactions against the original AL method, criticisms of the PGs began surfacing soon after publication of the "provisional" version in 1982; the critique was spearheaded by Savignon (1985), who pointed out the document's narrow concept of language use and opposed the suggestion by Higgs and Clifford (1982) that language programs develop two tracks: terminal ("survival") and regular, articulated. Kramsch (1986) has called attention to the PGs' oversimplification of illocutionary acts and lack of emphasis on discourse cohesion, and Lantolf and Frawley (1985) have objected to the PGs' classification of various language functions into levels, which may lead to an achievement rather than a proficiency test.

The role of grammatical development in the learner is also a subject of controversy. Magnan (1988) claims that a relationship exists between the percentage of grammar errors and the OPI rating. Conversely, Pienemann et al. (1988) discount the PGs' assumption that a relationship exists between syntactic development and proficiency, and Raffaldini (1988), with some empirical data, attempts to disprove the PGs' notion that rudimentary linguistic competence cannot manage complex speech acts in a sociolinguistically appropriate manner. Bachman and Savignon (1986), Kramsch (1986), and Raffaldini (1988) all argue that the OPI and the PGs are too preoccupied with speech analysis at the sentential rather than the discourse level and that they are not sensitive to other communicative factors; these critics have all offered modifications of or alternatives to the ratings. Clark and Lett (1988) outline numerous questions that must be answered about reliability, validity, and the variables involved. The advantages and disadvantages of the PGs and the OPI can be argued for years without a definitive conclusion, since "proficiency" means different things to different people, and we may not reach a consensus. All the more reason, then, that teachers need better guidelines for teaching and testing in order to guarantee that their students improve their oral skills.

Oral Proficiency Interview

Once situational and behavioral objectives are established, some kind of instrument is needed to assess the proficiency of the learners to determine whether they have achieved these goals. It is in this area that the OPI's measurements of various language competencies have been criticized most heavily, especially on the grounds that the OPI lacks proper validation as a criterion-referenced test (Bachman, 1988; Bachman & Savignon, 1986). Admittedly, measuring skills in speaking is an elusive thing; Lowe (1986, p. 392) recognizes that quantifiable outcomes in listening, reading, and writing are attainable more readily than in speaking.

The OPI attempts to approximate real-life verbal interaction as closely as possible by using interviewers trained in the technique through the ACTFL-sponsored workshops; however, it can replicate only a small sampling of normal conversations in the real world, by no means all of which are predicated on the presence of only two speakers or on an exchange of questions and answers. As noted by Lantolf and Frawley (1985) and Raffaldini (1988), the testees are at the mercy of the interviewer (who initiates situations) and can neither propose new topics or subjects of their own interest nor switch formality levels. Interviews, no matter how friendly and informal, are unable to elicit voluntary linguistic and sociocultural speech acts, such as suasion, proposals and counterproposals, negotiation, counseling, and rejoinders to statements in all kinds of socializing contexts. As Raffaldini (1988, p. 200) states, even the role-play phase of the interview tends to lapse into elicitation of opinions and information so as to evaluate the scope of vocabulary and structure. Moreover, the OPI does not evaluate what Thomas (1983) calls cross-cultural understanding—that is, the ability to comprehend not only the surface meaning of a message but also the tones and accompanying facial expressions and gestures with all their implications, and the extent to which the speaker can avoid giving a stereotyped impression.

Researchers such as Bachman and Savignon (1986), Freed (1987), Savignon (1985), and VanPatten (1986) have also criticized the emphasis on grammatical accuracy placed by the PGs and the OPI in the early developmental stages of communicative competence. Pienemann et al. (1988) have noted the OPI's "false authenticity," which assumes that syntactic complexities and proficiency levels are interrelated and progress in a linear fashion, and which fails to evaluate various other elements, such as sociolinguistic, pragmatic, and strategic competence. The notion of "accuracy" in the PGs is probably the result of error analyses of the late 1970s that often concluded that the degree of "irritability" felt by native speakers was the highest for syntactic errors (at the sentential rather than the discourse level).[15]

There is something troubling about being rated through controversial competence descriptions and an imperfect testing instrument. Bachman and Savignon (1986) state that the outcome can become similar to the result of discrete-point testing. It is also likely that learners perform better on a task that was most recently acquired. In the field testing of a placement test, for example, I found through item analyses that first-year students did much better than their more advanced peers on recently taught items. We should also note that while learners may acquire vocabulary and expressions in certain curricular sequences, they eventually become more proficient in the area in which they are most interested – cooking, computers, stamp collection, military science, and so forth. Some professions (e.g., banking) may call for higher proficiency in specific tasks but are probably not concerned with lower attainment in "general" skills. We should also remember that the original scales developed by the Foreign Service Institute were somewhat job-specific: the ability to fulfill certain functions for the U.S. State Department. It may very well be that, following the argument of Kramsch (1986), the PGs and the OPI represent a "commercialization" of language skills. One could very well develop guidelines and interview techniques for specific purposes – say, for the potential employment of testees in certain business sectors; were that the case, then hypothetical situations testing general skills, such as asking a neighbor for tools to fix a broken doorknob, could remain in the background.

There is no doubt that OPI techniques constitute an enormous step forward as compared to the days when teachers interested in measuring oral competence used short questions and picture descriptions based on the MLA Cooperative Tests. But the OPI itself is not a suitable instrument for semester-by-semester achievement testing, except perhaps in a longitudinal study or in intensive courses. Besides, if the training of graduate assistants and secondary school teachers in the OPI is problematic, administering such a test is even more so. Interviews generally take 10 to 15 minutes and are increasingly longer beyond the intermediate-mid level. In small language programs, there is only one teacher for each language, and it is difficult for teachers testing their own students, after months of contact in class, to arrive at an objective judgment. Even in a large program, switching instructors and equalizing the number of examinees per instructor often presents logistical problems. Although, short, OPI-*like* tests are possible once or twice a semester, such tests should be kept in proper perspective and never become the dominant factor in determining course grades, which must also take other elements into consideration, such as reading, writing, cultural understanding, authentic sociolinguistic behavior, and humanistic goals.[16]

Conclusion

The PGs and the OPI are not only logical extensions of the emphasis on oral communication of the 1960s but a definite improvement on previous testing schemata. They give fairly concrete objectives but should be continually revised and refined. There are recurring doubts that the PGs, with their underlying assumption that language competence and communicative ability develop sequentially, and with their failure to include sociocultural, sociolinguistic, and pragmatic behavior, are able to represent convincing, empirically validated stages of language acquisition. As for the OPI, it is not the only method for measuring proficiency, however one defines it.

Instructional materials and teacher preparation constitute two very large missing links in the proficiency movement. Many texts assume that the PGs and the attainment of oral proficiency are *the* goal of language instruction and claim to incorporate them. Yet this paper has sought to show that written-language based grammar explanations and use of an artificial level of language indicate that true oral proficiency will be difficult to attain unless radical changes are made in organization and approach, with an inclusion of more sociolinguistic elements and a continuing effort to create suitable materials at more advanced levels.

The use made of any given material depends largely on the teacher. Experienced teachers can make good use of an inefficient text and achieve many of the guidelines' goals. Conversely, a well-intentioned text can be ruined by those who are excessively preoccupied with grammatical and phonological details and who give pages of "supplementary" drills to their students. Moreover, budgetary pressure has forced some secondary school programs to combine two levels in a single class and dilute the program so as to keep up enrollments. In such circumstances, it becomes even more strenuous to follow the PGs effectively.

Higgs (1984, p. 4) explicitly advocates that the PGs/OPI might serve as "an organizing principle," and Lowe (1986, p. 392) states that the "*Guidelines* were originally designed to outline, not to describe the system exhaustively" as a broad framework. Though the PGs provide useful criteria for *some* of the language learning objectives, and the OPI for *some* of the ways in which to evaluate communicative competence, there is concern among researchers about OPI advocates who view the oral proficiency movement as the only true way. Thus, Schulz (1986) points to the varied needs of students and questions the necessity of the OPI, cautioning the overzealous "missionaries" among not only educators but also public officials who consider the development of oral skills to be the sole objective of language instruction. Lantolf and Frawley (1985, p. 344) urge the profession to "delay any guidelines until researchers are able to develop a clear understanding of what it means to be a proficient speaker in a language" and warn elsewhere of the resultant "premature institutionalization" of oral proficiency (1988, p. 181). (It is unfortunate that the word *provisional* was removed from the PGs in 1986). Magnan (1986) and Freed (1987) report that some institutions of higher learning are already using PG-based rating systems and OPI-oriented speaking tests, along with discrete-point tests for other skills, as a means of fulfilling an entrance or graduation requirement. Phillips (1990, pp. 58-59) mentions that the institutions applying for U.S. Department of Education Title VI projects must now demonstrate how their proposals are based on proficiency and how their evaluative procedures are "compatible with developing national standards." The recent guidelines of the National Endowment for the Humanities Division of Education Programs, designed to encourage colleges and universities to strengthen foreign language education through summer institutes, are laden with the term *proficiency.*

Most arguments against the PGs and the OPIs have been constructive, offering modifications or alternatives. The PGs should be refined continually and remain always as *guidelines* rather than promoted as standards, especially since the OPI continues to be a controversial instrument. There is much work to be done, including the following:

1) Investigation should be made into the extent to which the PGs and OPI-*oriented* techniques have been adopted in each state and at which educational institutions, and what modifications, if any, are being made.
2) Further improvements in the PGs are possible only if more empirical data regarding language learning and development in competence are obtained and analyzed.
3) The validity of the OPI has often been questioned. Its validity must be established and supplementary instruments ought to be explored.
4) PGs for special purposes need to be proposed, and various measurements (including the OPI) and their correlation should be established with the "general" PGs.

5) Native speakers should not be left out of the picture. They show considerable variation in competence, depending on such factors as education, age, social class, residence patterns, intelligence, and experience. How will they score on the OPI, and in what skills? Most studies on native speakers' reaction to learners have focused on "degrees of irritability," especially in terms of grammatical and/or phonological errors. What would be their perception of learners' competence in various situations?

Notes

1. For concise summaries and discussions of various methodological trends, see Benseler and Schulz (1980) and Grittner (1981).

2. In particular, Byrnes and Canale (1986), Higgs (1984), and James (1985) present extensive discussions of the repercussions of the PGs on such wide-ranging areas as curriculum design and evaluation, instructional materials, classroom teaching and testing, and pre- as well as in-service teacher training.

3. As pointed out by Rusterholz (1990, pp. 255-56), the proliferation of informal speech patterns at the beginning level often necessitates a review of expressions for greeting and leave-taking and other simple situations at a more advanced level; even textbooks published in France that aim for communicative competence lack sociolinguistic authenticity. See, for example, the detailed analysis of De vive voix by Gschwind-Holtzer (1981).

4. None of the examples cited are considered "vulgar"; see Léon (1967) for a distinction between style familier and genre vulgaire, and Joseph (1988) for the pedagogical implications of the increasing gap between the formal and colloquial levels. Queneau (1965) as a nonlinguist wrote a series of highly amusing and insightful essays on language levels in the 1950s.

5. The general career satisfaction of language teachers as reported by Fitzpatrick and Liuzzo (1989) is misleading, since those authors surveyed only ACTFL members. According to a somewhat old but quite extensive survey (Brickell and Paul, 1982, p. 178), only 20% of language teachers attend national professional conventions annually, 40 to 50% attend state or regional conferences, and most go to an in-service workshop, often of very general nature, only once a year. Jarvis and Taylor (1990, p. 177) also report that a full 40% of language teachers in Ohio work in more than one certification area.

6. Lange (1986, p. 30) proposes a fifth year, as "an additional, trial year" for which only a temporary certification would be granted, and Mellgren and Caye (1989) describe a closely coordinated collaborative program between the University of Minnesota and a nearby public school district; this latter effort is based on Lange's model and is a bright exception to the general state of affairs.

7. Surveys of the past and present problems and case studies definitely indicate improvements in the training of instructors at the college level; see Hagiwara (1970), Nerenz, Herron, and Knop (1979), and Schulz (1980).

8. Herr (1982) makes precisely this point, and very little research appears to have been done in the field, though use of literature at lower rather than

higher levels is advocated by Schofer (1990) and has been the focus of the journal *Teaching Language through Literature.*

9. Brickell and Paul (1982, p. 179) report that the majority of teachers are engaged in the instruction of levels 1 and 2, in which the main components according to the teachers are 75% language, 20% culture/civilization, and 5% literature. On the other hand, their undergraduate coursework consisted of 35% in language, 45% in literature, and 15% in culture/civilization. (At the graduate level, 25% was in language and 65% in literature.)

10. For a detailed discussion of various issues in methods courses, see Lange (1983) and Phillips (1989), and for desiderata for teacher training and teacher educators, see ACTFL (1988), Hancock (1981), and Jarvis and Taylor (1990).

11. More recent studies, such as those by Cramer and Terrio (1985), Kaplan (1984), and Magnan (1986), though not based on mass data like Carroll's, indicate the range of advanced students' proficiency as intermediate-high to advanced-high in terms of the ACTFL-ETS Speaking Proficiency Scale.

12. For a survey and an excellent bibliography of the types of study abroad and the experiences gained by participating students, see Koester (1986). According to Brickell and Paul (1982, p. 174), only about 50% of foreign language teachers have ever studied during college in a country where the language is spoken. Carroll (1967, p. 137) reported that the amount of time spent abroad (even if it is only a summer) and the age of the student when first beginning to study the language were the two factors most strongly associated with second language competence.

13. Testing of college graduates, especially those in the teacher certification program, has been advocated by many (see Brod, 1983, p. 40; Lange, 1986, p. 29; and Muyskens, 1984, p. 183). The need to establish national proficiency standards is advocated by Joiner (1981, p. 21). Even Schulz (1986), who opposes testing all students, expresses agreement. Hammerly (1982, p. 134) advocates a proficiency level equivalent to at least 4 on the U.S. State Department Foreign Service Institute (FSI) scale. Muyskens (1984, p. 183) suggests that it should be equal to the "Superior level" of the ACTFL scale, and Lange (1986, p. 30), to "Advanced Plus" to "Superior." See Johnson and LaBouve (1984) and Magnan (1986) for discussions of a movement in some states to establish minimum proficiency standards in certification programs.

14. The initial high interest in speaking and subsequent disappointment in the lack of progress are frequently voiced in our surveys of students. Horwitz (1988, p. 292) found that upward of 40% of students in French, German, and Spanish felt they would be fluent in two years or less of college study, and points to the need to "disabuse students of deleterious misconceptions about language learning." Curiously, student preference for written rather than oral activities are reported by Swaffar (1989, p. 306).

15. For a review of error analyses from this period, see Ludwig (1982). Later studies, such as those by Fayer and Krasinski (1987), attempt to go beyond individual sentences.

16. That the OPI should not be used as an indicator of classroom achievement is emphatically asserted by Dandonoli (1986, p. 78), a proponent of the OPI, and Schulz (1980, p. 375), who is skeptical about the OPI. OPI-oriented achievement tests leading ultimately to a full-fledged OPI are advocated by

Magnan (1985, p. 117); Omaggio (1986, p. 313) shows how it is possible to convert traditional test procedures to PGs-oriented types, and gives numerous suggestions; Berrier (1991) and Rusterholz (1990) describe evaluation of various aspects of oral communication from the instructors' point of view.

Works Cited

ACTFL. *ACTFL Proficiency Guidelines.* Yonkers, NY: ACTFL Materials Center, 1986.

_____. "ACTFL Provisional Program Guidelines for Foreign Language Teacher Education." *Foreign Language Annals* 21 (1988): 71-82.

Bachman, Lyle F. "Problems in Examining the Validity of the ACTFL Oral Proficiency Interview. *Studies in Second Language Acquisition* 10 (1988): 149-64.

_____ & Sandra J. Savignon. "The Evaluation of Communicative Language Proficiency: A Critique of the ACTFL Oral Interview." *Modern Language Journal* 70 (1986): 380-90.

Balcom, Patricia. "Should We Teach Grammar? Another Look at Krashen's Monitor Model." *Bulletin of the Canadian Association of Applied Linguistics* 7 (1985): 37-45.

Barnes, Betsey K. "Apports de l'analyse du discours à l'enseignement de la langue." *French Review* 64 (1990): 95-107.

Benseler, David P. & Renate A. Schulz. "Methodological Trends in College Foreign Language Instruction." *Modern Language Journal* 64 (1980): 88-96.

Berrier, Astrid. "L'Evaluation de l'oral: quelles questions?" *French Review* 64 (1991): 476-85.

Brickell, Henry M. & Regina H. Paul. "Ready for the '80s? A Look at Foreign Language Teachers and Teaching at the Start of the Decade." *Foreign Language Annals* 15 (1982): 169-87.

Brod, Richard I. "The State of the Profession – 1983." *Modern Language Journal* 67 (1983): 319-29.

Byrnes, Heidi & Michael Canale (Ed.) *Defining and Developing Proficiency: Guidelines, Implementations and Concepts.* Lincolnwood, IL: National Textbook Company, 1986.

Calvé, Pierre. "Dislocation in Spoken French." *Modern Language Journal* 69 (1985): 230-37.

Carroll, John B. "Foreign Language Proficiency Levels Attained by Language Majors near Graduation from College." *Foreign Language Annals* 1 (1967): 131-41.

Clark, John L. D. & John Lett. "A Research Agenda." *Second Language Proficiency Assessment: Current Issues.* Ed. Pardee Lowe, Jr. & Charles W. Stansfield. Englewood, NJ: Prentice Hall, 1988: 53-83.

Cramer, Hazel & Susan Terrio. "Moving from Vocabulary Acquisition to Functional Proficiency: Techniques and Strategies." *French Review* 59 (1985): 198-209.

Dandonoli, Patricia. "ACTFL's Current Research in Proficiency Testing." *Defining and Developing Proficiency: Guidelines, Implementations and Concepts.* Ed. Heidi Byrnes & Michael Canale. Lincolnwood, IL: National Textbook Company, 1986: 75-96.

Fayer, John M. & Emily Krasinski. "Native and Non-native Judgments of Intelligibility and Irritation." *Language Learning* 37 (1987): 313-26.

Fitzpatrick, Richard C. & Anthony L. Liuzzo. "Demographics and Assessments of Career Satisfaction of Foreign Language Teaching Professionals." *Foreign Language Annals* 22 (1989): 61-66.

Freed, Barbara F. "Preliminary Impressions of the Effects of a Proficiency-based Language Requirement." *Foreign Language Annals* 20 (1987): 139-46.

_____. Review of Charles J. James (Ed.), *Foreign Language Proficiency in the Classroom and Beyond. Studies in Second Language Acquisition* 10 (1988): 269-71.

Grittner, Frank M. "How to Break out of the Never-ending Circle of Retraining: A Self-adjusting Mechanism for the 1980's." *Proceedings of the National Conference on Professional Priorities.* Ed. Dale L. Lange & Cathy Linder. Hastings-on-Hudson, NY: ACTFL Materials Center, 1981: 72-77.

_____. "Bandwagons Revisited: A Perspective in Foreign Language Education." *New Perspectives and New Directions in Foreign Language Education.* Ed. Diane W. Birckbichler. Lincolnwood, IL: National Textbook Company, 1990: 9-44.

Gschwind-Holtzer, Gisèle. *"Analyse sociolinguistique de la communication didactique"* in *Application à un cours de langue: De vive voix.* Paris: Hatier-CREDIF, 1981.

Guntermann, Gail & June K. Phillips. *Functional-Notional Concepts: Adapting the Foreign Language Textbook. Language in Education: Theory and Practice, No. 44.* Washington, DC: Center for Applied Linguistics, 1982.

Hagiwara, M. Peter. *Trends in Training and Supervision of Graduate Teaching Assistants.* New York: Modern Language Association, 1970.

_____. "Linguistics, Applied Linguistics, and Pedagogical Grammar." *Michigan Academician* 12 (1980): 309-19.

_____. "The Inversion of the Subject Noun and Verb in Modern French." *Romanitas: Michigan Romance Studies.* Ed. Ernst Pulgram. Ann Arbor, MI: Department of Romance Languages, University of Michigan, 1985: 77-108.

Hammerly, Hector. *Synthesis in Second Language Teaching: An Introduction to Languistics.* Blaine, WA: Second Language Publications, 1982.

Hammond, Robert M. "Accuracy versus Communicative Competency: The Acquisition of Grammar in the Second Language Classroom." *Hispania* 71 (1988): 408-17.

Hancock, Charles R. "Modest Proposals for Second and Foreign Language Teacher Education in the 1980's." *Action for the '80's: A Political, Professional, and Public Program for Foreign Language Education.* Ed. June K. Phillips. Lincolnwood, IL: National Textbook Company, 1981: 179-94.

Hefferman, Peter. "Questioning Communicativity in the Second Language Classroom." *Canadian Modern Language Review* 43 (1986): 108-16.

Herr, Kay. "The Role of Literature in Secondary and Post-secondary Language Instruction: Disparity or Unity?" *Foreign Language Annals* 15 (1982): 203-7.

Higgs, Theodore V. "Language Teaching and the Quest for the Holy Grail." *Teaching for Proficiency, the Organizing Principle*. Ed. Theodore V. Higgs. Lincolnwood, IL: National Textbook Company, 1984: 1-9.

_____ (Ed.). *Teaching for Proficiency, the Organizing Principle*. Lincolnwood, IL: National Textbook Company, 1984.

_____ & Ray Clifford. "The Push toward Communication." *Curriculum, Competence, and the Foreign Language Teacher*. Ed. Theodore V. Higgs. Lincolnwood, IL: National Textbook Company, 1982: 57-79.

Horwitz, Elaine K. "The Belief about Language Learning of Beginning University Foreign Language Students." *Modern Language Journal* 72 (1988): 283-94.

James, Charles J. (Ed.). *Foreign Language Proficiency in the Classroom and Beyond*. Lincolnwood, IL: National Textbook Company, 1985.

Jarvis, Gilbert A. & Sheryl V. Taylor. "Reforming Foreign and Second Language Teacher Education." *New Perspectives and New Directions in Foreign Language Education*. Ed. Diane W. Birckbichler. Lincolnwood, IL: National Textbook Company, 1990: 159-82.

Joiner, Elizabeth G. "Preservice Teacher Education: Some Thoughts for the 1980s." *Proceedings of the National Conference on Professional Priorities*. Ed. Dale L. Lange & Cathy Linder. Hastings-on-Hudson, NY: ACTFL Materials Center, 1981: 78-80.

Johnson, Carl H. & Bobby W. LaBouve. "A Status Report of Testing of Prospective Language Teachers for Initial State Certification." *Foreign Language Annals* 17 (1984): 461-72.

Joseph, John E. "New French: A Pedagogical Crisis in the Making." *Modern Language Journal* 72 (1988): 31-36.

Kaplan, Isabelle. "Oral Proficiency Testing and the Language Curriculum: Two Experiments in Curricular Design for Conversation Courses." *Foreign Language Annals* 15 (1984): 491-98.

Koester, Jolene. "A Profile of Foreign Language Majors Who Work, Study, and Travel Abroad." *Modern Language Journal* 70 (1986): 21-27.

Kramsch, Claire. "From Language Proficiency to Interactional Competence." *Modern Language Journal* 70 (1986): 366-72.

Lange, Dale L. "Teacher Development and Certification in Foreign Languages: Where Is the Future?" *Modern Language Journal* 67 (1983): 374-81.

_____. "The MLA Committee on Foreign Languages, Literature, and Linguistics: Comments and Advice." *ADFL Bulletin* 17 (1986): 28-31.

_____. "Sketching the Crisis and Exploring Different Perspectives in Foreign Language Curriculum." *New Perspectives and New Directions in Foreign Language Education*. Ed. Diane W. Birckbichler. Lincolnwood, IL: National Textbook Company, 1990: 77-109.

Lantolf, James P. & William Frawley. "Oral Proficiency Testing: A Critical Analysis." *Modern Language Journal* 69 (1985): 337-45.

_____. "Proficiency: Understanding the Concept." *Studies in Second Language Acquisition* 10 (1988): 181-95.

Léon, Pierre R. "Aspects phonostylistiques des niveaux de langue." *Français dans le monde* 48 (1967): 58-72.

Lowe, Pardee, Jr. "Proficiency: Panacea, Framework, Process? A Reply to Kramsch, Schulz, and, Particularly, to Bachman and Savignon." *Modern Language Journal* 70 (1986): 391-97.

_____ & Charles W. Stansfield (Ed.). *Second Language Proficiency Assessment: Current Issues.* Englewood Cliffs, NJ: Prentice Hall Regents, 1988.

Ludwig, Jeannette. "Native Speaker Judgments of Second-Language Learners' Efforts at Communication." *Modern Language Journal* 66 (1982): 274-83.

Magnan, Sally S. "From Achievement toward Proficiency through Multi-Sequence Evaluation." *Foreign Language Proficiency in the Classroom and Beyond.* Ed. Charles J. James. Lincolnwood, IL: National Textbook Company, 1985: 117-45.

_____. "Assessing Speaking Proficiency in the Undergraduate Curriculum: Data from French." *Foreign Language Annals* 19 (1986): 429-38.

_____. "Grammar and the ACTFL Oral Proficiency Interview: Discussion and Data." *Modern Language Journal* 72 (1988): 266-75.

Mellgren, Millie P. & Leslie Ann Caye. "School-University Collaboration in Second Language Teacher Education: Building a Successful Partnership." *Foreign Language Annals* 22 (1989): 553-60.

Muyskens, Judith A. "Preservice and Inservice Teacher Training: Focus on Pro-ficiency." *Teaching for Proficiency, the Organizing Principle.* Ed. Theodore V. Higgs. Lincolnwood, IL: National Textbook Company, 1984: 179-200.

Nerenz, Anne G., Carol A. Herron & Constance K. Knop. "The Training of Graduate Teaching Assistants in Foreign Languages: A Review of Literature and Description of Contemporary Progress." *French Review* 52 (1979): 873-88.

Omaggio, Alice C. "The Proficiency-oriented Classroom." *Teaching for Proficiency: The Organizing Principle.* Ed. Theodore V. Higgs. Lincolnwood, IL: National Textbook Company, 1984: 43-84.

_____. *Teaching Language in Context.* Boston: Heinle & Heinle, 1986.

Phillips, June K. "Teacher Education: Target of Reform." *Shaping the Future: Challenges and Opportunities.* Ed. Helen S. Lepke. Middlebury, VT: Northeast Conference on the Teaching of Foreign Languages, 1989: 11-40.

_____. "Language Instruction in the United States: Policy and Planning." *New Perspectives and New Directions in Foreign Language Education.* Ed. Diane W. Birckbichler. Lincolnwood, IL: National Textbook Company, 1990: 45-75.

Pienemann, Manford, Malcolm Johnson & Geoff Brindley. "Constructing an Acquisition-based Procedure for Second Language Assessment." *Studies in Second Language Acquisition* 10 (1988): 217-43.

President's Commission on the Teaching of Foreign Languages and International Studies. *Strength through Wisdom: A Critique of U.S. Capability.* Washington, DC: Government Printing Office, 1979.

Queneau, Raymond. *Bâton, chiffres et lettres.* Paris: Gallimard, 1965.

Raffaldini, Tina. "The Use of Situation Tests as Measures of Communicative Ability." *Studies in Second Language Acquisition* 10 (1988): 197-216.

Rivers, Wilga M. *Teaching Foreign-Language Skills.* 2d ed. Chicago: University of Chicago Press, 1981.

Rusterholz, Barbara Lomas. "Developing Oral Proficiency in the Business French Class." *French Review* 64 (1990): 253-59.

Savignon, Sandra J. "Evaluation of Communicative Competence: The ACTFL Provisional Proficiency Guidelines." *Modern Language Journal* 69 (1985): 129-34.

Schofer, Peter. "Literature and Communicative Competence: A Springboard for the Development of Critical Thinking and Aesthetic Appreciation or Literature in the Land of Language." *Foreign Language Annals* 23 (1990): 325-34.

Schulz, Renate A. "TA Training, Supervision, and Evaluation: Report of a Survey." *ADFL Bulletin* 12 (1980): 1-8.

_____. "From Achievement to Proficiency through Classroom Instruction: Some Caveats." *Modern Language Journal* 70 (1986): 373-79.

Swaffar, Janet K. "Competing Paradigms in Adult Language Acquisition." *Modern Language Journal*, 73 (1989): 301-14.

Teschner, Richard V. "A Profile of the Specialization and Expertise of Lower Division Foreign Language Program Directors in American Universities." *Modern Language Journal* 71 (1987): 28-35.

Thomas, Jenny. "Cross-cultural Pragmatic Failure." *Applied Linguistics* 4 (1983): 91-112.

Valdman, Albert. "Classroom for Language Learning and Language Variation: The Notion of Pedagogical Norms." *World Englishes* 7 (1988): 221-36.

VanPatten, Bill. "The ACTFL Proficiency Guidelines: Implications for Grammatical Accuracy in the Classroom?" *Studies in Second Language Acquisition* 8 (1986): 56-67.

Walz, Joel. "Is Oral Proficiency Possible with Today's French Textbooks?" *Modern Language Journal* 70 (1986): 13-20.

_____. "A Survey and Analysis of Tests Accompanying Elementary French Textbooks." This volume.

Testing in Foreign Language Programs and Testing Programs in Foreign Language Departments: Reflections and Recommendations

Elizabeth B. Bernhardt and Craig Deville
Ohio State University

One of Webster's (1983) definitions of a *test* is "a basis for evaluation." Crucially, this definition contains the word *a* and not *the*. In other words, a test provides information for evaluation; it is not *the evaluation*. In an ideal world, this close analysis of the word *test* might not be necessary, but in a world intent on quick, ostensibly objective accountability, a test (such as a chapter test, a midterm, or a final examination) frequently becomes *the* evaluation for a course of study.

Tests, however, not only serve to evaluate the performance of students in a particular course; they also reflect the knowledge and approach of those who require, design, and administer them. This paper takes up the dual theme of testing student performance in foreign language programs and of assessing the testing programs themselves in foreign language departments. In other words, this paper examines testing as a vehicle: that is, as a means for asking and answering questions about student performance and as a data-gathering device about program goals and directions.

To meet this goal, appropriate everyday workings of foreign language testing are examined within the theory of psychometrics. This bridging of reality and theory is an attempt to bring realism to bear on foreign language testing as well as to communicate to language departments many of the components of the science of testing. The relationship between reality and theory is often one of tension. On the one hand, the constraints placed on language programs (time, multiple sections, limited staffing, instructors who possess various degrees of interest in language teaching, and large enrollments) often do not permit the kinds of testing programs that are most theoretically appropriate. On the other hand, many directors of language programs or department heads are not equipped to implement theoretically viable language testing programs based on language acquisition research or to cope with the psychometric theories and applications they imply. Lack of such information and skills should not be the excuse for a primitive testing program. The ultimate goal of this paper is to suggest ways in which the tension between these two facets of language programs can be lessened.

This paper is thus divided into two sections. The first section outlines a set of characteristics of testing programs and of tests themselves that any language department must take into consideration. The second section provides specific suggestions for ways in which language departments can indeed be sensitive to the basic requirements of testing. These suggestions focus on particular kinds of tests that language departments should consider using, as well as on particular kinds of technological developments that could be utilized to improve and modernize any foreign language testing program.

Part 1

Characteristics of Good Testing Approaches

Honesty

Most papers on testing begin with discussions of reliability and validity. Indeed, this paper will get to those concepts, but not before a discussion of something much more fundamental. The most fundamental of all testing concepts is this: any test must be grounded in the objectives of a program. That is, any placement test must be written in terms of the implicit and explicit objectives of the language program. Any achievement test that purports to measure student progress within the program must be written and interpreted within the objectives of a program. Any proficiency test to which students are subjected must also be interpreted within the framework of a program. In other words, honesty should be the hallmark of testing.

These statements regarding the match between program objectives and tests are probably commonplace and mundane, yet they are also probably the most frequently violated concepts in language program testing. How many programs exist that purport to be communicative in nature and then test grammatical competence at every turn? How many courses spend time working with communicative activities and then test the verb forms? How many professional organizations encourage communicative competence and then provide nationally competitive achievement tests that lack even a speaking section? How many secondary teachers work actively with students to get them excited about using foreign languages only to find that the university placement test employs a grammatical, multiple-choice format? How many foreign language professionals talk about innovative methods of testing and then administer programs that use the most traditional and outdated methods of language assessment?

The match between explicit objectives and the reality of foreign language programs should be the most central concern in any testing program. Any testing mechanism must conform to the real objectives of any program. This implies that a program frankly admit to its real intentions. If the implementors of a program want explicit grammatical competence, they should teach and test for it. If they want communicative ability, they should teach and test for it. No student or scholar can denigrate a program whose objectives and evaluation measures are compatible. This is honesty. But both student and scholar should be unwilling to accept a program that states one objective and tests another. Dishonest is the only appropriate descriptor for such a program.

Objectives need, however, to be realistic. Many programs are trapped in the public rhetoric of what is currently valued in the profession – namely, oral communication skills – and the private reality of running a language program. The private reality of language programs was alluded to above. Language programs are constrained by the amount of time allocated to language learning (usually 150 to 200 minutes per week), the number of students assigned per class (usually 25 to 30), and the quality and competence of staff (at the college level, usually graduate students/teachers with minimal training and frequently little motivation for lower-level language teaching). These private realities invariably play a role in the formulation of any set of objectives and their eventual measurement. Even if oral communication is the goal, can it be accomplished given the possible constraints of 25 students allotted 150 contact minutes with a teacher who has little if any classroom experience? In like manner, if the goal of the program is to give students the ability to analyze authentic literature, is there any point in providing practice in oral communication and then assessing that?

The point is this: it is important that programs state realistic, not wished-for, objectives. Only after a language department has fully explicated those objectives and made them public, should it endeavor to develop and implement a testing program. The risks programs run when the stated objectives are inconsistent with the actual instruction both within courses and across levels are twofold: (1) students are deluded and ultimately feel frustrated and (2) faculty accuse colleagues of lack of rigor and competence because individual expectations are not met. The end result of these inconsistencies is students who do not wish to continue in language programs and faculty who do not wish to teach in them.

Seriousness of Purpose

One of the theses in this paper is that tests assess both students and programs. The purpose of tests is not simply to obtain a score to fill in on the grade sheet at the end of a term. Tests are meant to guide both students and teachers. A testing program should make it clear that assessment is a key component in examining the quality of the program in which students are placed as well as examining what students have learned from their courses.

The concept of a testing program is an important one. The word *program* implies that a coherent set of stages in test development, test application, and test reevaluation exists. It also implies that the results of tests are reviewed periodically as a whole in order to assess the degree to which program goals are met, to review program quality, and to diagnose student progress. If students are not progressing according to program goals, then there is a problem with the tests (they may not be appropriate instruments), with teaching (teachers may not understand the objectives of the particular program), or with student learning (the materials may be inappropriate for the student population for which they are being utilized), or with the students themselves.

To develop and maintain a serious testing program, each program should have a person responsible for testing. Traditionally, this responsibility is shouldered by the language program coordinator. Such need not be the case: a properly prepared advanced graduate student could be assigned this responsibility. The more central issue concerns the preparation and knowledge of the person placed in charge.

The suggested program setup implies a person who is equipped with the knowledge of the basic principles of psychometrics. This knowledge entails, first, concerns about validity issues (what do the tests actually measure?) and, second, concerns about the quality of that measurement (are the tests accurate measures?). In other words, the individual charged with testing must have an extensive background in the assessment of individual language skills and also have expertise in statistical skills that provide information about the accuracy and appropriateness of the tests administered.

Characteristics of Good Tests

The most important feature of a test is its validity. In fact, a joint commission of the American Psychological Association, the American Educational Research Association, and the National Council of Mathematics Educators agreed in 1985 on the following:

> Validity is the most important consideration in test evaluation. The concept refers to the appropriateness, meaningfulness and usefulness of the specific inferences made from test scores. . . . Validity . . . is a unitary concept. Although evidence may be accumulated in many ways, validity always refers to the degree to which that evidence supports the inferences that are made from test scores (p. 9).

Appropriateness and *meaningfulness* are critical words here. They imply that a successful test must match as closely as possible what is known about a process at any time. This is technically termed "construct validity." Messick (1988) comments:

> The heart of the unified view of validity is that appropriateness, meaningfulness, and usefulness of score-based inferences are inseparable and that the unifying force is empirically grounded construct interpretation. Thus, from the perspective of validity as a unified concept, all educational and psychological measurement should be construct-referenced because construct interpretation undergirds all score-based inferences – not just those related to interpretive meaningfulness but also the content- and criterion-related inferences specific to applied decisions and actions based on test scores. As a consequence, although construct-related evidence may not be the whole of validity, there can be no validity without it. That is, there is no way to judge responsibly the appropriateness, meaningfulness, and usefulness of the score inferences in the absence of evidence as to what the scores mean (p. 35).

Test validity, then, is the attempt to match the configuration of a test to what it attempts to measure. Stated in the simplest of terms, a test of speaking should test speaking; a test of listening should test listening; a test of reading should test reading; a test of writing should test writing. While these statements appear obvious, they must be made nonetheless, because it is not uncommon to find language tests that purport to measure one skill and actually assess another. That is, some reading tests are in reality grammar tests in a multiple-choice format; some listening tests are actually pronunciation or sound-discrimination tests; some speaking tests ask test takers to "choose" a response rather than to "speak"; many writing tests are sentence-repetition tasks in disguise.

A significant amount of work has been conducted in the past decade regarding the "skills" (in testing terminology, "constructs") of speaking, listening, reading, and writing in a second language. It is within the testing program that the knowledge gained from such second language acquisition research needs to be most critically applied. As Messick (1988) notes in the above quotation, test validity is a dynamic process. A test is not labeled valid and then ignored. Any test development must be responsive to new research and findings within an area. This mandates that the person in charge of testing in a language department must be apprised of recent developments in a variety of research areas. The next section of this paper highlights recent findings in second language research that are particularly relevant to test development. Once again, it is important to repeat that a test must be reflective of the objectives of a particular program. If the program does not take as an objective the teaching of a particular skill, it should not include the testing of that skill as a component.

Speaking

The construct of "speaking" is indeed multidimensional. In past practice, speaking was often defined as the ability to pronounce words or to read aloud. Currently, a more accepted notion is that speaking entails communication; that is, speaking is generally focused on a transaction of some kind of information from one person to another. In other words, "speaking" at its most basic level in contemporary terms usually means the ability to participate in a conversation.

"Ability to participate in a conversation" is a complex matter. It is no less easy to evaluate it. According to Nunan (1989), participating in a conversation assumes the following abilities:

1) The ability to articulate phonological features of the language comprehensibly.
2) Mastery of stress, rhythm, and intonation patterns.
3) An acceptable degree of fluency.
4) Transactional and interpersonal skills.
5) Skills in taking short and long speaking turns.
6) Skills in the management of interaction.
7) Skills in negotiating meaning.
8) Conversational listening skills.

9) Skills in knowing about and negotiating purposes for conversations.
10) Use of appropriate conversational formulas and fillers.

This list of skills defines the parameters of the construct of speaking. To assess speaking abilities, then, an assessment instrument must operationalize the qualities listed. In other words, a speaking test must be conversational; it must account for more than grammatical skills by including social and management skills; and it must assess the speaker's ability to understand a conversational partner.

If one of the objectives of a program is indeed to teach speaking, then the program must test speaking. Most recently, the Oral Proficiency Interview (OPI) adapted from the Foreign Service Institute's procedures has been advanced as an appropriate assessment device. It is clear, however, that the OPI is appropriate only under conditions whereby considerable instructional time has passed (i.e., the OPI is inappropriate for weekly, unit, or semester testing) and whereby there is plenty of personnel time to conduct such an interview.

Hence, speaking tests must be administered that make efficient use of both time and personnel but are also able to reflect progress from one assessment to another, that is, are able to measure the development of speaking ability from week to week or unit to unit.

Brown et al. (1984) suggest three different types of speaking tasks that lend themselves appropriately as speaking assessment devices. They mention static tasks, such as orally explaining a diagram or describing a picture; dynamic tasks, such as relating a story that "involves the description of relationships which change over time" (p. 86); and abstract tasks, such as those requiring the expression of an opinion. The authors provide examples of these types of tasks as well as of instruments used for scoring them.

Such verbal assessments can be tape-recorded by students in some central location for evaluation at the convenience of the instructor. With detailed scoring protocols, students can be provided with speaking profiles so that they are able to trace, on their own, their development in second language speaking abilities.

The tasks listed above are information transfer tasks. That is, they imply a listener and an audience; the audience must comprehend the message in order to complete a task, follow a story, or react to an opinion. These tasks meet as closely as possible the requirements of authentic speaking tasks given the constraints of any testing mechanism.

Listening and Reading

The constructs of listening and reading can be grouped together because listening and reading are in essence acts of comprehension

(Nunan, 1989). That is, they entail gathering information from spoken or written discourse. This view on listening and reading has been rather slow to emerge in language programs, let alone in language testing programs. That is, "listening" is still frequently perceived to be a perceptual process whereby students are asked to distinguish sounds by making choices between minimal pairs or by taking dictation. Reading is linked to listening in that it is frequently taught and tested as "oral reading." That is, fluent, well-pronounced oral reading is perceived to be evidence of the ability to read.

As viewed at present, listening and reading, like speaking, are acts of communication: in the former, an act of communication between a speaker and a listener; in the latter, between an author and a reader. All these acts of communication require knowledge about speakers or authors and their functional intent, as well as contributions from the listener or reader, in order to make the message comprehensible. As argued above, if this is the view of listening and reading taken in a particular language program, then assessment procedures must consider and thus account for these factors.

A successful assessment mechanism in listening or reading must be integrative in nature; that is, it must be one that examines the extent to which a text actually communicates a coherent message to a reader or listener. Critical in this regard is that comprehension is a constructive construct, not one that is a sum of a number of discrete points. Measuring discrete points provides only a partial reflection of the comprehension process. It is on this point exactly that traditional measures of testing reading and listening comprehension falter. Cloze, for example, fails to measure the integration of material across anything longer than a clause (Shanahan, Kamil & Tobin, 1982). Direct questioning, either open-ended or multiple-choice, inherently implies the answers to the questions. Hence, such questions interact with the understanding of the spoken or written text and in a sense "show the hand" of the tester. Moreover, multiple-choice questions involve years of test development that entail analyses of the choices offered as well as of their passage dependency (Pyrczak & Axelrod, 1976). Even the most integrative of questions reveals its answer and integrates information from a relatively small amount of text (Graesser & Goodman, 1985).

Immediate recall has shown to be an effective and valid integrative measure of comprehension (Bernhardt, 1991; Bernhardt & Berkemeyer, 1988; Bernhardt & James, 1987; Johnston, 1983; Lee, 1986). Recall protocols permit the analysis of the manner in which learners reconstruct messages from text as well as the observation of those components in texts which interfere with understanding. Recall provides a relatively direct view of the process of comprehension. This view is clearly in contrast to discrete measures from which researchers infer integration. The discrete approach to testing requires that the test constructor select given components for observation – components that may or may not be critical for comprehension and that may or may not indicate the students' level of comprehension. The recall procedure is not test-*maker* selective; it allows the test *taker* to select what he or she has comprehended from the text. Recall protocols are then scored by matching the propositions remembered against the total number of propositions in a given text.

Writing

Writing is generally the fourth and final component of any language program. In a traditional view, writing is that activity which taps the ability to use particular grammatical forms. That is, writing is used not as an objective within the language program but merely as an outward manifestation of grammatical competence. A contemporary view, parallel to the other language skills mentioned above, posits that writing is an act of communication whereby an author intends to express some content in a written form with some functional goal in mind. Nunan (1989) comments that the ability to write includes not only mechanical aspects, such as spelling, punctuation, and grammar, but also "organizing content at the level of the paragraph and the complete text to reflect given/new information and topic/content structures; polishing and revising one's initial efforts; selecting an appropriate style for one's audience" (p. 37).

Writing is a rather complicated task; in fact, Nunan notes that it is generally perceived to be the most difficult skill to acquire. He observes that many fluent oral language users are unable to write well. Given the parameters of "writing," it is possible that a language program actually teaches "writing" not as a communicative act but rather as a convenient demonstration mechanism for other competencies. If this is indeed the case, writing per se should not be tested. If in fact writing is taught as a language skill so that students learn to compose written compositions for communicative purposes to reflect on the foreign language literature, for example, then writing should indeed be assessed.

The most appropriate way to assess the writing skill is to assess a written composition. This implies very little in the way of test development. Students are simply asked to write an essay. The most critical feature in test construction is the nature of the topic given. If one topic is assigned and a particular student has a considerable knowledge about that topic, then he or she is able to write more; that is, the test is likely to be measuring content knowledge more than it is measuring writing ability. Parallel to this phenomenon is a student who is assessed in comparison with the above-mentioned student. He or she may have more writing ability in the foreign language than the former student does, but be unable to demonstrate it because of unfamiliarity with the particular topic. In other words, the actual writing ability of either student is not fairly assessed. Hence, topics must be chosen carefully, ensuring that all students have a fair chance at demonstrating their writing ability.

Measuring writing ability can be more problematic than is generally thought. Hughes (1989) distinguishes between analytic and holistic scoring procedures. Analytic procedures entail giving separate scores for grammar, mechanics, vocabulary, and organization. Hughes notes that the major problem with this kind of scoring is that it "may divert attention from the overall effect of the piece of writing" (p. 94). Hughes contrasts the analytic procedure with holistic scoring, a scoring procedure that can be accomplished relatively quickly. Holistic scoring involves awarding a score on the basis of overall impression of the communicative effect of the piece of writing. The fundamental disadvantage of this latter type of scoring is that several raters should be used to award a holistic score that is reliable. Thus, what is saved in time per essay is compounded by the need to have several scorers participate.

Part 2

The task of the second portion of this paper is to bring together the characteristics of good testing programs and the characteristics of good tests into a coherent set of workable suggestions that any language department can follow. This paper takes as its primary thesis that testing itself is an important academic, research-based endeavor and should be treated as such. Hence, any program must submit to the tenets of research in testing and at the same time be responsive to the real world.

Suggestions for Testing

Within the page constraints of a paper, it is impossible to outline a complete set of suggestions for every skill discussed in the previous pages. Rather, the set of suggestions to be outlined will use the assessment of speaking as its example. These suggestions are applicable to each skill because they focus on sets of scores generated by a test.

Table 1 contains the outline of a sample speaking test based on some of the suggestions given in Brown et al. (1984), as mentioned above.

The task is well defined, and the students are told how they will be assessed. The sample test is designed to be used in college foreign lan-

Table 1
Sample Speaking Test

Directions to the student: In this task you are given a sequence of line drawings and asked to tell the story that they illustrate. Your instructor will listen to and record your response. Your grade will depend on your pronunciation, grammar, and fluency, as well as the appropriate use of vocabulary. In your response, be sure to include the following: (1) clear reference to the characters and to where they are and what they are doing; (2) a description of any activities taking place and the proper sequence in which they occur; (3) any changes that take place in the characters or in their locations; (4) any obvious inferences one could make from the drawings. Be aware that attempts to communicate the message of the illustrations are also important. In other words, it is important to relate as much as you can from the pictures even if you make some linguistic mistakes. A total of ____ points are possible – ____ for pronunciation, ____ for grammar, ____ for vocabulary, and ____ for the information provided.

Adapted from G. Brown, A. Anderson, R. Shillcock, and G. Yule, *Teaching Talk Strategies for Production and Assessment* (New York: Cambridge University Press, 1984).

guage classrooms at the intermediate level. It can be used in large or small classes and administered individually or in a group. Grades are given according to criteria specified on a scoring grid, and these grades contribute to the overall assessment profile of each student.

Any assessment procedure should provide instructors with helpful feedback in several areas. Overall student performance on a test can indicate how well students have mastered the material. Instructors can compile a supply of test stimuli and exercises similar to the one suggested here that cover a broad range of student abilities. With such a supply, the instructor can select an instrument at the appropriate ability level for the given sample of students, and even one appropriate for individual students. This flexibility in instrument selection will challenge the better students and enable the weaker students to accomplish tasks at their level.

An examination of individual student response patterns may also provide the instructor with evidence as to how the students are accomplishing the task, that is, how the students are processing its demands. This information should give the instructors and testing specialists some insight into the construct being tested.

The sample test (Table 1) is based for the most part on a norm-referenced model, but aspects of the criterion-referenced model are also included. In the development stages, native speakers are used as a type of norm group, that is, a group that determines mastery criteria for nonnative speakers.

Native speakers are used as a hypothetical reference group when scoring the pronunciation ability of the students. Scorers must assess the degree to which a native speaker would comprehend a student's pronunciation. Not all scorers will themselves be native speakers, and thus will have to assess pronunciation according to their own nonnative ability but with the criterion of native ability in mind. Two interrater reliability measures will need to be established. For the development of the test, a measure will be needed to determine the consistency of the native speakers with regard to their use of the scoring grid. Past experience has shown that reliability coefficients of .95 for these tasks are not uncommon; therefore, tasks where raters cannot reach agreement at the .90 level should not be used.

The actual speaking tests should be recorded and then scored by two instructors/raters. The instructors/raters must be aware of the prescribed scoring procedure so that interrater reliability can be established here too. They should be trained not only in using a scoring grid but in using any rating scale where student ability is assessed. Simply handing teachers a scoring grid without providing them with proper guidance in its use will result in an unreliable evaluation. A speaking task that covers the range of student abilities and is reliably scored will discriminate more accurately and fairly among the test takers on the speaking construct.

If the tests are well developed, administering and scoring should prove relatively easy. The test can easily be given during class or lab hours, so that the instructor can retain a spoken (recorded) sample. Scoring, then, becomes a simple matter of coding the quality and adding up points.

A test such as that in Table 1 is used to help determine the student's grade in the course. Such grades represent specific measures of a skill area at one point in a given curriculum. As such, they must be viewed as one of many contributions to the grade of the student. Although the scoring procedure is determined by reference to the criteria established by the native speakers, the grade will be at least partly established with regard to the student's performance relative to that of others in the course.

Suggestions for Testing Programs

"Seriousness of purpose" was used earlier in this paper to capsulize one of the characteristics of a testing program. To keep testing serious, each language program should have a person whose job it is to write (and rewrite) the tests. In other words, if there is indeed a *program*, each individual instructor should not be quizzing and testing in a free-form style without guidance and responsiveness to the program at large. In addition, individual instructors should not be expected to teach a course according to their own designs but then be forced to administer a test that is not reflective of their teaching.

To shoulder this portion of a language program, the person charged with the responsibility must have some schooling in psychometrics. That is, this person should have basic statistical skills that accommodate data analysis via computer and should be reasonably informed about the theory and practice of psychometrics. This individual should also be capable of performing data analysis via several readily available, PC-based assessment programs. Tables 2-5 illustrate the direction suggested here. After tests across the program are appropriately designed, administered, and scored, scores should be entered into a computer program for systematic analysis. In this manner, data regarding class performance could be submitted for cumulative assessment purposes. The scores of major unit tests could be collated, analyzed, and reported in section meetings. To maintain an esprit de corps, only group data could be reported so that no individual teacher or instructor could be singled out for merit or failure. The purpose of analyzing the program data would be to assess overall effectiveness of the program itself.

Tables 2-5 illustrate the data generated by a hypothetical (and fictitious) foreign language class on a given measure. (The data have no relation to the speaking test used in the previous example.) An examination of these figures indicates just some of the information that an appropriate test analysis computer program offers. Such data could be obtained from discrete measures as well as from more integrative mea-

Table 2
Sample Class Score on a Given Test and on the Subscales

Identification	Score	Culture	Grammar	Vocab.	Reading
Baker, Judy	53	16	13	12	12
Burner, Stacy	34	10	8	8	8
Coaster, Paul	45	8	12	12	13
Fenbert, Jim	47	11	13	10	13
Hairston, Beth	26	10	5	6	5
Jordan, Michelle	50	11	14	10	15
Richards, Sue	50	13	13	10	14
Smith, Elmer	28	9	8	6	5
Smith, Tom	39	10	11	8	10
Wilson, Mike	45	14	11	8	12
TOTAL SCORE	62	16	17	14	15

Table 3
Sample Printout of Combining Scores, Either
from Subscales or from Total Test Scores

Identification	Grammar	Vocab.	Vocgramm
Baker, Judy	13	12	2
Burner, Stacy	8	8	-1
Coaster, Paul	12	12	2
Fenbert, Jim	13	10	1
Hairston, Beth	5	6	-3
Jordan, Michelle	14	10	2
Richards, Sue	13	10	1
Smith, Elmer	8	6	-2
Smith, Tom	11	8	0

sures, such as the protocol. (The printouts come from the Test and Question Answer Scan [TQAS] program, Small Systems Associates.) The program gives the total test score and breaks this down into subscales, providing total scores for the subscales as well (Table 2). Should the instructor wish to combine scores either from subscales or from any testing (Table 3), the program allows this option and standardizes the scores to any scale specified, thereby enabling broad comparisons across classes. Table 4 shows a diagnostic report for an individual student, Judy Baker. Such reports can be especially helpful in illustrating the weaknesses the student may have. Summary statistics (Table 5) are available; they give reliability estimates for the total test as well as for the different subscales.

Accordingly, each instructor can be informed as to class performance. Further, each instructor can be provided with learner profiles, which specify individual test performance by item as well as predicted performance. Many computer programs also accommodate the development of individual student profiles. Students should be given printouts of their profiles at least twice a term. These profiles should include all quiz and major unit tests. In other words, the profiles can focus on all language skills assessed, as well as on any cultural material included in the goals of the language program.

Programs such as this offer many functions and are uncomplicated to use. One additional function deserving mention is the detailed item analysis, a useful and necessary function that enables the supervisor to construct better instruments and even to build an item pool for future use. It is the responsibility of the test supervisor to implement such

Table 4
Sample Diagnostic Report for a Student (Baker, Judy)

Subscale	No. of Items	No. Correct	Percent Correct
Culture	16	16	100
Grammar	17	13	76
Vocabulary	14	12	86
Reading	15	12	80
TOTAL TEST	62	53	85

Item No.	Subscale (if any)	Your Answer	Correct Answer
6	Reading	C	B
7	Vocab	D	B
17	Grammar	C	A
43	Vocab	C	A
44	Grammar	B	E
47	Grammar	B	A
52	Grammar	A	B
61	Reading	B	C
62	Reading	D	C

Note: Incorrect items are listed along with the subscale to which they belong.

Table 5
Summary Statistics of the Total Test and for Each Subscale

	Culture	Grammar	Vocab.	Reading	Total
No. of Items	16	17	14	15	62
Means	11.200	10.800	9.000	10.700	41.700
Standard Devs.	2.440	2.898	2.160	3.592	9.522
Standard Errors	0.772	0.917	0.683	1.136	3.011
Minimum Scores	8.000	5.000	6.000	5.000	26.000
Maximum Scores	16.000	14.000	12.000	15.000	53.000
Reliabilities	0.665	0.691	0.514	0.848	0.901

technology and to instruct the teachers on how to take advantage of it so as to facilitate record keeping and evaluate the testing program. The one obvious caveat is that technology alone will not create a better testing program; it is but one facet of a well-conceived and honest program.

Depending on the size of a department, it may or may not be feasible to have just one individual in charge of testing. In this case, all staff members should be trained in computer skills for testing purposes. If all staff have access to a computer for data input and analysis, they can conduct their own class analyses as well as individual learner profiles. The language program director should be privy to all class analyses and student profiles for discussion purposes with the staff members.

Conclusion

A testing program must be characterized by honesty and integrity. Honesty means that students are assessed according to the objectives of the language program; integrity means that the tests are valid assessments of what they purport to measure. Both of these features of testing programs can come about if a language department invests monetary and human resources into the development and maintenance of such a program. Without such an investment, a testing program does not exist. What does exist is a set of trials for students to survive.

Works Cited

American Psychological Association. *Standards for Educational and Psychological Testing*. Washington, DC: American Psychological Association, 1985.

Bernhardt, E. B. *Reading Development in a Second Language*. Norwood, NJ: Ablex, 1991.

_____ & V. B. Berkemeyer. "Authentic Tests and the High School German Learner." *Die Unterrichtspraxis* 21 (1988): 6-28.

_____ & C. J. James. "The Teaching and Testing of Comprehension in Foreign Language Learning." *Proficiency, Policy, and Professionalism in Foreign Language Education*. Ed. D. W. Birckbichler. Lincolnwood, IL: National Textbook Company, 1987: 65-81.

Brown, G., A. Anderson, R. Shillcock & G. Yule. *Teaching Talk: Strategies for Production and Assessment*. New York: Cambridge University Press, 1984.

Graesser, A. C. & S. M. Goodman. "Implicit Knowledge, Question Answering, and the Representation of Expository Text." *Understanding Expository Text*. Ed. B. Britton & J. B. Black. Hillsdale, NJ: Lawrence Erlbaum, 1985.

Hughes, A. *Testing for Language Teachers*. New York: Cambridge University Press, 1989.

Johnston, P. H. *Reading Comprehension Assessment: A Cognitive Basis*. Newark, DE: International Reading Association, 1983.

Lee, J. F. "Background Knowledge and L2 Reading." *Modern Language Journal* 70 (1986): 350-54.

Messick, S. "The Once and Future Issues of Validity: Assessing the Meaning and Consequences of Measurement." *Testing Validity*. Ed. H. Wainer & H. S. Braun. Hillsdale, NJ: Lawrence Erlbaum, 1988: 33-45.

Nunan, D. *Designing Tasks for the Communicative Classroom*. Cambridge: Cambridge University Press, 1989.

Pyrczak, F. & J. Axelrod. "Determining the Passage Dependence of Reading Comprehension Exercises: A Call for Replications." *Journal of Reading* 19 (1976): 279-83.

Shanahan, T., M. Kamil & A. Tobin. "Cloze as a Measure of Intersentential Comprehension." *Reading Research Quarterly* 17 (1982): 229-55.

Webster's Ninth New Collegiate Dictionary. Springfield, MA: Merriam-Webster, 1983: 218.

Two Philosophies of Language Program and Language Testing Design

Hector Hammerly
Simon Fraser University

Two major philosophies of language program design – the holistic approach and what I call the "cumulative mastery" approach – are largely incompatible, as are their testing design correlates. This essay will define and briefly discuss both philosophies and then consider their implications for testing, with examples from oral testing.

Holism versus Cumulative Mastery

The holistic (or global) philosophy holds that a second or foreign language (FL) is best "acquired" as a whole, the way the native language is acquired. Free communication is seen not as an eventual goal but as the essential activity from which grammaticality emerges via negotiation. If there is enough communication, errors will gradually disappear, or so it is claimed. (See, among many others, Krashen & Terrell, 1983; Savignon, 1983; and Swaffar, 1991.) According to this philosophy, FL acquisition in the classroom will be successful if it re-creates the natural communication conditions under which a language is acquired in early childhood or in the field.

For years, communicative syllabi have been opposed to sequential grammatical syllabi (Wilkins, 1976), but I think this is a false dichotomy. A structural sequence can be combined with integration and attention to communication (Hammerly, 1982). I am not aware of any language program in which what is taught one week is no longer important the next. Moreover, there seem to be few FL programs left in which communication is not (at least in theory) a major goal.

The opposite of holism is the philosophy I call cumulative mastery. This is a concept that can be applied to the guided learning of all complex skills. In the FL field, it means teaching and learning a language step by step, bottom-up, while integrating and using (top-down) what is learned, for gradually freer communication, as it is learned, together with everything taught and learned to that point.

Tests based on the holistic philosophy tend to be holistic too, such as the Oral Proficiency Interview (OPI). On the other hand, tests that agree with the cumulative mastery philosophy concentrate on measuring control and meaningful use of what the students have specifically been taught and have had adequate opportunity to study and master. (This measuring is done first in context-free or limited-context formats and gradually in context-richer and eventually free formats.)

The most highly developed pedagogical manifestation of the holistic philosophy – praised as "most successful" by, for example, Krashen (1984) – is the so-called immersion approach (e.g., Lambert & Tucker, 1972; and Swain & Lapkin, [n.d.]). In this approach, students are not taught the FL as such, but the entire curriculum is (initially) in the FL.[1] The results, though ballyhooed for many years as outstanding, have always been poor, even with the original St. Lambert group whose "success" started the whole movement (Spilka, 1976). The pseudo-immersion approach assumes that one can learn an FL quite well in the classroom while doing something else. Approaches based on the holistic philosophy are misguided in putting the communicative cart before the linguistic horse. While very young children who are surrounded by native speakers and are free of linguistic interference succeed in acquiring their native language "simply" by using it, older children and college students in FL classrooms find themselves under radically different conditions: they already know a language, and they have to share the attention of only one native speaker (if that) with 20 or 25 other students.

Thus, it is naive to even try to reproduce in a FL classroom, crowded with older children or young adults, the process of native language acquisition by young children, which is a once-in-a-lifetime event. Second language acquisition in the field is usually quite successful up to about age 12 or 13, but again, the sociolinguistic environment in a German classroom in Cincinnati is very different from that in the city of Bonn. A FL classroom can be neither a playground nor a foreign country.

Since the immersion approach is the most highly developed manifestation of the holistic philosophy, it should also be its litmus test (Hammerly, 1987). Immersion programs are sociopolitically successful. In Canada, parents have high expectations of French immersion and assume these programs will help their children secure good bilingual positions. Demand has been so great that many parents have stood in line all night to register their children in French immersion. Not only that: parents hear their children speak rapidly, and so they assume they are speaking excellent French. The students themselves have high expectations, and most assume they speak very good French – until further studies or work experience brings them face to face with their ungrammaticality, with the fact that what they speak is really "Frenglish."

Linguistically, pseudoimmersion has always been a failure. Much of the research supporting this conclusion is summarized in Hammerly (1989), especially chapter 2. Suffice it to refer here to the results of three studies:

1) Spilka (1976) found that after six and seven years in French immersion, 40 children in the much-praised original St. Lambert experimental groups had one or more grammatical or vocabulary errors in 52% of their spoken sentences during story retelling. Only about 6% of the sentences of francophone children the same age were incorrect. Further, there was no evidence of progress in accuracy among the immersion pupils from grades 1 to 6, and the gap in correctness between them and francophones increased over the years.

2) Pawley (1985) administered Foreign Service Institute interviews to 97 Grade 11 students in early (6,600 hours) and late (3,000 hours) French immersion. The great majority received a rating of 2 or 2+ (on a scale of 0 to 5). In short, it took many years to get a very faulty 2/2+. Compare this to the six months it takes many well-motivated young adults to reach level 3 in speaking in intensive, systematic French or Spanish programs at the Foreign Service Institute and to similar results that can be attained in two or three years in good-quality university language programs.[2]

3) Pellerin and Hammerly (1986) reported on interviews with a small number of French immersion students after 13 years in the program. Although most questions in the interviews were easy, on the average these students had one or more grammatical or lexical errors in 53.8% of their simple sentences.[3] Pseudoimmersion evidently doesn't work. It produces not "functional" – as it is claimed – but dysfunctional bilinguals.[4]

The crucial difference between the holistic and the cumulative mastery philosophies lies in how the development of FL competence is viewed. Holists see the whole system as gradually becoming more and more nativelike, as errors slowly disappear.[5] The problem with this view is that one can communicate successfully in a language classroom (if success consists in just conveying meaning) while speaking quite ungrammatically. Important distinctions in languages like Spanish or French are communicatively redundant and thus not the object of negotiation; for example, one can communicate quite successfully in these and other languages without ever mastering (and only rarely having to negotiate) noun gender. When the ability merely to convey messages is stressed, the incentive to communicate grammatically either doesn't develop or is soon lost.

In contrast, cumulative mastery is based on the view that FL competence can be successfully developed in the classroom only when the language system is built up and integrated cumulatively a small part at a time, through careful teaching. Once part A has been taught and learned, it is used to communicate to the extent that it allows; then part B is taught and learned, followed by the meaningful use of A and B together; then part C is taught and learned, followed by controlled communication using A, B, and C, but no more; and so forth. (Of course, as each part is added the relationship between the parts becomes more complex.) Students are discouraged from using partial systems for global ends, and errors are not allowed to become habitual. At the same time, the range and variety of communication gradually increase.

With a cumulative mastery philosophy, students need frequent diagnostic feedback on how well they have learned what they have been taught and are expected to learn. Thus, tests are essential, at least in their diagnostic function. But before we can discuss the design of oral language tests that foster cumulative mastery, we need to consider briefly two points: the proficiency movement and the relationship between language programs and language testing.

The Proficiency Movement

The proficiency movement (PM) has had a mixed effect on FL teaching. Had the PM strongly emphasized control of specific language structures rather than stressing communication so much, its effect on the profession would have been entirely positive. As it is, many programs have abandoned the unseaworthy ship of grammar-translation only to land on the shores of ungrammatical babble.

By calling a rating of 2 on the 5-level ILR scale "advanced" proficiency, ACTFL has institutionalized as normal the poor results that were reported on a quarter-century ago by Carroll (1967). Thus, an opportunity to inspire the profession to improve its performance was lost. It would have been far better to identify those few programs which were producing level 3s and higher, to determine what made them more successful and to make those characteristics known to the rest of the profession.

The PM has also severely distorted the purpose of proficiency interviews, which are at the heart of the ACTFL ratings. The proficiency interview was initially designed – and is still used, at least by the government (as the ILR interview) – to determine whether a person can function in a job that requires proficiency in an FL, without any reference to an instructional program. To determine the limits of the interviewee's proficiency, interviewers lead interviewees into situations in which they must try to survive linguistically well beyond their control of the language. While this procedure seems desirable to evaluate proficiency for job placement purposes after a language has been learned formally or acquired naturally, a linguistic-survival mentality is unnecessary and indeed linguistically harmful to students within FL programs. It encourages them to try to survive communicatively in interviews – and in general – regardless of grammaticality. The technical difficulties in using such "a very blunt instrument" as the OPI (Meredith, 1990, p. 295) within FL programs might someday be overcome, but the fact that the OPI rewards premature survival skills makes it completely unsuitable for our classrooms.[6]

A high level of proficiency is, of course, the aim of any serious language program; however, the word *proficiency* has become so distorted in its use that I prefer to emphasize the concept and goal of second language competence (*second* being any tongue other than the native language or languages of the student). This is achieved when linguistic competence – structural accuracy, at the core of the model – can be used to communicate (communicative competence) in culturally appropriate ways (cultural competence). (Of course, the PM is a coalition that loosely unites people with very different points of view – those who strongly believe in linguistic accuracy not too comfortably together with those who think that communication is all that matters. And that is the reason the word *proficiency* has lost much of its original meaning, which was strongly oriented toward language structure.) "Teaching for proficiency" à la ACTFL guidelines seems to mean helping students progress from holistic communicative survival in which numerous errors are made, through a long series of holistic stages of communication with fewer and fewer errors, until more or less error-free communication is achieved. This is a fundamentally incorrect view of how to develop a high level of second language competence in the classroom. ILR interview ratings were never meant to be the basis for an instructional sequence or plan. Some improvement will occur despite a holistic emphasis on communicative survival, but students will soon settle for hard-to-remediate "Spanglish," "Frenglish," and so on.

How can communicative fluency and linguistic accuracy be attained? Both can be attained by emphasizing accuracy first, keeping communicative activity under control, and only gradually allowing communication to become freer and more fluent as control of structure expands and by not placing students in the position of making far more errors that can be effectively corrected, and thereby forming poor linguistic habits. The design of tests can support or negate the design of programs, and vice versa. Since students give the impression of directing much effort toward meeting the demands of tests, it is essential that tests match program aims and philosophy at every step.

Tests can contradict the aims of the FL program in a variety of ways. Primary reliance on written tests, for example, negates an oral-emphasis goal, no matter how often this supposed goal is stated. (If the main aim of the program really is to develop oral fluency and accuracy, the listening and speaking skills should always–even at the very advanced level–constitute at least 50% of the course grade.) Fill-the-blank test formats, which allow students to largely ignore even the sentences in which the blanks appear, negate the fact that language occurs in context and should therefore be taught, practiced, used, and tested in the context of, at least, short sentences.

Use of OPIs for a grade–anywhere within or at the end of courses or programs–contradicts the aim of grammaticality, for such interviews virtually guarantee that students will concentrate on surviving communicatively rather than attaining linguistic control. Grammar is no doubt part of the OPI–some might say too much a part of it (Bachman & Savignon, 1986; Kramsch, 1986)–but it is such a general, fuzzy part of the OPI that no specific structures can be mastered by the students in preparation for the interview. Thus, it is bound to be perceived as a holistic communicative evaluation. And, so while OPIs may help make any FL program look impressive, their use within programs makes specific cumulative mastery difficult or impossible to attain.

Two Oral Progress Tests

I will now discuss two other ways of testing the speaking skill, which I believe remains the weakest aspect of language test design, especially in terms of cumulative mastery.

These two types of oral tests are complementary. Both are guided-output tests; that is, they direct the students to produce oral output that makes use of the sounds, structures, or vocabulary the examiner wants to hear. I am referring to laboratory oral tests and progress (not proficiency) interviews. They both focus on the specifics of FL learning, the more objective laboratory test concentrating more on language rules and elements, the more subjective progress interview allowing some expression of personal meaning. (In "objective" items, only one or a few predetermined answers are acceptable; in "subjective" evaluations, student output can be quite varied.) Colleges and universities that have listen/record laboratories can offer laboratory oral tests; all can offer progress interviews.

Laboratory Oral Tests

In laboratory oral tests (see Appendix A for an example), the students (1) listen to simple directions, models, cues, and so on; (2) are given pauses to think after most cues, and (3) record their output during short pauses. In laboratories with remote or teacher-directed student control, only (3) above is recorded onto the student cassette. This means that from a 20-minute speaking test, an approximately 3-minute tape of student answers would have been recorded, one right after the other, in each booth. Trained teaching assistants, with the help of answer keys, can then score the day's speaking test. In larger programs, several versions of each test may be necessary. Thus, mass testing of the speaking skill is possible.

Laboratory oral tests have four sections. Section 1 involves pronunciation. Here students are asked to record their imitation of a series of short phrases they hear, without being told which particular sounds in the phrases will be evaluated. After the second laboratory oral test in the program, the pronunciation section could be replaced by other activities involving close attention to sounds, such as some forms of dictation. Of course, even after pronunciation ceases to be formally tested, students are held to a high standard of pronunciation on all speaking tests.

Section 2 measures control over a sample of the specific grammatical structures that have been taught, practiced, and used meaningfully since the last test. Structures learned earlier can and should be used too, though not tested directly. The grammar section can take the form of correlation, replacement, transformation, or, when necessary, oral translation frames. While the pronunciation section, if any, is best handled without pauses to think, the grammar section requires pauses both to think before responding and, of course, to record the answers. (My many years' experience with this type of test shows that with short sentences these pauses need not be longer than about eight seconds.)

Section 3 measures control of a sample of the vocabulary learned since the last oral test. I have found that visuals are unreliable in eliciting specific lexical items and that oral translation of short, simple sentences (following an FL model) works much better. A short model FL sentence with simple structure is presented auditorily with its native-language equivalent, and the FL sentence provides the structural pattern for the testing exercise that follows. In effect, the native-language sentence that cues each frame simply provides the lexical pointers the student needs to modify the FL sentence lexically.

Consonant with the goal of developing not just linguistic but also communicative competence, laboratory oral tests go beyond "mechanical" context-free output to require the students to generate meaningful (though not perhaps personally meaningful) sentences under guidance. This is done in section 4, which consists of directions for FL dialogue between the student and one or more native speakers on tape. Directions are given in the native language so as not to give away words and structures and are presented in an indirect manner so that they merely indicate what idea is to be expressed and cannot be "translated" word for word. The students have to generate their own sentences in the FL, quickly referring mentally, as needed, to previously learned FL sentences, and so forth. Directions have to be such that the student cannot totally ignore what the native speakers on the tape are saying.

Detailed, diagnostically useful feedback should be provided after laboratory oral tests, including points per section.

Progress Interviews

The second type of speaking test based on cumulative mastery is the progress interview (see Appendix B for an example). This may look like any other interview, but the questions are carefully chosen to evaluate control over specific structures, vocabulary, and situational contexts that have been taught and practiced and should have been mastered since the last oral test. A series of alternate questions must be prepared on each point, to help prevent students from learning through the grapevine what questions are being asked.

As a check against inconsistency, it is better (but not essential) that two trained interviewers conduct progress interviews and add up or average the scores. With skillful interviewers, about five or six minutes per student, plus a minute or so for scoring, are enough. Feedback is essential: once students have been evaluated, they should each be given a chart that points out specific strengths and weaknesses and directs them to sources of remediation.

When facilities and personnel allow it, I have found it best to use both laboratory oral tests and progress interviews within the same school term, since the former deals with specifics and the latter is a little more global. For example, in a regular semester of Spanish as an FL one can give two laboratory tests and one or two interviews, as it is unfair to the students and unconducive to regular study to have just one make-or-break speaking test at the end of the term. I would suggest that no more than about four or five weeks should pass without one or the other type of speaking test being given; by so doing, the students' attention is drawn consistently and continuously to the importance of oral performance.

The weight given to each section of the laboratory test or to each evaluation criterion for the progress interview is also based on the over-all cumulative mastery design. Each aspect of second language competence should be emphasized in testing as it is taught and expected to be learned in the program, with an early focus on linguistic competence gradually shifting to communicative competence, and cultural competence instruction interspersed all along.

Control over sounds is stressed early in a cumulative mastery program. Mastering morphological and syntactic structures is a major concern through the intermediate level (usually the second year in college) and to a lesser extent beyond that level. While vocabulary is learned throughout the program, it would be a mistake to emphasize it early, as such premature lexicalization is linguistically harmful – students whose knowledge of vocabulary exceeds their structural control will still want to use that vocabulary freely, which results in fluent ungrammaticality. Fluency itself should not be given significant weight in oral testing until the advanced or very advanced level, for an early or intermediate focus on fluency is detrimental to linguistic accuracy. (Pseudoimmersion students characteristically speak very rapidly.) "Slow-normal" speed is perfectly acceptable.

A cumulative mastery program must be carefully paced; if it is too fast, students will never quite master anything and will emerge from the program speaking as poor a classroom "pidgin" as those taught with holistic approaches like pseudoimmersion. (And as the language is learned it must be used for communication, or students will emerge, as did many in misguided audiolingual programs, speaking nothing at all.) Most college or university FL programs try to "cover" all of the structure of the language much too quickly – and, as a result, superficially. English-speaking students need at least three, and preferably four, semesters for the once-through-but-thorough cumulative mastery of the structure of languages like Spanish or French. With faster "coverage" there is no mastery, and in the second and third years students require remediation "reviews" instead of being able to build on what they have learned. (Of course, making the language program semi-intensive or intensive reduces its time frame accordingly, enabling students to take courses taught in the language earlier.)

The construct validity of these two types of speaking tests depends on the validity of the cumulative mastery philosophy. Their content validity derives from making sure that only what has been adequately taught, practiced, and meaningfully used is tested; this content will, of course, have to be established separately for programs and materials that follow different content sequences. The reliability of these two types of tests will have to be established through empirical research.

FL program and test design demand much thought and effort. But it is all worth it when one sees – and hears – young people complete a cumulative mastery language program as transitional bilinguals who can speak (and write) the language at level 3, that is, with accuracy (without poor linguistic habits) and with reasonable fluency. From there, they can move beyond the program – by residing in the foreign setting – to become true bilinguals.

Notes

1. I say "so-called immersion" because it isn't immersion at all, as the student is surrounded by 25 other students whose performance in the target language is as poor as his or hers. This is pseudoimmersion. True immersion or, simply, immersion is the situation in which the learner is surrounded by native speakers of the target language. This, depending on the learner's background, level of language training, and age, either can result in a "terminal 2+" or can be very successful. It seems especially successful after a solid foundation in the FL has been established in the student's country.

2. My experience includes teaching Spanish for three years at the Foreign Service Institute and serving as a proficiency interviewer for the last half of that time. I have also taught Spanish at the university level for many years. See also charts in Cleveland et al. (1960).

3. A transcript of these interviews appears in Hammerly (1989).

4. Other relevant studies are Adiv (1980), Gustafson (1983), Hamm (1988), Lister (1987), and Tatto (1983).

5. The assumption seems to be that one can start with many linguistic "holes" (as in Swiss cheese?), gradually fill the holes, and end up with no holes (as in Gouda?). I claim that with this approach many of the linguistic holes will refuse to disappear and the outcome will almost invariably be unappetizing.

6. Why should FL students be encouraged to survive communicatively at the expense of linguistic competence long before they need to engage in real

communication with native speakers? On the other hand, in my opinion the original ILR interview rating scale should be used for hiring (teachers would have to be at least level 4s to be able to bring their students up to level 3), and it would surely prove invaluable for such research purposes as comparing the outcomes of different programs or methods.

Works Cited

Adiv, Ellen. "An Analysis of Second-Language Performance in Two Types of Immersion Programs." *Bulletin of the Canadian Association of Applied Linguistics* 2, ii (1980): 139-52.

Bachman, Lyle F. & Sandra J. Savignon. "The Evaluation of Communicative Language Proficiency: A Critique of the ACTFL Oral Interview." *Modern Language Journal* 70 (1986): 380-90.

Carroll, John B. "Foreign Language Proficiency Levels Attained by Language Majors Near Graduation from College." *Foreign Language Annals* 1 (1967): 131-51.

Cleveland, H., G. J. Mangone & J. C. Adams. *The Overseas Americans*. New York, McGraw-Hill, 1960. (Reproduced in Ringbom, Håkan. *The Role of the First Language in Foreign Language Learning*. Clevedon, Avon, England: Multilingual Matters, 1987: 66-67).

Gustafson, Rosanna L. "A Comparison of Errors in the Spoken French of Grades Two, Four and Six Pupils Enrolled in a French Immersion Program." Unpublished project, Master of Arts – Teaching of French, Simon Fraser University, 1983.

Hamm, Christiane. "The ACTFL Oral Proficiency Interview in a Canadian Context: The French Speaking Proficiency of Two Groups of Ontario High-School Graduates." *Foreign Language Annals* 21 (1988): 561-67.

Hammerly, Hector. *French Immersion: Myths and Reality: A Better Classroom Road to Bilingualism*. Calgary, Alberta: Detselig, 1989.

_____. "The Immersion Approach: Litmus Test of Second Language Acquisition Through Classroom Communication." *Modern Language Journal* 71 (1987): 395-401.

_____. *Synthesis in Second Language Teaching: An Introduction to Linguistics*. Blaine, WA: Second Language Publications, 1982.

Kramsch, Claire. "From Language Proficiency to Interactional Competence." *Modern Language Journal* 70 (1986): 366-72.

Krashen, Stephen D. "Immersion: Why It Works and What It Has Taught Us." Ed. H. H. Stern. *The French Immersion Phenomenon*, Special Issue No. 12 (1984) of *Language and Society*: 61-64.

_____ & Tracy C. Terrell. *The Natural Approach: Language Acquisition in the Classroom*. Oxford: Pergamon Press/Alemany Press, 1983.

Lambert, Wallace E. & G. Richard Tucker. *Bilingual Education of Children: The St. Lambert Experiment*. Rowley, MA: Newbury House, 1972.

Lister, Roy. "Speaking Immersion." *Canadian Modern Language Review* 43 (1987): 701-17.

Meredith, R. Alan. "The Oral Proficiency Interview in Real Life: Sharpening the Scale." *Modern Language Journal* 74 (1990): 288-96.

Pawley, Catherine. "How Bilingual Are French Immersion Students?" *Canadian Modern Language Review* 41 (1985): 865-76.

Pellerin, Micheline & Hector Hammerly. "L'expression orale après treize ans d'immersion française." *Canadian Modern Language Review* 42 (1986): 592-606.

Savignon, Sandra J. *Communicative Competence: Theory and Classroom Practice.* Reading, MA: Addison-Wesley, 1983.

Spilka, Irène V. "Assessment of Second language Performance in Immersion Programs." *Canadian Modern Language Review* 32 (1976): 543-61.

Swaffar, Janet. "Articulating Learning in High School and College Programs: Holistic Theory in the Foreign Language Curriculum." *Challenges in the 1990s for College Foreign Language Programs: Issues in Language Program Direction.* Ed. Sally Sieloff Magnan. Boston, MA: Heinle & Heinle Publishers, 1991: 27-54.

Swain, Merrill & Sharon Lapkin. *Evaluating Bilingual Education: A Canadian Case Study.* Clevedon, Avon (England): Multilingual Matters, n.d. [1983?].

Tatto, Mabel A. "A Comparative Analysis of Grammatical Errors in the Written Code Between Grade Eleven Immersion French and Grade Eleven Core French." Unpublished project, Master of Arts – Teaching of French, Simon Fraser University, 1983.

Wilkins, D. A. *Notional Syllabuses.* London: Oxford University Press, 1976.

Appendix A
Sample Laboratory Oral Test after About
120 Hours of College Spanish

Note: Comments to readers of this article appear between brackets. What the student is expected to say appears between slashes. Specific items being scored are underlined. What the student hears appears in quotation marks. The student does not read anything.

[This speaking test would be preceded by a listening comprehension test and followed by a short, simple reading comprehension test, all within 50 minutes.

This type of test, except to some extent for section 4, makes no pretense of being communicative. Its exercises frankly and openly measure oral control over rules and elements of structure in sentence context. Making such a test "more communicative" would destroy its effectiveness in efficiently and objectively evaluating language specifics.]

"SPEAKING TEST AFTER UNIT __."

"Section 1: Pronunciation."
[By this point – 120 hours of instruction – there would be no pronunciation section but perhaps some form of dictation. Thus, this is a sample of the format the pronunciation section in early tests would have.]
   "After you hear each phrase twice, record once your imitation of it." [Given the possibility of extraneous noise, each item throughout a laboratory oral test should be presented twice. As several responses would greatly complicate scoring, only one – the first, if several are given – is scored; students are informed to that effect.]

   [1.] *"¿Qué bora es?"* / *¿Qué bora es?*/   0 1 2
   [2.] *"=/No sé, Manuel.*/   0 1 2
   [3.] *"=/¿Por qué no miras el reloj?*/   0 1 2
   [4.] *"=/Está parado.*/   0 1 2
   [5.] *"=/Preguntémoselo a Paco.*/   0 1 2
   Pronunciation Total   /10

   [Ten likely pronunciation trouble spots have been identified in advance and should each be scored on a 0/1 basis – 1 if the sound is pronounced the way a native Spanish speaker would pronounce it, 0 if it isn't. (As there are two trouble spots per phrase, up to 2 points per phrase are possible.) Trying to establish various degrees of pronunciation acceptability for each sound makes the scoring task so slow that it becomes onerous and unmanageable. For the benefit of assistant scorers with limited experience, the answer key should list the most likely substitutions. There need not be a meaningful relationship between the phrases.]

"Section 2: Grammar."

[In the last 20 hours, the following grammatical structures, among others, have been studied: periphrastic future (*ir* + *a* + infinitive), morphology and usage of the two past indicative tenses (preterite and imperfect), and positive and negative constructions using commands and object pronouns.]
   "In the following exercises, listen carefully to the instructions and examples; think – don't speak – during the pauses provided for you to think, and record each answer only once when asked to record."

"Exercise 1: Future Construction."
"Change the following sentences from the present tense to the future construction:"
   [The periphrastic future might not be communicatively derived from the present indicative, but all that is being determined here is whether

the students can form it. Any tense the students have already mastered would do in the cue sentences, as long as the infinitive is not given to them, for this would make it too easy. The examinees should have to produce the infinitive, as well as the rest of the construction, in their minds.]

"Example: You hear: *Tenemos un examen.* [2] Think; don't speak yet. [Short pause.] You would change it to (record): [short pause] *Vamos a tener un examen.*"

"Now the exercise begins."

"1. *Pepe conversa con ella.*" [2]

[Pause to think.]

"Now record." [Pause.] [Same instructions throughout.]

/Pepe *va a conversar* con ella./   0   1

(Etc.)

[Scoring: the underlined part of each sentence must be correct for the student to get any credit. A full point is given when the whole sentence is correct; a half-point, if there are one or more grammatical or lexical errors or omissions outside the underlined part.]

"Exercise 2: Preterite."

"Change the following sentences to the preterite."

[Examples, cues, and pauses as above to produce five test sentences such as these:]

"1. *No venden los muebles.*"

/No *vendieron* los muebles./   0   1

(Etc.)

"Exercise 3: Commands."

"Change the following sentences into commands, substituting pronouns for nouns."

[Examples, cues, and pauses as above to produce five sentences such as:]

"1. *Ud. quiere dejar el auto.*"

/*Déjelo* (Ud.)/   0   1

(Etc.)

"Section 3: Vocabulary."

[All of the grammatical structures used in the vocabulary exercises are thoroughly known to the students. Only their ability to produce some of the most recently learned lexical items is being tested.]

"Translate the following sentences, using as a model the structure of the latest Spanish sentence you hear."

"Example: Repeat: *Vamos a leer un libro.* This means: We're going to read a book. [2] Now translate: We're going to buy a record player."

[Pause to think.] "You would say: [pause to respond] *Vamos a comprar un tocadiscos.*" [Note that the correct answer in Spanish is given as the model for the next sentence.]

"Exercise 1."
"Repeat: *Acaba de salir.*" /*Acaba de salir.*/
   "She's just left. *Acaba de salir.*" [2]
   [1.] "Now translate: He's just lied again." [2]
   [Pause to think.] Record."
   /*Acaba de <u>mentir</u> otra vez.*/   0   1
   "Repeat: *Acaba de mentir otra vez.*"
   (Etc.)

"Exercise 2."
[Directions, etc., as in exercise 1 above. Model sentence: *¡Qué viaje tan lindo!* = What a beautiful trip!]
   "*¡Qué viaje tan lindo!*"
   [1.] "What an expensive gift!"
   /*¡Qué <u>regalo</u> tan <u>caro</u>!*/   0   1   2
   (Etc.)

"Section 4: Dialogue"
[This dialogue calls on the students to use meaningfully, in an integrated manner, what they have learned so far, with emphasis on the past tenses.]
   "In this part you will participate in a guided conversation with *los señores Iglesias,* whose voices are on tape. Follow the usual directions for pauses to think and to record."
   (*Sr. Iglesias:*) "...*y, ¿qué le parece San Antonio?*"
   "Answer that you like it very much; add that you especially like the parks, the restaurants, and the Spanish colonial buildings." [2] [Fairly long pause to think.]
   "Record." [Pause to record; about 12-15 seconds are needed to record a rather long sentence like this one.]
   /*Me gusta mucho; especialmente me gustan los parques, los restaurantes, y los edificios coloniales.*/   0 1 2 3
   (*Sra. Iglesias:*) "*Dígame . . . ¿es usted del este de los Estados Unidos?*"
   "Answer that you're from Wisconsin. Add that when you were a child you lived in the country."
   /*Soy de Wisconsin. Cuando era niño(a) vivía en el campo.*/
                                            0 1 2 3
   "But add that you were a little bored and tired of the cold."
   /*Pero estaba un poco aburrido(a) y cansado(a) del frío.*/

0 1 2 3

"So explain that when there was an opportunity for a good job, you came here."

/(Así que, De modo que) cuando hubo (una) oportunidad de un buen empleo (trabajo), (me) vine aquí./   0 1 2 3

(Sr. Iglesias:) "Y, ¿de dónde cree que es mi esposa?"

"Say you think she's Chilean, but you're not sure."

/Creo que es chilena, pero no estoy seguro(a)./   0 1 2 3

/15

[Scoring is 3 points for a complete sentence without errors or omissions; 2 points if it has 1 error; 1 point if it has 2 or 3 errors; and 0 points for more than 3 errors or no response. Alternate forms considered correct in educated standard Spanish are accepted.]

Test Totals
Listening Comprehension:___ /30
Speaking ability:
  Pronunciation:___ /10
  Grammar:___ /15
  Vocabulary:___ /10
  Dialogue:___ /15
  Subtotal:___ = ___ /50
Reading comprehension: /20
Overall test total:___ /100

Other, shorter tests involving listening and reading comprehension and simple written tasks can be administered between the longer tests and/or interviews that emphasize speaking ability.

Appendix B
Sample Progress Interview after About
120 Hours of College Spanish

By carefully selecting questions in advance and improvising a little, interviewers can get students to use those grammatical structures whose control needs to be evaluated (because they have recently been taught, practiced, etc.) at each point in the program. This plan doesn't always work, however, for unlike the directed dialogue just discussed, the more open-ended questions of an interview give students a chance to display their keen ingenuity for talking around the structures they should have mastered but have not. After seeking to put the student at ease in English, if necessary, the interviewers would ask a total of five or six questions of the sort exemplified below, plus a few short follow-up questions as needed. (Four or five alternative questions for each of the questions listed would be used with different students.)

(1. *Gustar, parecer, and present tense in general*:)
"*¿Le gusta más el campo o la ciudad?*"
(Follow up:) "*¿Por qué?*"
(2. *Commands*:)
"*Deme instrucciones en cuanto a qué hacer:*"
"*Tengo hambre. ¿Qué hago?*"
[E.g., /*Vaya a la cafetería*, etc./.]
(Follow up:) "*Y entonces, ¿qué hago?*"
(3. *Periphrastic Future*:)
"*¿Qué va a hacer Ud. el fin de semana?*"
(Follow up/expansion:) "*¿Y sus amigos/amigas?*"
(Follow up:) "*¿Y entonces?*"
(4. *Preterite and Imperfect*:)
"*Díganos qué hizo, etc., esta mañana desde que salió de su casa hasta que llegó aquí.*"

(Be sure to follow up with questions that require the student to shift tense aspect, such as "*¿Qué pasó entonces?*" "*¿Cómo era(n)?*" "*Y entonces, ¿qué hizo?*" "*¿Puede describirlo/la?*")

[5. A topical question for a longer answer could also be asked.]

While the above interview is in progress, the two interviewers should each be marking a criteria sheet cum structure list such as the one illustrated below. The students know quite well that they are being tested; still, it helps them if these sheets are not filled out in full view (the sheets can be kept, for instance, inside the covers of large books). At the end of the interview, each interviewer should have decided on one point for each criterion line and an indication (e.g., numbers or check marks, agreed on in advance) of which of the structures on the list the student needs to work on further.

Sample Progress Interview Evaluation Sheet

Course: SPAN 101 (second semester)

Name:						Date:
Comprehension	0	2	4 / 6	8	10: ___	
Pronunciation	0	2	4 / 6	8	10: ___	
Grammar	0	5	10 / 15	20	25: ___	
Vocabulary	0	2	4 / 6	8	10: ___	
Fluency	0	1	2 / 3	4	5: ___	

Subtotal 1: ___/60
Subtotal 2: ___/60
  Total: ___/120

Structure Checklist	Comments and/or Examples

Present, irregular forms
– – – – –, usage
Gender/number agreement
........(Etc.)........
Imperfect, forms
Preterite, regular forms
– – – – –, irregular forms
Imperfect and preterite, usage

(Only the structures emphasized since the last oral test or progress interview and those which tend to present ongoing difficulties need be listed.)

The criteria given above would be weighted differently at different points in the program, in accordance with the program's teaching philosophy. Students should be informed in advance of what the various criteria are and how they will be weighted.

Each question should not be asked more than twice at a slow speed within normal range. Of course, if a student doesn't understand a question, he or she fails that portion of the interview. Other than that, comprehension need not be emphasized within progress interviews provided that it is measured often and in other ways, that is, via listening and reading comprehension activities and tests.

The Development of a Foreign Language Placement System at the University of Iowa

Irene Wherritt, Cynthia Druva-Roush, and Joyce E. Moore
The University of Iowa

In keeping with the national concern for language testing, the University of Iowa (U of I) established the Foreign Language Assessment Project (FLAP) in 1988. The present report relates recent efforts to establish a new process for assessing the language abilities of incoming freshmen at the U of I. First, background information will be given about the way FLAP fits into national testing activities and agendas and about the goals, accomplishments, and future directions of the project. Then, four issues will be addressed:

1) What is the quality of the placement test for incoming freshmen?
2) Is the test the best predictor of success in foreign language study?
3) What other factors are important in predicting success in foreign language study?
4) Is an incentive program effective in encouraging advanced-level students who have satisfied the language requirement to continue language study?

Background

In the 1980s, much attention was given to the development and implications of the American Council on the Teaching of Foreign Languages (ACTFL) proficiency guidelines and the Oral Proficiency Interview (OPI). Many authors have since concluded that the guidelines and the OPI, although helpful as a first step, have oversimplified the process of assessing language abilities (Bachman & Clark, 1987; Lantolf & Frawley, 1985; Shohamy, 1990).

Also during the 1980s, several institutions and organizations began developing alternatives to the OPI. To date, universities that have published articles on their assessment instruments include Brigham Young University (Larson, 1989), the University of Iowa (Wherritt, Cleary & Druva-Roush, 1990), the University of Minnesota (Barnes, Klee & Wakefield, 1990; Lange, 1987), the University of South Carolina (Mosher, 1989), and the University of Texas at El Paso (Teschner, 1990). In addition, the Center for Applied Linguistics has developed Simulated Oral Proficiency Interviews in Chinese, Portuguese, Hausa, Hebrew, and Indonesian. The Educational Testing Service has developed a listening and reading comprehension test in Japanese and Russian (Stansfield, 1990). The expense of such endeavors in both money and time has prohibited any of these projects from following through on a large scale to serve other institutions. Exceptions include the BYU computer-adaptive test, S-CAPE, which has been marketed nationally, and the U of I Spanish test, which has been sold to other institutions.

At the national level, however, little coordination for testing exists and funding for research on test development has been scarce (Stansfield, 1990). The broadest forum for language testing continues to be the Language Testing Research Colloquium, held each year prior to the annual Teaching English to Speakers of Other Languages convention. This colloquium, while useful to researchers of second language testing, has always emphasized English as a Second Language. To date, the main forums for foreign language testing have been journal articles and general conference sessions.

In recent issues of *Foreign Language Annals* the topics of testing and articulation have been discussed as a national priority for the 1990s. For example, Byrnes (1990) argues that articulation between high school and college will increasingly deal with students of higher language ability or at least students who have had longer exposure to foreign languages. Differences may also be greater in the language abilities of students because of the growing but incomplete implementation of new programs. Regarding false beginners, Byrnes states, "The practice of placing students with extensive previous instruction into beginners' classes . . . is not only devastating from the standpoint of learner motivation and, thus, educationally totally unsound, it is ultimately fiscally irresponsible" (p. 289). Stansfield (1990, p. 395) emphasizes the critical need to develop usable language tests now. Henning (1990, p. 379) stresses the importance of going beyond simple test validity: he says we cannot just ask, Is this test valid? but rather What is this test valid for? Shohamy (1990, p. 387), in discussing the limits of the OPI, asserts that tests must be based on a broader and more expanded view of the area they are testing.

The Foreign Language Assessment Project (FLAP)

FLAP is funded by the U of I Center for International and Comparative Studies, the Evaluation and Examination Service, and the College of Liberal Arts. The goals of the project are to improve articulation in foreign languages between high schools and the university and to develop outcome measures for (1) exiting from the language requirement, (2) the language major itself, and (3) teacher certification. To date, because of the large enrollments in first- and second-year level classes, program activity has focused on placing incoming freshmen.

As a beginning assessment, in the first year of the project a survey (Wherritt & Cleary, 1990) was conducted at post-secondary institutions to determine placement practices in Spanish language. Spanish was chosen because it has the largest enrollments at both the secondary and the college levels of study. The survey revealed that foreign language placement testing procedures are neither systematic nor satisfactory for most institutions.

During the first two years of the project, a Spanish-language placement test was developed and field-tested (Wherritt, Cleary & Druva-Roush, 1990). Since that time, similar tests have been developed in French and German. In this report, emphasis will be placed on the quality of the Spanish exam and the tracking of students enrolled in an incentive program.

As another step toward improved articulation between study at the high school level and that at the college level, FLAP has sponsored annual workshops for high school and college teachers and has participated in conferences and workshops throughout the state and nation. As a follow-up to test development, FLAP sent to each secondary school district in the state copies of public test forms, accompanied by a letter explaining the university's new language requirements and procedures and inviting inquiries about the new incentive program. High school teachers were given permission to photocopy the tests for use with their students. Future plans include assessment at higher levels of language study and testing for lesser-taught languages.

Quality of Placement Test: Reliability and Validity

The Spanish, German, and French tests are machine-scoreable and can be administered in a 50-minute period. Most freshmen (approximately 90%) take the test during summer orientation. Test results are available at the advising center about two hours after administration.

Although the tests are limited to machine scoring and a 50-minute administration, they do attempt to meet Shohamy's (1990, p. 387) desire for a broad-based test. The Spanish FLAP test has 6 sections and includes 7 item types for a total of approximately 40 items. For writing, a 25-word, tape-recorded dictation is used as a warm-up; in the Spanish field trials, these dictations correlated favorably (r = .60) with the over-all test scores. Simulated authentic tape-recorded listening comprehension items include dialogues, radio advertisements, and announcements in public places (approximately 30% of the test). Grammar items are contextualized in a modified cloze multiple-choice reading passage (approximately 20%). Reading comprehension items include simulated authentic newspaper, magazine, or general informational reading with items of global comprehension in English (approximately 18%) and modified cloze passages in which all five foils fit into the individual sentence, but only one fits into the meaning of the entire passage (approximately 18%). The test ends with a drawing or diagram in which multiple-choice items appear in the target language (approximately 14%). Five hundred items are stored in an item bank and can be retrieved randomly for the creation of new tests.

The Spanish FLAP test was administered to 1,203 entering freshmen during summer orientation in 1990. The average difficulty of 46.15 reflects a moderately difficult test; on the average, only 46% of the examinees got any single item correct. The average item discrimination is .37 (anything above .40 is high). This figure indicates whether the students who got the item correct also tended to receive a higher score on the test as a whole. The higher the index, the more discriminating the item. The KR-20 reliability coefficient of .84 indicates that the items correlate quite well with one another. The score distribution for the Spanish FLAP test is shown in Table 1.

Of those individuals administered the test, the largest percentage placed into a third-semester course. The average number of years of Spanish study among all students taking the test was 2.72, which verifies

Table 1
**Distribution of Spanish FLAP Test Scores
for Fall 1990 Entering Freshmen**

Placement Level	Number	Percent
First semester	1	.08
Second semester	138	11.47
Third semester	481	39.98
Fourth semester	293	24.36
Fifth semester	290	24.11
TOTAL	1203	100.00

the reasonableness of the suggested entrance guide that one year of high school study is roughly equivalent to one semester of university study.

The criterion validity, or how well performance on the test predicts performance in the class, was examined initially in the spring of 1989 using intact Spanish classes at the U of I. Course grades were chosen as the criterion. These grades are calculated using 50% oral comprehension and production, 25% reading comprehension, and 25% vocabulary and grammar. The test was administered near the end of the semester so that the results would reflect the abilities of individuals who had completed each semester of instruction. A clear positive relationship between test scores and grades existed among this set of data. The correlations ranged from .62 to .66 from the end of the first semester through the end of the fourth semester. Individuals doing less well in the course scored lower on the test.

Prediction of Performance of Incoming Students

A loss function for each course was created to establish cut scores for placement into the first four semesters of Spanish taught at the U of I. A loss function is an analysis of the possible errors to be made by setting a cut score at a specific level. Four cut scores were statistically determined, three for placement into three higher-level courses and one for exemption from the language requirement. Success was defined as receiving at least a C+ in a course; failure, as receiving a C or lower. Two types of errors were counted for the loss function: either (1) predicting failure for individuals who in fact succeeded in the course (false negative) or (2) predicting success for individuals who in fact failed (false positive). To set a cut score, one looks for that score for which the sum of the two types of error is minimized.

For the spring-1989 semester students, the loss function minimum was a score of 53 for the end of the fourth semester. This score can be used for exemption. For placement into the fourth semester, the loss function minimum for the end of the third semester was in the range of 42 to 46. The end of the second semester reached a minimum at 39; the end of first semester at 30.

A similar analysis was performed for those entering freshmen who had taken the Spanish FLAP test during summer orientation in 1990 (n = 529). Only those entering freshmen who had both a Spanish FLAP score and a final grade in a Spanish course during the fall 1990 semester were included in the analysis. The cutoff scores for three out of the four courses were validated by these data. The loss function for first-semester students was minimized at a score of 30; for third semester students, a score of 45; and for fourth semester students, a score of 53. Verification of the cutoff scores for the second-semester course proved more problematic. The loss function was minimized at the much higher score of 51. Only those students who had a higher FLAP placement score succeeded with a C+ or above.

The loss function approach was not effective because a majority of the entering students did not succeed (with a C+ or above) in the second-semester class. A cross-tabulation was performed between number of years of high school Spanish study and placement score. The results indicated that of those students who had completed between two and three years of study, who placed at a third- or fourth-semester level but who took the second-semester course, 50% did not succeed with a C+ or above. A cross-tabulation of a student's year by success or failure in the course indicated a strong relationship (chi squared = 19.98, df = 3, p <.01). These data indicate that a much larger proportion of freshmen is not succeeding in the course, and a much larger number of sophomores is succeeding. Whether or not students took their first semester of Spanish at the U of I is a better predictor of how well they will do in second-semester Spanish than either the number of years of Spanish taken in high school or how well students do on the Spanish placement test.

Problems in Prediction of Success

Generally, the instruments developed to date by FLAP have succeeded in assisting advisers in the appropriate placement of students. Some unanswered questions about prediction of success are discussed here to demonstrate the complexity of test development for several languages at a large university.

Spanish

Although a strong correlation exists (.62 - .66) between placement test results and course grades for intact classes, the correlations between placement test scores and course grades for entering freshmen is much lower (.05 - .46). This low correlation may result from a restriction of range, since 63% of those individuals taking the Spanish FLAP test during freshmen orientation fail to take a course during the fall semester. When a stepwise multiple regression was performed using high school background, university admission scores, and FLAP scores, overall high school grade point average was the strongest predictor of course grade. The FLAP placement test score and number of years of high school Spanish did not enter into the prediction equation. For purposes of adequate placement, a decision rule involving more variables than the FLAP score may have to be developed.

French

A French FLAP test was constructed and piloted in both the fall 1989 and the spring 1990 semesters. Four forms were administered. The overall test statistics were excellent. The test difficulties ranged from 56.68 to 69.29, test item discrimination from .28 to .36, and internal consistency from .73 to .85. An attempt to set cut scores using the loss function approach employed for Spanish, however, proved unsuccessful. Although the cut scores for the first three semester courses were clearly set, the cut score for the fourth semester fell far below the cut scores for the first three semesters. An attempt to rescore using only those items which discriminated well between first- and second-year students (that is, second-year students on the average were more likely to get the item right than first-year students) also proved unsuccessful. New items were written during the fall 1990 semester, five forms constructed, and the test administered to all of the first five semester classes in French. On the average, the tests were more difficult (45.96-53.06), with approximately the same level of internal consistency (.73-.84). This set of data resulted in a cleaner cut score for fourth-semester French, although falling very close to the third-semester cutoff. An examination of the course grades for fourth semester French indicates that almost all students receive a C+ or above in this course. A loss function approach to setting cut scores based on finding the score where prediction error is minimized is ineffective when one type of error (false negative) is nonexistent. Unless another measure of course proficiency can be found, this problem will continue to exist.

German

Five forms of a German FLAP test were developed during the spring 1990 semester. Cut scores were set and the test administered to fall 1990 entering freshmen (n = 175). The test difficulty was 67.74, with an average item discrimination of .26 and an internal consistency index of .76. The test appears to be doing very well at placement. Individuals placed into courses by the FLAP German test (54 entering freshmen taking the FLAP German test also took a German course during the fall semester) are succeeding in the course with a C+ or above. The curriculum is currently under revision, and the next research question will be whether a new test must be written to reflect curricular changes.

Foreign Language Incentive Program (FLIP)

Two important parts of developing a comprehensive foreign language assessment program concern addressing the issue of false beginners and communicating to high school students the need for language study prior to college enrollment. Toward these ends several steps have been taken at the U of I: (1) a foreign language admissions policy was established for entering students; (2) a Foreign Language Incentive Program (FLIP) was developed; and (3) intensive review courses have been created to eliminate false beginners from the regular first-semester courses.

Foreign Language Admissions Policy

A foreign language admissions policy that requires all incoming students to have completed two years of study of the same foreign language in high school was put into effect in the fall 1990 semester. In addition to the admissions policy, the university has a four-semester graduation requirement that students can satisfy by completing the fourth-year level of a foreign language in high school, by completing the fourth-semester level of college language, by completing a combination of high school and college study, or by obtaining an exemption-level score on a FLAP test. Freshmen are required to take a FLAP test if they have studied French, German, or Spanish in high school. Students who have completed four years of a single foreign language in high school are exempt from this requirement unless they wish to participate in the incentive program. The admission policy sends a message to students about the importance of foreign language study prior to enrolling in the university and, in combination with the graduation requirement, encourages students to complete four years of high school study. The FLAP committee and the Office of Admissions have spent considerable time communicating foreign language policy changes to high school teachers.

Foreign Language Incentive Program

FLIP has both incentive and penalty components. The incentive program provides that students who place into a fourth-semester language course and earn at least a B- receive credit for the prerequisite third-semester course. Students who place into a course at the fifth-semester level or higher and receive at least B- receive credit for both the prerequisite third- and fourth-semester courses. Incentive credit is ungraded but counts toward the hours required for graduation. The incentive program, put into effect for the fall 1990 semester in conjunction with the admissions policy, is available to all entering students.

Intensive Review Course

After the incentive program was created, a policy to prohibit false beginners from entering normal sequenced language classes was proposed. This policy allows students who place at the second-semester level or higher to continue study in the same language for full credit or to begin study of a different language for full credit. Students placing below the second-semester level who opt to continue study in the same language are required to complete an intensive review course for less credit than would be received in the normal sequence. Registration for normal sequenced classes is blocked electronically for students who place below the second-semester level of language studied in high school. The intensive review requirement is still under development, with a projected implementation date of fall 1992.

This gradual approach to adopting more stringent policies will allow for incoming students, language departments, and high schools to accommodate to the new requirements. It is hoped that the combination of incentive credit for advanced study, with penalties for false beginners, will provide an impetus for higher enrollments in advanced courses, study beyond the two-year requirement, and a decrease in the numbers of students in beginning-level university courses.

Fall 1990-Semester Foreign Language Incentive Program (FLIP)

This section of the paper looks at what happened to the first group of students enrolling for incentive credit at the U of I and the impact FLIP has had on enrollment patterns.

Table 2
Students Registered for and Receiving Incentive Credit

	Registered/ Total	Grade > B-	Grade < B-	Missing Data
French	51 / 89	44 (86%)	7 (14%)	
German	27 / 38	18 (67%)	7 (26%)	2 (7%)
Spanish	173/259	109 (63%)	53 (31%)	11 (6%)

Two hundred and fifty-one students enrolled in the fall 1990 semester registered for the opportunity to earn incentive credit. Of those 251, a total of 171, or 68%, met the criterion of a B- or better course grade. Table 2 shows the number of students who registered for incentive credit out of the total number of students eligible to register and the number of students receiving credit, by language. The missing-data category represents students for whom records were unavailable.

Until the program has been in effect for several semesters, it is not possible to predict whether the percentages of students receiving credit for the fall 1990 semester represent reasonable expectations for the future. One indicator of the impact of FLIP is the number of fourth- and fifth-semester sections that were added to the fall schedule to accommodate students who were placed by the FLAP tests into higher-level courses. The Department of Spanish and Portuguese opened an additional seven course sections at the fourth-semester level and five at the fifth-semester level, while the Department of French and Italian added three upper-division courses.

To get a clearer picture of FLIP, students earning incentive credit were compared with students who had registered for incentive credit but failed to receive at least a B- in Spanish, German, and French (see Table 3).

The statistics for German and French are somewhat unstable because of the small number of students involved. In addition, the average range of placement test scores for French appears slightly different from that for Spanish and German because the scores for French are based on Modern Language Association tests as opposed to FLAP tests.

Several trends are apparent in the data for all three languages. Students who earn incentive credit tend to have higher average placement test scores and cumulative grade point averages across all three languages. Most encouraging are the high percentages of students who are succeeding at the incentive credit level. At the beginning of the semester, language instructors questioned the validity of the cut scores

Table 3

Credit and Noncredit Earners by Course, XPTS, XCumGPA, and XHSU

Course	(N)	XPTS		XCumGPA		XHSU	
		Credit	No Credit	Credit	No Credit	Credit	No Credit
Spanish							
35:012	(43/29)	56	53	3.19	2.32	3.6	3.4
35:107	(64/24)	63	61	3.12	2.36	4.0	4.0
35:108	(2/-)	67	– –	3.66	– –	4.0	– –
German							
13:022	(8/1)	53	– –	3.29	– –	3.75	– –
13:101	(3/5)	65	62	3.76	2.73	3.6	2.7
13:103	(7/-)	61	– –	3.18	– –	3.7	– –
13:114	(-/2)	– –	55	– –	2.70	– –	3.5
French							
9:012	(15/-)	74	– –	3.20	– –	4.0	– –
9:106	(20/7)	75	71	3.28	2.14	4.0	4.0
9:108	(1/-)	79	– –	2.87	– –	4.0	– –
9:111	(7/-)	83	– –	3.79	– –	4.5	– –
9:112	(1/-)	74	– –	3.19	– –	4.0	– –

Note: Courses numbered under 100 are fourth semester and courses numbered above 100 are fifth or sixth semester; XPTS = mean placement test score; XCumGPA = mean cumulative University of Iowa grade point average; XHSU = mean high school units or years of language study.

on the FLAP tests because large numbers of students were enrolling in upper-division courses; there was some concern that these students would really not have had adequate high school preparation. At the close of the semester, however, course instructors who had taught in the program for more than one year indicated that there were no discernible differences in the background skills of students placed by the FLAP tests and those of students from previous years placed by other criteria. The years-of-language-study statistic is somewhat meaningless at this level since almost all the students have had four years of high school language.

The data show that 63% of the students in Spanish, 67% of the students in German, and 86% of the students in French who enrolled for incentive credit were successful. In considering grade distributions, section 4.1.2 of the 1990 classroom manual for the College of Liberal Arts recommends that for intermediate courses, 49% of the grade distribution be represented by A's and B's; for advanced courses, the percentage increases to 55%. If the FLIP enrollees for each language are viewed as a class, the grade distributions are quite high as compared with the recommendations of the College of Liberal Arts. There is every indication, both from the descriptive statistics and from anecdotal information, that the FLAP tests are placing students appropriately, and that more students are opting to continue language study beyond the two-year requirement.

Conclusion

The initial survey; the development, validation, and research on assessment instruments; and the universitywide consultations have already shown several benefits: greater outreach and communication have been extended to Iowa high schools; a new placement policy has been developed; and new placement instruments are being used successfully at the U of I. FLAP has been successful in achieving its initial goals. From the experience, four preliminary observations can be made to help other institutions embarking on language assessment projects.

1) Test scores alone cannot be used to make placement decisions. Other factors must be considered, such as high school grade point average and lapse time from last course enrollment. Further research at other institutions will help to corroborate the findings discussed here.

2) An incentive program such as the one developed at the U of I can be very successful in encouraging good high school language students to continue in college-level courses.

3) Policymakers at other institutions may want to consider a penalty for students who elect to start over. At the U of I, the penalty component of the entrance requirement was more difficult for the faculty to agree on than the incentive policy was, since recruitment of students has become a university issue.

4) The experience at the U of I has taught the FLAP committee that inclusion of high school teachers in FLAP meetings, workshops, and activities has been an essential part of policy and test development.

In the past decade, language enrollments at the college level have been increasing and students enter college-level courses with more complex and varied language experience. It is imperative that postsecondary institutions do more research on test development and that they collaborate on the use of different assessment procedures and instruments.

Works Cited

Bachman, Lyle & Clark, J. "The Measurement of Foreign/Second Language Proficiency." *The Annals of the American Academy of Political and Social Sciences* 490 (1987): 20-33.

Barnes, Betsy K., Carol A. Klee & Ray M. Wakefield. "A Funny Thing Happened on the Way to the Language Requirement." *ADFL Bulletin* 22 (1990): 35-39.

Byrnes, Heidi. "Priority: Curriculum Articulation. Addressing Curriculum Articulation in the Nineties: A Proposal." *Foreign Language Annals* 23 (1990): 281-92.

Henning, Grant. "Priority: Testing. Priority Issues in the Assessment of Communicative Language Abilities." *Foreign Language Annals* 23 (1990): 379-84.

Klee, Carol & Elizabeth Rogers. "Status of Articulation: Placement, Advanced Placement Credit, and Course Options." *Hispania* 72 (1989): 264-74.

Lange, Dale L. "Developing and Implementing Proficiency-oriented Tests for a New Language Requirement at the University of Minnesota: Issues and Problems for Implementing the ACTFL/ETS/ILR Proficiency Guidelines." *Proceedings of the Symposium on the Evaluation of Foreign Language Proficiency*. Ed. A. Valdman, Bloomington, IN: Indiana University, 1987: 275-90.

Lantolf, James P. & William Frawley. "Oral-Proficiency Testing: A Critical Analysis." *Modern Language Journal* 69 (1985): 337-45.

Larson, Jerry W. "S-CAPE: A Spanish Computerized Adaptive Placement Exam." *Modern Technology in Foreign Language Education: Applications and Projects*. Ed. W. F. Smith. Lincolnwood, IL: National Textbook Company, 1989: 277-89.

Mosher, Arthur. "The South Carolina Plan for Improved Curriculum Articulation between High Schools and Colleges." *Foreign Language Annals* 22 (1989): 157-62.

Shohamy, Elana. "Reaction: Language Testing Priorities – A Different Perspective." *Foreign Language Annals* 23 (1990): 385-94.

Stansfield, Charles W. "Reaction: Some Foreign Language Test Development Priorities for the Last Decade of the Twentieth Century." *Foreign Language Annals* 23 (1990): 395-401.

Teschner, Richard V. "Spanish Speakers Semi- and Residually-Native: After the Placement Test Is Over." *Hispania* 73 (1990): 816-22.

Wherritt, Irene & T. Anne Cleary. "A National Survey of Spanish Language Testing for Placement or Outcome Assessment at B.A.-granting Institutions in the United States." *Foreign Language Annals* 23 (1990): 157-65.

_____, Anne Cleary & Cynthia Druva-Roush. "Development and Analysis of a Flexible Spanish Language Test for Placement and Outcome Assessment." *Hispania* 73 (1990): 1124-29.

Self-Assessment and Placement: A Review of the Issues

L. Kathy Heilenman
The University of Iowa

One way of looking at placement is to view it as an attempt on the part of an educational institution to find the best fit between the previous preparation of incoming students and the courses and programs it has to offer them. On the surface, this task appears deceptively easy – one has only to assess students' current level of skill and/or knowledge and then identify the course or sequence that best meets their needs. This apparent simplicity, however, conceals several thorny problems. First, the assumption that a test (or an interview or an equivalency formula) can determine students' present status vis-à-vis a certain program assumes the ability to articulate that program's goals in terms that are measurable. Second, the ability to measure those goals assumes the availability of the time, commitment, and expertise necessary to construct a reliable and valid placement instrument. Third, such an instrument should, insofar as possible, reflect actual classroom tasks that learners will perform. And finally, placement procedures must operate efficiently and effectively under existing budgetary, time, and personnel constraints. The first two requirements – measurable goals and adequate test development – are possible to achieve, albeit with some difficulty. The latter two – essentially face validity/positive backwash and practicality – are frequently contradictory.

Traditionally, language departments have relied on various combinations of formulas equating secondary study to postsecondary study, personal interviews, and locally or externally developed tests to place students (Hagiwara, 1983; Klee & Rogers, 1989). Recently, however, a surge of interest in the use of self-report or self-assessment to assess learners' competencies in a second or foreign language has led to speculation about the suitability of self-assessment as a placement instrument (e.g., Dickinson, 1987; LeBlanc & Painchaud, 1985b; Oskarsson, 1978).

Evaluation versus Certification

Such speculation assumes recognition of the difference between evaluation and certification. Evaluation (here self-assessment) and certification (here the determination that a student has reached a certain ability level or has fulfilled a certain requirement) are not identical (Aleamoni, 1979; Holec, 1979). That is, evaluation can occur without certification, but the reverse is not possible. As a matter of professional integrity, certifying bodies (e.g., language departments) cannot abdicate the responsibility of externally evaluating and thus certifying or not certifying a certain level of competence in students who successfully meet their requirements.

Nevertheless, current practice frequently uses the same test both to certify proficiency or achievement at a certain level (or to exempt students from certain courses) and to place students in courses below that level. It is obvious that self-assessment cannot be used for certification purposes, since it pits students' best interests against their integrity (Dickinson, 1987; Painchaud, 1989; Upshur, 1975). A reasonable proposal, then, would be to use a more extensive and well-developed direct and indirect testing program for those relatively few students presenting themselves for certification (or exemption) and to reserve a self-assessment instrument for the majority of students who need to be placed in courses.

Such a scheme effectively removes the temptation to better one's lot; it does not, however, prevent students from deliberately underestimating their abilities in order to receive credit for a first-semester language course. This problem seems to be one whose solution lies less in test development than it in educational policy and practice. It would be possible, for example, to simply disallow "starting over" as a blanket policy. Students would then have the option of continuing in the language at a more advanced level or "beginning at the beginning" in another language. Alternatively, of course, such students could be shifted into a special review course designed for false beginners (Klee & Rogers, 1989; Loughrin-Sacco et al., 1990).

Self-Assessment and Placement

Given acceptance, then, of the difference between evaluation and certification, the advantages of self-assessment in the context of placement are evident. First, such tests are efficient and economical. There is little or no concern with test security and, as long as there is no incentive for learners to either over- or underestimate their abilities, dishonesty is not a problem. In addition, a self-assessment questionnaire can efficiently sample more language behavior more quickly than a direct or even indirect test of such behavior can. Thus, areas that are normally left untested because of time constraints (speaking and writing) or lack of facilities (listening) can become part of the placement procedure.

Increased learner involvement is a second advantage. Learners whose opinions and judgments have been sought and valued are less likely to feel manipulated by what often seem arbitrary placement levels decided by machine-mediated procedures. As Canale (1985, p. 250) has pointed out, language testing is all too often "a crude, contrived, confusing, threatening, and above all intrusive event," with learners cast as "obedient examinees" rather than active participants. Self-assessment, on the other hand, has the potential of being both humane and learner-centered, with students being asked to participate in a process rather than being dictated to as the result of a product.

Finally, a self-assessment instrument will communicate a program's goals and expectations much more effectively than a decontextualized test score will. The process of developing an effective self-assessment instrument will, of necessity, involve faculty in an internal discussion of what they expect learners to achieve at various levels. Such discussion, in turn, will cause curricula and tests to be more closely and obviously linked.

Yet before rushing to embrace self-assessment as the magic solution to all problems, several questions must be raised. First, what exactly does it mean to ask learners to self-assess? Second, is it possible to produce self-assessment instruments that are reliable, valid, and instructionally sound within the context of placement? Third, what evidence do we have that learners can indeed accurately assess their capabilities? And fourth, does the existing literature provide guidance in the development of a self-assessment placement test and/or give examples of such instruments?

Self-Assessment: What Is It?

Self-assessment involves asking learners to make judgments about their own abilities. That is, instead of asking students to write a narrative about last weekend and then evaluating it, holistically or otherwise, students are asked how easily or how well they *could* write such an essay if they were asked to. Or, instead of using multiple-choice questions over a reading passage, students are asked to look at the passage and respond "yes," "probably," or "no" to the question, "I can understand the basic ideas." (See the Appendix for examples of various self-assessment formats.)

In other words, a self-assessment instrument is an overtly indirect measure of language ability. In addition, it is a self-report of a belief or judgment concerning one's own language behavior. As such, self-assessment can deal with potentially observable behaviors (e.g., how well students can narrate last weekend's activities) or with constructs that for all intents and purposes are difficult to observe (e.g., the ability to speak German in various contexts).

Such self-reports or assessments have long been common in educational, psychological, and social research. Self-reports have been used to facilitate data collection (e.g., asking people their age), to measure behavior (e.g., the number of times a doctor was visited within the past month), to assess attitudes (e.g., anxiety, satisfaction with life), and to solicit opinions (e.g., for or against animal rights). Given the effort, reports of behavior can be verified by objective observation: birth certificates can be checked or an observer can be posted in the doctor's office. Attitudes and opinions, however, cannot – one cannot directly observe "anxiety" or "pro-animal rights." It is possible, though, to measure and compare other, equally indirect indices. Thus, people who rate themselves as "very anxious" will be expected to behave in ways that are commonly assumed to denote anxiety (worried expressions, increased heart rate, observed anxiety attacks, etc.); people who declare themselves pro-animal rights will be more likely to pat than to kick stray dogs; and so forth. In other words, reports of private states and beliefs will be borne out by public and observable behaviors (Evans, 1986).

In terms of language, such self-report measures as "experience in a Spanish-speaking country" are common. Likewise, the use of self-report to gather data on such attitudes and opinions as "foreign language anxiety" or "attitude toward speakers of Japanese" is also well accepted. Less familiar, though, are self-assessment measures of language ability. Such measures do, however, hold promise in terms of sampling power, efficiency, and student involvement; they should be seriously evaluated.

In general, researchers and testing and evaluation experts have been suspicious of the "subjective" nature of self-report data and have proceeded to validate such measures against extrospective, observable, direct, and indirect measures. But there is no logical reason for self-report data to be any more subject to experimental contamination than data gathered by the "objective" sampling of a particular domain (Howard, 1981). In fact, the case can be made that self-report data, which effectively sample respondents' total experience, should be used as the criterion for less face- and content-valid indirect measures (Barrows et al., 1981). Finally, as Howard and his colleagues (1980) argue, the fact that in many cases self-report measures are found to correlate rather modestly with a behavioral criterion measure casts doubt on both, since error variance in either or both measures could be contributing to the low correlation.

Characteristics of Self-Assessment as a Test

It is important to realize that self-assessment refers to a type of measurement rather than to a particular testing instrument. There are many possible ways to gather learners' perceptions of their abilities, some of which are discussed later (see the Appendix for examples). In addition, the items included in a self-assessment instrument will differ according to situational constraints and demands. Thus, it is not possible to talk about the reliability or validity of self-assessment instruments in a general sense. There are likely to be valid and invalid self-assessment instruments, reliable and unreliable self-assessment instruments, just as is the case in other testing formats. It is possible, however, to discuss the advantages and disadvantages of self-assessment in regard to reliability and validity and to survey the existing literature for evidence of test characteristics of particular self-assessment tests.

Reliability

Reliability is the degree to which a measuring instrument is accurate and consistent (Aleamoni, 1979; Hughes, 1989). Thus far, reliabilities reported for self-assessment instruments have been high, ranging from .54 to .96, with the majority being greater than .80 (see Bachman & Palmer, 1981, 1989; Davidson & Henning, 1985; Heilenman, 1990; Hilton et al., 1985; Weltens et al., 1989).

Validity

Validity, or how well a test does what it is supposed to do (Oller, 1979), can be viewed in several ways. Face validity, the acceptability of the test to those involved, seems to pose little or no problem. In general, learners react positively to self-assessment items (e.g., von Elek, 1985), although there has been one report of a small number of students who felt that "someone" should place them (LeBlanc & Painchaud, 1985b).

Content validity, in reference to placement tests, requires evidence of the extent to which a test reflects the content and task types found in the curriculum it serves. This aspect is obviously a function of test development but does not seem to pose any particular difficulties. In fact, self-assessment alleviates the problem of not being able to test certain areas because of time or equipment constraints, thereby increasing the number of potential domains that can be sampled.

Construct validity focuses on the test score as a measure of an underlying construct, and, all else being equal, is less important within the pragmatic context of a placement test than it might be elsewhere (Schaefer, 1982). Instead, for a placement test it is more important to consider predictive validity (how well a test predicts later performance) and concurrent validity (how well a test agrees with the results of other, accepted measures). The issue of predictive validity is addressed by several studies. LeBlanc and Painchaud (1985b) and Painchaud (1989) describe an ongoing placement program at the University of Ottawa that depends on self-assessment for placement. They report that changes in placement are less frequent using self-assessment than previously. In addition, Jannssen-van Dieten (1989) describes pilot work indicating that had self-assessment scores been used for placement, only 3 of the 25 persons involved would have been placed in a group different from that indicated by the criterion measure. Finally, Heilenman (1989), using four 11-point scales, asked university students of French to rate their global ability in listening, reading, writing, and speaking (n = 327). Overall differences among levels (first semester, second semester, second year, above second year) were significant (F = 27.24, p < .001). Post hoc tests, however, indicated no significant differences between judgments of students enrolled in the second semester and those of students enrolled in the second year. In other words, although overall student judgments could differentiate among levels, this effect was primarily due to differences between judgments of students at beginning levels and those of students at more advanced levels.

The concurrent validity of self-assessment instruments has been addressed by a number of studies comparing performance on a self-assessment instrument with performance on another measure of language ability. Given the variety of learners tested, the wide range of self-assessment instruments used, and the various criterion measures chosen, it is difficult to draw any general conclusions. Nevertheless, correlation coefficients between self-assessment instruments and other measures seem to cluster between .30 and .60, with a few reaching around .90 and a few being very low (for reviews, see Blanche, 1988; Blanche & Merino, 1989; Heilenman, manuscript). According to Aleamoni (1979) concurrent validity coefficients frequently lie between .40 and .68, and so this range is not surprising. Another way of looking at the issue, however, is to view these correlations as neither (1) low enough to reject completely various self-assessment instruments as substitutes for other measures nor (2) consistently large enough to accept certain self-assessment instruments as totally satisfactory alternatives. Nevertheless, as Oller (1979) has pointed out, low correlations in and of themselves do not indicate that two tests are not measuring the same thing; nor do they in and of themselves establish low concurrent validity. Such correlations may result from, among other possibilities, inherently poor measures, low reliability, or a restricted range of scores (Hatch & Farhady, 1982). It is encouraging, however, that the most consistently high correlations with behavioral criterion measures are found for those self-assessment instruments which have a history of conscientious test development (e.g., see Barrows et al., 1981; Hilton et al., 1985; LeBlanc & Painchaud, 1985b).

Instructional and Curricular Concerns

Beyond a concern with reliability and validity, test developers need also to consider a test's effects in terms of utility, feasibility, and fairness (Shohamy, 1990). Utility involves ascertaining that a test is indeed useful in a practical sense. For a placement test, this element would involve the prompt and useful reporting of scores, the backwash effect of the test on teaching and curriculum, and perhaps the possibility of acquiring diagnostic information. Here there seem to be no real disadvantages and several actual advantages in the use of self-assessment. If the self-assessment placement test is constructed so as to faithfully reflect the goals of a program, then instructors can be supplied with students' assessments in various areas in order to plan instruction better. Similarly, by having program goals and objectives that are clearly defined and delineated as part of an open placement procedure, teachers at the secondary level can make more informed decisions regarding the articulation of their programs with those of postsecondary institutions.

Both feasibility and fairness are also issues that self-assessment procedures can address satisfactorily. As already outlined, self-assessment instruments are easier to administer, take less time, and are more cost-effective than comparable direct and indirect measures of language ability. Finally, fairness – whether a test is ethical, legal, and in the best interests of the learner – would not seem to be a major issue, except perhaps in the case of students who feel that such assessment is more properly and correctly done by those in charge of instruction.

Accuracy of Learner Self-Assessments

The question of whether learners can accurately assess their language abilities depends on the manner in which accuracy is defined. There is, as Barrows et al. (1981) point out, no logical reason to think that the evaluation provided by a particular extrospective test is more accurate than the assessment given by learners themselves. Nevertheless, if the assumption is made that instructor ratings and/or standardized test scores represent a closer approximation of the so-called true value of learners' language proficiency, then it makes sense to assess such accuracy by comparing learner self-assessment with instructor judgments or test scores. To the extent, then, that learners' self-assessments approximate these measures, learners will be said to be accurate. To the extent to which they diverge, learner self-assessments will be said to be under- or overestimations of ability.

Evidence provided in several studies is mixed, with some pointing to quite good matches between self-assessment and other measures (e.g., Barrows et al., 1981; Hilton et al., 1985; LeBlanc & Painchaud, 1985b; Oskarsson, 1981; von Elek, 1985), while others find that learners, particularly less proficient ones, tend to overestimate their abilities (Anderson, 1982; Blue, 1988; Janssen-van Dieten, 1989; Oller & Perkins, 1978; Wesche et al., 1990). Heilenman (1990) found clear evidence of overestimation among less proficient learners, thought because of the research design it was not possible to measure the degree of overestimation. It should be noted here that a tendency for beginners to overestimate is a not-uncommon finding in other areas (Garhart & Hannafin, 1986; Olson & Martin, 1980; Pohl, 1982; Reed, 1988) and may simply reflect such learners' inexperience with what it means to be proficient. Note also that, for placement tests, a tendency toward overestimation may be reduced since, as Martin (1984) points out, tendencies toward favorable self-presentation in surveys (comparable here to tendencies toward overestimation) are minimized when subjects are aware that their claims will be verified by external evidence. That is, learners who are aware that their judgments will help to determine the class into which they will be placed may tend to be less likely to overestimate their abilities.

In summary, it seems that overestimation on the part of less proficient learners may serve to mitigate the usefulness of self-assessment as a placement procedure. Still, the fact that such overestimation is not a general finding (as well as the possibility of controlling or minimizing it through instructions and question selection/wording) should encourage test developers to proceed with some caution but to proceed nevertheless in investigating self-assessment as a useful placement procedure.

Developing a Self-Assessment Placement Instrument

Many of the steps for developing a self-assessment placement instrument will be quite similar to those for developing any language test. The following outline of test development is based on materials provided in Aleamoni (1979) and Hughes (1989), with specific suggestions regarding self-assessment.

Step 1: State the Problem/Define the Purpose

Placement/Certification

Will this be a placement test or will it serve as both a placement and an exemption instrument? If the latter, self-assessment is not a viable option, since students will find themselves forced to weigh integrity against self-interest. To paraphrase Upshur (1975, p. 58), it is neither fair nor reasonable to ask people to in effect cut their own throats.

Results

How detailed and accurate must results be? It will in all likelihood be easier to develop a self-assessment instrument (or other test) that will divide students into three groups rather than into four or into four groups rather than eight. Will a global score suffice or is it necessary to sort students according to abilities in particular areas (conversation, writing, etc.)? How difficult will it be for students to change their placement? It is probably unrealistic to expect any test to place all students accurately, and in fact there is likely to be a significant amount of overlap in score distributions between contiguous quarters or semesters (Dizney & Gromen, 1967; Heilenman, 1983). Thus, it will be important to establish and monitor the degree of change or number of placement misses that are acceptable. For example, if it is relatively easy to move from level to level (e.g., classes are not full), then less accuracy is needed than if the reverse is the case.

On the other hand, if movement among levels is administratively feasible, then one might consider a scheme something along the lines proposed by Shaw (1980), whereby students are provided with a package of materials and encouraged to visit classes before settling on the appropriate level.

Backwash

How important is the backwash effect? Self-assessment instruments lend themselves well to positive backwash effects because there is little concern for test security and since they can efficiently sample domains normally difficult to test. As long as care is taken in the selection of content, a positive backwash effect is to be expected.

Constraints

Are there constraints resulting from lack of time (for construction of the test as well as for administration and scoring), expertise, or personnel? Valid self-assessment instruments are no less time-consuming to construct than more traditional measures are. They are, however, less mystifying. As a result, faculty input and effort may be easier to procure than is usually the case. From an administrative point of view, once concern with test security is eliminated, several possibilities open up. Self-assessment placement tests could be sent to students before they enroll (cf. Painchaud, 1989). Similarly, secondary students could complete such instruments during their last language class rather than waiting to arrive at the college or university. In addition, it seems feasible to adapt such instruments to computer administration and scoring so that students could be evaluated on a walk-in basis.

Step 2: Determine Instructional Objectives and Curricular Goals

This may well be the most problematic step in the process. As Byrnes (1990, p. 75) has pointed out, foreign language curricula are at present in an untidy state of "unarticulation" and/or "disarticulation" that makes it difficult to clearly specify the content of courses and programs in terms useful for either testing or placement. This situation is less the fault of language faculty than it is a reflection of a lack of consensus on a conceptual plane. Jakobovits' assessment of the situation in 1970 bears repeating today:

> The question of what it is to know a language is not yet well understood and consequently the language proficiency tests now available and universally used are inadequate because they attempt to measure something that has not been well-defined (p. 75).

(See also Hagen, 1990, and Stevenson, 1981, for similar views.)

Luckily for those involved in placement testing, this state of affairs, although troublesome, is not fatal. As Schaefer (1982, pp. 75-76) has put it:

> A [placement] test used in the real world to make practical decisions is primarily justified not by its theoretical foundations but by the

degree to which it improves the decision-making process, making it more effective or more efficient.

This does not mean that theory can be ignored. Developing a placement test, however, does not necessarily entail validating a construct; nor does it necessarily imply the development of a curriculum. It does mean identifying those features which differentiate among various course levels. Such information may be gathered by looking at written course objectives and course achievement tests, as well as by polling instructors and inspecting materials used. Of course, insofar as the people involved in test development are the same people involved in instruction, test development and curriculum development are likely to proceed in tandem. The advantage in such a case is that many unspoken assumptions on the part of the teaching staff are likely to be made explicit and become subject to discussion, thus leading to better-articulated goals and objectives as well as to closer ties between testing and curriculum.

Step 3: Determine the Content for the Self-Assessment Instrument

A set of test specifications is needed such that many possible tests could be developed. Actual test items will be samples of these specifications. At a minimum, the following should be specified: tasks students are expected to carry out, types of texts (oral and written), and people to whom student output is to be addressed (Hughes, 1989). An example of how this task might be done is given by LeBlanc and Painchaud (1985a, 1985b) in their description of the development of a placement test for which reading and listening were the skills to be evaluated. LeBlanc and Painchaud asked instructors to write descriptors they felt were representative of each of the six existing levels of reading and listening comprehension courses. This effort produced more than 1,000 descriptors that varied quite widely. It was nevertheless possible to establish rough levels. Subsequently, a matrix was developed, taking into account types of texts, genres, registers, length, and type of presentation (speed, number of repetitions for oral texts). The result was formal descriptions of each level that could be used to develop actual self-assessment items. Reproduced below is the description for level 2 listening (LeBlanc & Painchaud, 1985b, p. 683):

> Is able to understand, in a dialogue of the social conversation genre between two students at the familiar register and spoken at regular speed, the topic of the conversation with one or two details.

At this point, it will also be necessary to establish test format (types of items, scales, multiple-choice versus forced choice or free response, etc.), time to be allowed, difficulty level, and scoring procedures. Here, choices made may have consequences for the test's reliability or validity. Outlined below are suggestions based on the literature concerning the construction of survey, interview, and self-report instruments (see also Molenaar, 1982). In the case of self-assessment of language skills, however, much work remains to be done as to how these issues impinge on the reliability, validity, and accuracy of self-assessment of second language abilities.

Item Type

Items may consist of global evaluations of ability or may focus on discrete behaviors. Global questions may ask for an overall evaluation of ability or may query distinct skill areas. Questions focusing on discrete behaviors may ask learners to assess their abilities by describing the task or may give learners actual examples (see the Appendix). Although studies asking for global judgments have produced acceptable correlations with other measures (Oskarsson, 1981; Wangsotorn, 1981), studies that have directly compared the use of global scales with that of behavioral descriptions indicate that the latter are preferable (Janssen-van Dieten, 1989; LeBlanc & Painchaud, 1985b). Taken in conjunction with the advice commonly given survey writers to avoid overly general, vague questions (Turner, 1984), the exclusive use of global questions would seem inadvisable.

Learners have been asked to assess their abilities using descriptions of tasks (e.g., LeBlanc & Painchaud, 1985b), as well as to give their judgments after looking at actual samples of the task (e.g., Janssen-van Dieten, 1989; von Elek, 1985). To date, there has been no direct comparison of these two formats. Learners asked to judge their abilities based on a concrete task sample may well be more accurate than learners whose judgments are based on what they interpret the task to be. On the other hand, by using actual texts (written and oral), test developers run the risk of having learners' judgments focus on the characteristics of that one task *sample*, rather than on the more general question of how they deal with that *type* of task.

Type of Scale Used

Learners may be asked to respond using labeled rating scales calibrated with varying numbers of points. Technically, such scales produce ordinal- rather than interval-level measurement, thus limiting the statistical analyses that can be performed (for discussion of this general issue, see Bass et al., 1974; Borgatta & Bohrnstedt, 1980; Newstead & Collis, 1987). From a practical standpoint, however, the majority of scales can be treated as if they produced interval-level data (Guilford, 1985; see

Bass et al., 1974, for examples of statistically optimal scales). On the other hand, scales for which the underlying construct is not logically measurable on an interval scale (e.g., the ACTFL-ETS proficiency ratings), scales that are restricted to dichotomous answers ("yes" or "no"), and scales that deliberately have more positive labels than negative ones (or vice versa) should be treated as producing ordinal rather than interval data.

Order of Items

Items may be presented in a random order or they may be ordered in a Guttman-like scale ranging from least to most difficult (see Barrows et al., 1981, and Hilton et al., 1985, for examples). The use of the latter may help learners to assess their abilities more realistically, since in effect it provides a sort of macroscale along which learners can align their judgments (Schwarz & Hippler, 1987). In other words, beginning learners will be less likely to assess themselves as highly capable on items toward the difficult end of the scale simply because they will realize that beginners should not be able to do things toward the top of the scale. On the other hand, the use of such an ordered scale implies the ability to establish a satisfactory rank order of difficulty prior to and independent of the self-assessment instrument.

Instructions

Within the context of survey/interview methodology, Cannell et al. (1981) emphasize the importance of clarifying the purpose of the test as well as attempting to increase the respondents' commitment to give accurate and well-thought-out answers. For a self-assessment placement instrument, students should be given a rationale for the use of self-assessment, told that items represent a range of abilities, and encouraged to use the complete range of the scale. Practice items, perhaps including one or two filled out by fictitious learners at various levels, could be provided.

Language of Test

If at all possible, the language of the test should be the students' first language. Asking learners to rate themselves using a language in which they are not proficient increases the risk of inaccurate self-assessment (Oller & Perkins, 1978). If this arrangement is not possible, questions should be extensively pretested, including having actual students read and revise them. Reid (1990) reports that using small numbers of structural and vocabulary patterns seems to produce a more understandable, if rather repetitious, instrument.

Step 4: Item Writing

Writing the actual items is demanding. Test developers will probably want to write many more items than they think will be needed in order to eliminate those which are unclear or otherwise troublesome. Here, developers of self-assessment instruments will want to take heed of experience incurred in writing survey, interview, and other self-report measures.

Avoid Negatively Worded Items

Such items are often found to introduce error owing to respondents' difficulties in processing (Schmitt & Stults, 1985). Bachman and Palmer (1989) may be right in their contention that learners are better able to discern what they cannot do than to report what they can do. Nevertheless, inquiring about a lack of skills confounds this issue with that of negatively worded questions and should be avoided. (For further discussion, see Heilenman, 1990.)

Attempt to Write Items That Are Directly Relevant to Learners' Experiences

If at all possible, questions asking students to speculate about what they *might* be able do but have never before done (e.g., order a meal in a restaurant, buy a train ticket) should be avoided. Learners whose experience is largely limited to the classroom are unlikely to be able to give accurate or even well-informed judgments in these cases. (For further discussion and examples, see Heilenman, 1990.)

Allow Sufficient Time for Revision

The development of a self-assessment instrument appears simple. In reality, however, it may prove difficult to write items that consistently elicit the expected responses. Wording effects (changes in response caused by changes in wording) can present unpredictable and frustrating challenges. It is also dangerous to assume that the frame of reference of the test developers (usually experienced language learners and teachers) is shared by learners. Students may legitimately judge themselves able to "hold a conversation" based on their ability to do so within the sheltered confines of their classrooms. On the other hand, test developers may be quite aware of these same students' limitations (see Heilenman, 1990, for discussion and illustrations). In sum, the use of self-assessment in placement is not a substitute for the time and effort required to develop a valid and useful testing instrument. Many of the problems are the same; some are different. The time involved, however, is likely to be substantial.

Step 5: Pretest

This is essential for self-assessment instruments in which ambiguities, differing frames of reference, and question vagueness may combine to produce error and confusion. It may be extremely helpful to discuss a preliminary draft of the test with a stratified, random sample of the students for whom it is destined. Open discussion of questions among colleagues may also reveal unforeseen problems. In addition, Converse and Presser (1986) suggest the following:

1) Create split-sample (split-ballot) comparisons. That is, ask the "same" question twice using different wording. Then compare learners' performance on the supposedly identical questions.
2) Use follow-ups to closed questions. Ask learners to explain their answers.
3) Use multiple indicators. If the ability to read literary works is an important goal, ask students several questions in this area.

Of course, it is assumed that appropriate statistical analyses will be performed (item analysis, reliability, and validity), either at this point, if sufficient data is available, or later, as part of the first administration (Hughes, 1989). Here, too, decision scores can be determined (Aleamoni, 1979).

Step 6: Develop a Plan for Evaluation, Review, and Modification

Are students actually being placed satisfactorily? How many students were misplaced and had to be moved? Were any students obviously underplaced? It may be advantageous to look more closely at those cases of misfit with an eye toward later test modification. Finally, all tests should be reviewed periodically and formally revalidated on a regular basis. Aleamoni (1979) suggests a three-year cycle of yearly review and revalidation.

Conclusion

Two final questions remain. The first returns to the problem of construct validity, or "the extent to which scores are consistent with theoretical expectations" (Yaremko et al., 1986, p. 40). Although, as already pointed out, placement tests are most appropriately validated against either the accurate assignment of students to courses (Hughes, 1989) or perhaps against another test whose validity is satisfactory (i.e., predictive and concurrent validation), concern with construct validity is not misplaced.

What exactly is a self-assessment or self-report instrument measuring? A commonsense approach would be to say that it is measuring respondents' perception of their own abilities based on self-observation in a variety of situations. But as Evans (1986) points out, perceived competence also reflects self-image and will not necessarily be congruent with another measure of reality. Thus, self-assessment of language ability may reflect learners' self-confidence, experience, ability to judge, or other factors not necessarily directly related to their language ability (Oskarsson, 1978). Wesche et al. (1990), for example, found a substantial negative correlation between scores on a scale constructed to measure anxiety in using French and self-assessment scores. This finding, however, is preliminary and should not be exaggerated; it could result from the fact that both the self-assessment instrument and the anxiety scale were Likert-type instruments, with the correlation being, then, at least partly, the result of a method effect (cf. Campbell & Fiske, 1959). Another possibility is that lack of anxiety in language use is actually related in predictable ways to success in using that language, a supposition supported by MacIntyre and Gardner's (1989, pp. 272-73) demonstration of "a clear relationship . . . between foreign-language anxiety and foreign-language proficiency."

The second question is more practical and concerns the use of self-assessment within ongoing language programs. Dickinson and Carver (1980) point out the many advantages of helping students learn how to learn. To become truly self-directed learners, however, students have also to become successful monitors and evaluators of their own progress (Dickinson, 1987). In this sense, the development of self-assessment instruments for use in placement represents a step toward a larger goal.

Works Cited

Aleamoni, Lawrence M. *Methods of Implementing College Placement and Exemption Programs*. Princeton, NJ: College Entrance Examination Board, 1979.

Anderson, Pamela L. "Self-Esteem in the Foreign Language: A Preliminary Investigation." *Foreign Language Annals* 15 (1982): 109-14.

Bachman, Lyle F. & Adrian S. Palmer. "The Construct Validation of Self-Ratings of Communicative Ability." *Language Testing* 6 (1989): 14-29.

_____. "The Construct Validation of the FSI Oral Interview." *Language Learning* 31 (1981): 67-86.

Barrows, T., S. M. Ager, M. F. Bennett, H. I. Braun, J. L. D. Clark, L. G. Harris & S. F. Klein. "College Students' Knowledge and Beliefs: A Survey of Global Understanding. The Final Report of the Global Understanding Project." New Rochelle, NY: Change Press, 1981. ERIC ED 215 653.

Bass, Bernard M., Wayne F. Cascio & Edward J. O'Connor. "Magnitude Estimations of Expressions of Frequency and Amount." *Journal of Applied Psychology* 59 (1974): 313-20.

Blanche, Patrick. "Self-Assessment of Foreign Language Skills: Implications for Teachers and Researchers." *RELC Journal* 19 (1988): 75-93.

_____ & Barbara J. Merino. "Self-Assessment of Foreign-Language Skills: Implications for Teachers and Researchers." *Language Learning* 39 (1989): 313-40.

Blue, George M. "Self-Assessment: The Limits of Learner Independence." *ELT Documents* 131 (1988): 101-18.

Borgatta, Edgar F. & George W. Bohrnstedt. "Level of Measurement Once Over Again." *Sociological Methods and Research* 9 (1980): 147-60.

Byrnes, Heidi. "Addressing Curriculum Articulation in the Nineties: A Proposal." *Foreign Language Annals* 23 (1990): 281-92.

Campbell, Donald T. & Donald W. Fiske. "Convergent and Discriminant Validation by the Multitrait-Multimethod Matrix." *Psychological Bulletin* 56 (1959): 81-105.

Canale, Michael. "Language Assessment: The Method is the Message." *Georgetown University Round Table on Languages and Linguistics 1985*. Ed. Deborah Tannen & James E. Alatis. Washington, DC: Georgetown University Press, 1985: 249-62.

Cannell, Charles F., Peter V. Miller & Lois Oksenberg. "Research on Interviewing Techniques." *Sociological Methodology*. Ed. Samuel Leinhardt. San Francisco: Jossey-Bass, 1981: 389-437.

Clark, John L. D. & Eleanor H. Jorden. "A Study of Language Attrition in Former U.S. Students of Japanese and Implications for Design of Curriculum and Teaching Materials." 1984. ERIC ED 243 317.

Converse, Jean M. & Stanley Presser. *Survey Questions: Handcrafting the Standardized Questionnaire*. Beverly Hills, CA: Sage, 1986.

Davidson, Fred & Grant A. Henning. "A Self-Rating Scale of English Difficulty: Rasch Scalar Analysis of Items and Rating Categories." *Language Testing* 2 (1985): 164-79.

Dickinson, Leslie. *Self-Instruction in Language Learning*. Cambridge: Cambridge University Press, 1987.

_____ & David Carver. "Learning How to Learn: Steps towards Self-Direction in Foreign Language Learning in Schools." *ELT Journal* 35 (1980): 1-7.

Dizney, Henry F. & Lauren Gromen. "Predictive Validity and Differential Achievement on Three MLA-Cooperative Foreign Language Tests." *Educational and Psychological Measurement* 27 (1967): 1127-30.

Evans, Ian M. "Response Structure and the Triple-Response-Mode Concept." *Conceptual Foundations of Behavioral Assessment*. Ed. R. O. Nelson & S. C. Hayes. New York: Guilford Press, 1986. 131-55.

Garhart, Casey & Michael Hannafin. "The Accuracy of Cognitive Monitoring during Computer-Based Instruction." 1986. ERIC ED 267 768.

Guilford, J. P. "A Sixty-Year Perspective on Psychological Measurement." *Applied Psychological Measurement* 9 (1985): 341-49.

Hagen, L. Kirk. "Logic, Linguistics, and Proficiency Testing." *ADFL Bulletin* 21, 2 (1990): 46-51.

Hagiwara, M. Peter. "Student Placement in French: Results and Implications." *Modern Language Journal* 67 (1983): 23-32.

Hatch, Evelyn & Hossein Farhady. *Research Design and Statistics for Applied Linguistics*. Rowley, MA: Newbury House, 1982.

Heilenman, L. Kathy. Self-Assessment of Second Language Ability. Manuscript.

_____. "Self-Assessment of Second Language Ability: The Role of Response Effects." *Language Testing* 7 (1990): 172-98.

_____. "The Use of a Cloze Procedure in Foreign Language Placement." *Modern Language Journal* 67 (1983): 121-26.

_____. "Use of Self-Assessment in Placement Testing." Paper presented at the Modern Language Association, Washington, DC, 1989.

Hilton, Thomas L., Jerilee Grandy, Roberta Green Kline & Judy E. Liskin-Gasparro. *Final Report: The Oral Language Proficiency of Teachers in the United States in the 1980s – An Empirical Study*. Princeton, NJ: Educational Testing Service, 1985.

Hippler, Hans-J. "Response Effects in Surveys." *Social Information Processing and Survey Methodology*. Ed. Hans-J. Hippler, Norbert Schwarz & Seymour Sudman. New York: Springer-Verlag, 1987: 102-22.

Holec, Henri. *Autonomy and Foreign Language Learning*. Oxford: Pergamon Press, 1979.

Howard, George S. "On Validity." *Evaluation Review* 5 (1981): 567- 76.

_____, Scott E. Maxwell, Richard L. Weiner, Kathy S. Boynton & William M. Rooney. "Is a Behavioral Measure the Best Estimate of Behavioral Parameters? Perhaps Not." *Applied Psychological Measurement* 4 (1980): 293-311.

Hughes, Arthur. *Testing for Language Teachers*. Cambridge: Cambridge University Press, 1989.

Jakobovits, L. A. *Foreign Language Learning: A Psycholinguistic Analysis of the Issues*. Rowley, MA: Newbury House, 1970.

Janssen-van Dieten, Anne-Mieke. "The Validity of Self-Assessment by Inexperienced Subjects." *Language Testing* 6 (1989): 30-46.

Klee, Carol A. & Elizabeth S. Rogers. "Status of Articulation: Placement, Advanced Placement Credit, and Course Options." *Hispania* 72 (1989): 763-73.

LeBlanc, Raymond & Gisèle Painchaud. "Self-Assessment as a Placement Test." 1985a. ERIC ED 259 584.

_____. "Self-Assessment as a Second Language Placement Instrument." *TESOL Quarterly* 19 (1985b): 673-87.

Loughrin-Sacco, Steven J., Sylvia A. Matthews, Wendy M. Sweet & Jan A. Miner. "Reviving Language Skills: A Description and Evaluation of Michigan Tech's Summer Intensive French Course." *ADFL Bulletin* 21, 2 (1990): 34-40.

MacIntyre, P. D. & R. C. Gardner. "Anxiety and Second-Language Learning: Toward a Theoretical Clarification." *Language Learning* 39 (1989): 251-75.

Martin, Elizabeth. "Appendix H: Scheme for Classifying Survey Questions According to Their Subjective Properties." *Surveying Objective Phenomena.* Ed. Charles F. Turner & Elizabeth Martin. New York: Russell Sage Foundation, 1984: 1: 407-31.

Molenaar, Nico J. "Response Effects of 'Formal' Characteristics of Questions." *Response Behaviour in the Survey-Interview.* Ed. W. Dijkstra & J. van der Zouwen. New York: Academic Press, 1982: 49-89.

Newstead, Stephen E. & Janet M. Collis. "Context and Interpretation of Quantifiers of Frequency." *Ergonomics* 30 (1987): 1447-62.

Oller, John W. *Language Tests at School.* London: Longman, 1979.

_____ & Kyle Perkins. "Language Proficiency as a Source of Variance in Self-Reported Affective Variables." *Language in Education: Testing the Tests.* Ed. John J. Oller Jr. & Kyle Perkins. Rowley, MA: Newbury House, 1978.

Olson, Margot A. & Diane Martin. "Assessment of Entering Student Writing Skill in the Community College." 1980. ERIC ED 235 845.

Oskarsson, Mats. *Approaches to Self-Assessment in Foreign Language Learning.* Oxford: Pergamon Press, 1978.

_____. "Self-Assessment of Language Proficiency: Rationale and Applications." *Language Testing* 6 (1989): 1-13.

_____. "Subjective and Objective Assessment of Foreign Language Performance." *Directions in Language Testing: Selected Papers from the RELC Seminar on "Evaluation and Measurement of Language Competence and Performance."* Ed. John A. S. Read. Singapore: Singapore University Press, 1981.

Painchaud, Gisèle. Personal communication. 1989.

Pohl, Norval F. "Using Retrospective Pre-Ratings to Counteract Response-Shift Confounding." *Journal of Experimental Education* 50 (1982): 211-14.

Reed, Keflyn X. "Expectation vs. Ability: Junior College Reading Skills." 1988. ERIC ED 295 706.

Reid, Joy. "The Dirty Laundry of ESL Survey Research." *TESOL Quarterly.* 24 (1990): 323-38.

Schaefer, Carl F. "The Cloze Procedure for Placement Testing." *Glottodidactica.* 15 (1982): 75-82.

Schmitt, Neal & Daniel M. Stults. "Factors Defined by Negatively Keyed Items: The Result of Careless Respondents?" *Applied Psychological Measurement* 9 (1985): 367-73.

Schwarz, Norbert & Hans-J. Hippler. "What Response Scales May Tell Your Respondents: Informative Functions of Response Alternatives." *Social Information Processing and Survey Methodology.* Ed. Hans-J. Hippler, Norbert Schwarz & Seymour Sudman. New York: Springer-Verlag, 1987: 163-78.

Shaw, Peter A. "Comments on the Concept and Implementation of Self-Placement." *TESOL Quarterly* 14 (1980): 261-62.

Shohamy, Elana. "Language Testing Priorities: A Different Perspective." *Foreign Language Annals* 23 (1990): 385-94.

Stevenson, Douglas K. "Language Testing and Academic Accountability: On Redefining the Role of Language Testing in Language Teaching." *IRAL* 19 (1981): 15-30.

Turner, Charles F. "Why Do Surveys Disagree? Some Preliminary Hypotheses and Some Disagreeable Examples." *Surveying Subjective Phenomena*. Ed. Charles F. Turner & Elizabeth Martin. New York: Sage Foundation, 1984, 2:159-214.

Upshur, John A. "Objective Evaluation of Oral Proficiency in the TESOL Classroom." *Papers on Language Testing 1967-1974*. Ed. Leslie Palmer & Bernard Spolsky. Washington, DC: TESOL, 1975: 52-65.

von Elek, Tibor. "A Test of Swedish as a Second Language: An Experiment in Self-Assessment." *New Directions in Language Testing*. Ed. Y. Lee, A. Fok, R. Lord & G. Low. Oxford: Oxford University Press, 1985: 47-57.

Wangsotorn, Achara. "Self-Assessment in English Skills by Undergraduate and Graduate Students in Thai Universities." *Directions in Language Testing: Selected Papers from the RELC Seminar on "Evaluation and Measurement of Language Competence and Performance."* Ed. John A. S. Read. Singapore: Singapore University Press, 1981: 240-60.

Weltens, Bert, Theo J. M. Van Els & Erik Schils. "The Long-Term Retention of French by Dutch Students." *Studies in Second Language Acquisition* 11 (1989): 205-16.

Wesche, M. B., F. Morrison, D. Ready & C. Pawley. "French Immersion: Postsecondary Consequences for Individuals and Universities." *Canadian Modern Language Review* 46 (1990): 430-51.

Yaremko, R. M., Herbert Harari, Robert C. Harrison & Elizabeth Lynn. *Handbook of Research and Quantitative Methods in Psychology: For Students and Professionals*. Hillsdale, NJ: Erlbaum, 1986.

Appendix
Sample Self-Assessment Items

Following are actual items used in various reported studies and projects.

■ Global, writing (Heilenman, 1989).

Imagine that you have been given the job of writing a detailed (3 to 4 page) account about yourself in French. It would include your life from when you were small up to the present day (childhood memories, games, school, friends, youth, present occupation, interests, personal qualities, relatives and friends, memorable experiences, future plans, etc.). You have plenty of time but there's no dictionary available. How well would you manage?

_____ I wouldn't be able to write anything at all.
_____ I would be able to write only a few simple sentences about my life.

_____ I could give a bare-bones account of my life, but it wouldn't be very long or sophisticated.

_____ I could write about most of the major events of my life but I would probably have to leave out some things that I wouldn't know how to say.

_____ I would be able to give a fairly accurate account of my life but I probably would have some trouble being very elaborate (giving lots of details, etc.) I might have some trouble with particular vocabulary or grammar.

_____ I would be able to write a fairly complete and coherent account of my life with only minimal difficulty.

■ Global, difficulty (Davidson & Henning, 1985, p. 178).

Speaking fluently

none / very little / some / average / more than avg. / much / extreme

■ Can-do, speaking, 3-point scale, rough difficulty ordering (Barrows et al., 1981, p. 164)

Give simple biographical information about myself (place of birth, composition of family, early schooling, etc.).

quite easily / with some difficulty / with great difficulty or not at all

■ Can-do, various skills, 4-point scale (Clark & Jorden, 1984, p. 77)

Teaching a class using Japanese as the language of instruction.

extreme difficulty / considerable difficulty / some difficulty / little or no difficulty

■ Can-do, listening comprehension, 4-point scale (Hilton et al., 1985)

Understand movies without subtitles.

quite easily / with some difficulty / with great difficulty / not at all

■ Can-do, listening comprehension, 5-point scale, rough difficulty ordering (Painchaud, 1989)

Je peux comprendre des directives données en anglais dans un cours sans avoir à les faire répéter.

jamais / rarement / moitié / souvent / toujours

■ Can-do, task provided (von Elek, 1985)

Do you understand this sentence?

yes, absolutely / I think so / no

■ Difficulty, grammar, 4-point scale (Bachman & Palmer, 1989, p. 27)

How many different kinds of grammar mistakes do you make in English?

(BAD) I make grammar mistakes in almost everything / many kinds / only a few kinds / I almost never make grammar mistakes (GOOD)

■ Descriptor matching, reading (Barrows et al., 1981, p. 268)

This question asks you to judge your own level of reading ability in your MPL [most proficient language]. Please read each of the six paragraphs below and decide which paragraph best describes your ability to read the MPL. Circle the number preceding only one of the paragraphs below.

1) I cannot really read anything in the language, or can read only a few words that I have "memorized."

2) I can recognize the letters of the alphabet or the very common characters or printed syllables of the language. I can read some personal and place names, street signs, office and shop designations, numbers, and some isolated words and phrases.

. . .

6) I can read extremely difficult and abstract prose, as well as highly colloquial writing and the classic literary forms of the language.

Using an Exit Requirement to Assess the Global Performance of Undergraduate Foreign Language Students

Ken Fleak
University of South Carolina

The organizing principle of proficiency has been instrumental in the restructuring of the beginning-level foreign language curriculum at many universities since the mid-1980s. At the University of South Carolina, the major impetus began in 1984 with the South Carolina Educational Improvement Act, which mandated that all state high schools must offer minimally two years of one foreign language. Shortly thereafter, a decision at the University of South Carolina-Columbia to require two units of study in the same foreign language for admission starting in the fall of 1988 lead to a serious revision of the placement procedures, the beginning sequence of courses, and the previous policy of viewing the university requirement only in terms of credit hours. It is clear that the new concepts of a mandatory placement test based on listening and reading comprehension, a cloze-type measure of contextualized discrete grammar and vocabulary at the phase 1 level, and an oral interview, along with writing samples in the second phase for those students scoring at a higher level, all served to prompt a new course structure in first-year Spanish and other languages.

In consequence, students are now able to demonstrate university-required minimal proficiency in two ways. First, a passing grade on the second phase of the Spanish placement test is an acceptable means of demonstrating such proficiency. If this occurs, students are not required to take any additional courses in the second language, but if they do, retroactive credit is given for a grade of B or better in the course that the phase 2 test stipulates. The second way to fulfill the language requirement is to complete all course work through Spanish 122 and to pass the exit exam, which is an integral part of that course.

Implementation of the exit exam began in the fall semester of 1988, as part of the final course in the sequence of required Spanish courses. Students who are placed in the 100-level program now need to satisfy their language requirement through the demonstration of minimal functional skills, which are tested by means of the exit exam in speaking, listening, reading, and writing. While quizzes and chapter exams remain achievement tests in their orientation, the standards for the exit exam differ significantly because it is proficiency-based. Just as the Oral Proficiency Interview (OPI) is used as a measure of the language learner's speaking level in order to demonstrate what students can do with the language rather than what they know about it (Magnan, 1986, p. 119), the exit exam provides a parallel type of assessment of overall, or global performance, that exceeds the parameters of a specific course. For Heilenman and Kaplan (1986. p. 59), a proficiency-based curriculum "aims at global evaluation of learners' performance in the various skill areas." In the case of exit exam testing, a valid instrument indicates to both instructor and students that learning is something more important than the number of pages covered in a class. The idea of accumulative knowledge is firmly in place, and the concept of accountability in foreign language instruction is evident through this new testing procedure.

In summary, proficiency is shown via (1) passing both phases of the Spanish placement test or (2) passing the third-semester exit exam. By necessity, the two tests, although not the same, are very similar and must test all of the basic language modalities. A failure on the phase 2 placement tests means that students have not yet attained minimal performance levels that should be reached by the end of Spanish 122.

Implementation of the New Testing Procedure

To initiate a testing format of this magnitude and have it favorably accepted by both faculty and students, a period of pretesting is advisable. The original design for the exam was piloted for three semesters at the 200 level, before it actually began to count as part of the requirement in the Spanish 122 course, thus providing adequate time for an evaluation of the format and the expectations for student performance levels. The creation of a Testing and Curriculum Committee was a major step that proved crucial in (1) formulating important decisions for the course in which the exam would be given and (2) in establishing uniformity in its application in all languages. Issues considered related to the timing of the exam during the semester, the part it would play in the course grade, and the retake policy. In a typical semester of 14 or 15 weeks, the ideal period for the initial testing should occur during week 10 or 11, with the retakes following in 2 or 3 weeks, at which time students are allowed one opportunity for retaking each section they failed. While all of the initial testing takes place within the classroom, the retake testing is conducted outside class at an announced time and place.

If the exit exam is to be seen as a valid testing procedure by both students and faculty, its integration with a course must be carefully studied. As part of the Spanish 122 requirement, the exit exam directly reflects the course goals because it represents an overall assessment of each student's performance level from the initial contact with the language up to this point. One possible format would establish the concept of giving a minimal passing grade when students have passed each section of the exam. For students failing to meet this requirement, no course credit would be given, whereas for students passing the different sections of the exit exam, the remaining course grades for such components as chapter tests, compositions, quizzes, and participation would be activated to determine the course grade above that of the minimal passing grade (a D) for a successful completion of the exit exam requirement.

Designing an Exit Exam

Since the initial piloting period, minor changes have occurred in the exit exam from semester to semester in order to standardize and improve its different sections. The American Council on the Teaching of Foreign Languages (ACTFL) proficiency definitions have been used as a point of departure in the creation of the course structure and the testing instruments. If a department establishes a level (such as "novice high" or "intermediate low") as the goal to be reached by the end of a course, the progression toward that point is easier because the focus is clearly on what students are able marginally to achieve in each skill area before they successfully complete or continue with their language study. The emphasis for instructional purposes has been placed directly on use of the language instead of on a sequencing of grammatical rules.

Rationale for Oral Testing

What it means to know a foreign language is a frequent point of discussion in pedagogical circles. The ACTFL speaking guidelines have provided our profession with a much-needed direction in developing an adequate measure of the language learner's speaking skill through identifying of global tasks/functions, context, content, accuracy, and text types. Omaggio (1986, p. 175) reports that many students designate speaking as the most important skill they wish to develop. Despite the problems that frequently exist regarding large class size, multiple sections taught by instructors and graduate students, inadequate tester training, and poor logistics for test administration, language departments that are truly proficiency-based have often adopted at least some form of oral evaluation. In a recent study, Harlow and Caminero (1990, p. 491) report that 57% of the language programs surveyed at large universities test speaking proficiency in at least some form. The reasons most often cited for not testing this skill were time restraints, testing logistics, lack of interest, lack of staffing/training, and testing formats. These results would indicate a need to suggest alternative formats for oral testing that might encourage more language programs to adopt some type of measurement of the student's speaking progression, even when such obstacles are obvious.

Designs for the Oral Testing Component

In the planning stages before the fall semester of 1988, the Spanish Testing and Curriculum Committee at the University of South Carolina struggled with an acceptable design for the speaking phase, which was highly problematic because of the burden that the format of an extended OPI-type oral interview would place on colleagues teaching multiple sections of the course. Consequently, an innovative format was developed that allowed students to be tested in the classroom itself.

The speaking segment of the Spanish exit exam has included several creative formats, which represent a response to the problems most often associated with oral testing by most instructors. In order to test specific skills, two or three evaluations using a two-minute design have been effectively used. On the day of the oral test, students are placed in pairs in order to work with practice materials while they are waiting for the exam. Each student is evaluated individually. The first student is called forward and given the evaluation form. Students are given two minutes to gather their thoughts; when one student is ready to be tested, another should be going through the same two-minute warm-up so that no time is wasted between tests. Students have two minutes to express what they are asked to say. When finished, students leave the classroom in order to avoid any contact with partners still waiting to be interviewed. For this format, three chairs are placed in a corner of the classroom, one for the instructor, one for the student being tested and, at a distance, the third chair for the student who is waiting to be tested. Several forms of the test are used so that the student who is waiting will not overhear the responses from the student being tested. For example, when description is tested, five or six different pictures are accessible. All tests are recorded. When the passing grade for the performance is questionable, a second colleague evaluates the test. If two evaluators' judgments conflict, a third evaluator acts as arbitrator, and the two concurring grades constitute the final decision.

Description, survival situations, and past-tense narration were cited as three areas in which students needed to demonstrate proficiency. Underhill (1987, p. 66) speaks of the use of visual material as "an economic and effective way of providing a topic of conversation without giving the learner words and phrases to manipulate and give back." Students receive no target-language clues. Responses to both pictures and situation cards are effective measures of speaking because the vocabulary and the structures must be produced entirely by the students. During the two-minute testing period, students are given a picture and asked to describe what they see. (See Table 1.) Using this format, it is possible to complete the testing of an average class in 50 minutes.

Table 1
Descriptive Oral Evaluation

You have two minutes to look over these materials and gather your thoughts. Please take this time to read the suggestions below and to look at the picture(s).

During your test, you will have two minutes to describe the picture(s) to your instructor. Try to say as much as you can; use complete sentences in the present tense and avoid using English. Include information such as the following:

Who the people are (their relationships, professions, etc.)
Where they are
What they are doing
What the people look like; what they are wearing
How the people feel; what they are probably thinking
What the people might be saying to one another
The weather, time and season, when these are obvious
Some common objects you see in the picture

A second format that advances the same goals is a situation that places an emphasis on narration. The significance of this procedure is that it allows the tester to combine an evaluation of functional topics and structures. (See Table 2.)

A third format is a situation-based role-play, which is important because it represents a required testing procedure at the intermediate range of the OPI. The student is required to simulate surviving a situation, such as going out with friends, dining at a restaurant, making travel plans, asking for directions, shopping for food and clothing, or making a hotel reservation.

Since the situation-based oral evaluation does not take long (see Tables 3 and 4), two minutes are not always required. It has thus been decided to combine narration in the past with the situation-based oral evaluation, thereby reducing the frequency of the oral tests from three to two; in any event, three evaluations per semester proved interruptive to the flow of the course.

Table 2
Narration in the Past

Tell me about a recent date or evening out with your friends. Include information such as the following:

> What day you went out and with whom
> Where you went
> What you did there
> What you talked about
> Anything interesting that happened *or* that you found out about your date/friends
> Whether or not you had a good time
> What time you returned home

Table 3
Situation-Based Oral Evaluation

You are at a travel agency in Mexico City, and you wish to fly to San José, Costa Rica.

1) Find out when there are flights to San José.
2) Indicate whether or not you want a round-trip ticket.
3) Find out how much a first class ticket costs.
4) Find out what documents you need, and when you have to confirm the reservation.

If more interaction is desired, another approach is to use a series of survival topic cards. (See Table 5.) With this testing procedure, four minutes are required in order to create the additional interactive step. Students have four minutes to look at the topic card and plan what they are going to say. They then have two minutes to talk on the subject, following the suggestions listed on the card. If time permits, students may add additional comments. This section is followed by another two-

---

Table 4
Situation 1

When you arrive in Mexico City, you go to the Hotel María Cristina to look for a room. Indicate the following to the hotel receptionist:

1) You would like a room for tonight.
2) You prefer a single room with a shower on the third floor.
3) You want to know how much the room costs and whether breakfast is included.

Situation 2

You are staying at the Hotel Presidente while vacationing in Mexico City. During the early morning hours, a robbery has occurred in the hotel room next to yours. Since you had easy access to the room, a police officer comes to question you about your early morning activities. Tell him that:

1) You got up at 6:30 A.M.
2) You took a shower around 6:45 A.M.
3) You had breakfast and got dressed.
4) You left at 8:00 A.M.

Table 5
Topic Card Evaluation

Shopping for Clothing

1) How often, where, and with whom do you go shopping?
2) Do you prefer to go downtown or to the shopping malls? Why?
3) What type of clothing do you need to buy now?
4) What colors do you prefer?
5) Where do you find good bargains?
6) How do you usually pay for things?
7) Where are you going to travel during your next vacation? What clothing are you going to buy for that trip?
8) Indicate anything else you would like to say on this subject.

minute period during which the instructor asks the individual student a few follow-up questions. Because of the increased time, two days are advisable.

The exit exam's speaking format was recently revised so as to make the testing approach even more interactive. With the OPI as a model, a mini-interactive, four-to-five-minute oral test was initiated. Significantly, this design eliminates the need for a preparatory period. The entire test is interactive and consists of three sections: the warm-up, the thematic questions/answers, and the wind-down. Identified are nine or ten lexical areas that students should control, with several suggested questions for each. Instructors select three or four different lexical groupings per student so that each student has a different series of questions.

Rationale for Listening Comprehension

In the past, the receptive skills of listening and reading have largely been overlooked for active development. Nevertheless, myriad recent studies on listening and reading comprehension, along with the publication of Spanish textbooks that integrate active listening and reading components, point to a change in the treatment of these skill areas in the beginning language classroom. The introduction of video and interactive video emphasizes the increasing focus on these language modalities. Long (1989, p. 38) cites more than 200 articles in her study on the "schema-theoretic perspective" of listening. Larson and Jones (1986, p. 119) state a rationale for including a systematic program to develop the listening skill when they assert that most of the situations a language learner faces in the real world involve listening much more than speaking. A greater concentration on listening additionally brings with it an enhancement of the language learner's speaking performance. When listening is seen as an active skill that needs to be developed and integrated with other skill areas, new possibilities for progress in language learning emerge.

Listening not only should be incorporated as a dynamic part of classroom practice but must form an essential component of the test. Authenticity in the selection of the listening materials represents yet another principal concern. Rogers and Medley (1988, p. 468) share the view that authentic selections are "best suited for the development of skill in listening and reading comprehension." The passage used for listening development should reflect a real-life environment as closely as possible. The listening descriptions from the 1986 *ACTFL Proficiency Guidelines* indicate a need for a program that reflects the contexts in which people function on a day-to-day basis in the world of the target language. Such an intention is made clear by the guidelines themselves, which "assume that all listening tasks take place in an authentic environment at a normal rate of speech using standard or near-standard norms" (*ACTFL Proficiency Guidelines*, 1986, p. 2). If the listening goals for an exit exam aim toward the intermediate range, students may realistically be expected to grasp the comprehension of some of the details in a short selection of connected discourse that deals with basic personal background and interests, survival needs, routine tasks, and social conventions.

Design of the Listening Comprehension Phase of the Exit Exam

The selection of the listening segments of an exit exam should parallel the description of the range that represents the instructional goal at that point in the learner's development. In the testing format at the University of South Carolina, two or three short listening activities that reflect authentic functions and contexts are chosen for the Spanish test. Since the entire written exam is 50 minutes long, the listening section should last a maximum of 10 minutes. Topics have included advertisements for travel plans, restaurants, rental apartments, and the like, as well as short interviews and conversations about someone's daily life and interests. Since selective listening is an important component of receptive skill development, language learners should have expectations for what they are going to hear. Chamot and Kupper (1989, p. 17) speak of the importance of "establishing a mind set in listening comprehension tasks." In the same way that native speakers have certain expectations for what they will hear in a certain environment or situation, students should be provided with some advance organizers in order to have an idea of the topic, the register, and/or the context.

First, advance organizers are always used as part of the testing procedure to provide students with an idea of the content. These organizers consist of a classification of the type of listening segment, such as labeling sections of the test as an interview, a conversation, an advertisement, or a daily survival situation. Next, a short description of the context is provided. Finally, students are given time to read the questions (which are in English) before hearing the passage, thereby obtaining a clear focus for the three or four pieces of information they must obtain. (See Tables 6 and 7.)

Authenticity of materials and selective listening form the bases for the listening section of the exit exam. The questions should derive from a functional context, which requires an understanding of the general topic along with some supporting pieces of information.

Table 6
Part 2: An Advertisement

Context: As you are listening to the radio, you hear the following advertisement for a restaurant. Since you are interested in finding a place to dine and the restaurant is close to your hotel, you take notes about the restaurant's facilities. Listen to the advertisement and record your answers on the answer sheet. You will hear the selection twice.

1) The restaurant
   a) serves Mexican as well as American food.
   b) serves seafood.
   c) is vegetarian.
2) On Tuesdays *La Habichuela* offers
   a) specials on margaritas.
   b) a buffet.
   c) fajitas for only 400 pesos.
3) The restaurant is located
   a) downtown.
   b) near the beach.
   c) convenient to the arts center.
4) Which of the following statements is true?
   a) The restaurant accepts only cash.
   b) You must make a reservation.
   c) The restaurant is open Tuesday through Saturday.

Listening text:

Para lo mejor en comida mexican venga al Restaurante La Habichuela. En La Habichuela servimos lo mejor en platos regionales, mexicanos y americanos a precios razonables. En su próxima visita pruebe nuestros tacos y fajitas de pollo y nuestras deliciosas enchiladas. Para acompañar su comida, le ofrecemos una variada selección de vinos y cervezas del país. Los martes es nuestro día familiar con un buffet delicioso por sólo 400 pesos por persona. Los miércoles es día de damas y ofrecemos margaritas y sangría gratis. Y, claro está, los viernes y sábados tenemos música en vivo. Además de nuestro comedor familiar tenemos salones privados para celebrar cumpleaños, bodas y aniversarios. El Restaurante La Habichuela está localizado en el centro de la ciudad y abre de martes a domingo y días feriados de 11:00 de la mañana a 12:00 de la noche. Aceptamos toda clase de tarjetas de crédito. No se necesita hacer reservación. El Restaurante La Habichuela, para usted y su familia.

Table 7
Part 3: Situations

Context: A man is traveling in Mexico and has just arrived in Mexico City. The taxi driver takes him to a downtown hotel, where he wants to find out if a room is available.

1) Which of the following statements is true?
   a) There is no room available in the hotel.
   b) There are five rooms available.
   c) The man needs one room.
2) The hotel clerk asks to see
   a) his passport.
   b) his driver's license.
   c) his airplane ticket.
3) The hotel room is
   a) number 474.
   b) on the fifth floor.
   c) on the third floor.
4) There is a restaurant
   a) in the hotel.
   b) next to the hotel.
   c) two blocks from the hotel.

Listening text:

–*Buenas noches. ¿En qué puedo servirle?*
–*Necesito una habitación.*
–*Bueno. ¿Tiene Ud. una reservación?*
–*No, señor. Lo siento mucho.*
–*No importa, tenemos dos habitaciones. ¿Para cuántas personas?*
–*Sólo uno.*
–*¿Y por cuántas noches?*
–*Cinco noches. Cuánto cuesta?*
–*50.000 pesos por noche.*
–*¿Aceptan las tarjetas de crédito?*
–*Sí, aceptamos* Visa *y* Mastercard. *Por favor, necesito ver su pasaporte.*
–*Sí, cómo no, aquí lo tiene.*
–*Muy bien, gracias. Aquí tiene la llave de su habitación. Está en el tercer piso, número 374.*
–*¿Hay un restaurante en el hotel?*
–*No, señor, pero hay uno muy cerca. Yo le recomiendo "La Barraca"; está aquí al lado del hotel.*
–*Muchos gracias.*
–*De nada. Adiós.*

Rationale for Reading Comprehension

As with listening, reading comprehension is now receiving more attention in the foreign language classroom. Larson and Jones (1986, p. 127) point to this interest and call for the creation of measurements of effective global reading proficiency. In a study on reading comprehension at the University of Virginia, Barnett (1988, p. 115) concludes that "students given special training in reading skill and strategy development at an earlier level will demonstrate greater progress in reading comprehension than those following a more traditional approach emphasizing reading beginning in the third semester."

Authentic material is necessary when working with reading development. Campbell (1990, p. 91) states that it is impossible to write a valid proficiency-based reading comprehension test without using authentic passages. Therefore, appropriate passages may include advertisements, news items, literary readings, forms, schedules, menus, and so on.

Design of the Reading Selection for the Exit Exam

At the University of South Carolina, two or three different selections are used for testing students' proficiency level. The kinds of materials chosen have included a portion of a short story, a news item, and/or an advertisement. Advance organizers are provided in a manner parallel to that of the listening section. The type of reading and the context are identified for students.

Students can thus anticipate what they are going to read. The questions – multiple-choice items in English – provide an additional preview of the content. Students are not expected to understand everything. Selective reading development and guessing from the context are important strategies at this level. (See Table 8.) The basic principle inherent in the reading section of the exit exam is that the results of the testing must demonstrate the student's ability to comprehend the main ideas and some supporting details in simple authentic text types.

Rationale for Testing Writing

With the writing skill, we once again need to focus on what students are able to write and at what level of linguistic accuracy. Are language learners able to fill out travel documents? Can they write notes, mes-

Table 8

Part 1: An Advertisement

You are planning a trip during spring break. Read the advertisement (see page 128) that describes different travel packages to Mexico, the Dominican Republic, Orlando, and Costa Rica. Answer the three questions below in order to decide which is the best trip for you.

1) All five packages include
   a) the use of a compact car.
   b) the airfare.
   c) a continental breakfast.
2) Which feature does the Bavaro Beach Resort have that the other packages do not?
   a) a city tour.
   b) a complimentary gift.
   c) breakfast and dinner.
3) Which of the following does the trip to Orlando offer that the other packages do not?
   a) meals.
   b) the use of a car.
   c) a city tour.

sages, and postcards? For writing to be effective at the beginning and intermediate levels, it should consistently reflect needs of a practical and personal nature. Omaggio (1986, p. 225) distinguishes between writing as a support skill and writing as a communicative task. With the increased emphasis on speaking, listening, and reading in the first-year foreign language classroom, it appears inevitable that postlistening and reading activities should encompass written tasks as a natural and frequent classroom activity. Writing, then, initially develops out of other skills and will continue to do so until it is sufficiently advanced to merit separate consideration.

As a highly individualized activity, writing may be improved through the use of such strategies as planning and revising. In Table 9 I indicate the components of an effective writing assignment when it is viewed as a process.

As an effective follow-up to listening and reading, writing in the years to come may form a more integral part of classroom activities than it has in the past. In Table 10 I establish a design for linking the use of authentic materials in the writing process.

EXCURSIONES

MEXICO CON MEXICANA

POR PERS.
HAB. DOBLE

MEXICO 6 DIAS: Incluye: tarifa aérea, 5 noches de alojamiento, impuestos de hotel, traslados, visita de ciudad recorriendo El Zócalo, Palacio Nacional, Catedral Metropolitana, Plaza de Las Tres Culturas, Chapultepec y zonas residenciales. Visita a la Basílica de Nuestra Señora de Guadalupe.   **$399.**

REPUBLICA DOMINICANA

BAVARO BEACH RESORT: 4 días, 3 noches Incluye: impuestos, tarifa aérea, traslados, desayunos y cenas estilo buffet.   **$299.**

ORLANDO

PASAJE, HOTEL Y AUTO: Incluye pasaje aéreo directo a Orlando. 5 días, 4 noches de hotel y auto subcompacto. Precio por persona ....   **$394.**

COSTA RICA CON LACSA

COSTA RICA 4 DIAS: Incluye tarifa aérea, alojamiento con impuesto, traslados, city tour, Volcán Irazú, Valle Orosis y Cártago con almuerzo.   **$399.**

COSTA RICA 7 DIAS: Incluye tarifa aérea, alojamiento con impuestos, traslados, city tour con Fábrica de Cuero, Volcán Irazú, Cártago con Almuerzo, Ojo de Agua, Sarchi y Volcán Poas.   **$499.**

Table 9
Establishing a Design for Writing Assignments

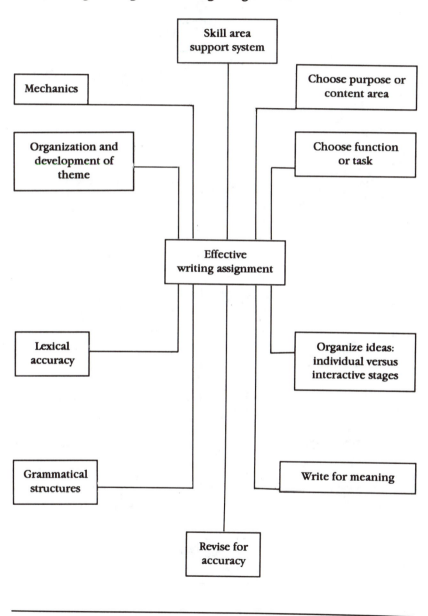

Skill area support system

Mechanics

Choose purpose or content area

Organization and development of theme

Choose function or task

Effective writing assignment

Lexical accuracy

Organize ideas: individual versus interactive stages

Grammatical structures

Write for meaning

Revise for accuracy

Table 10
Linking Authentic Materials

```
                         ┌──────────────────┐
                         │    Follow-up     │
                         │ interaction and  │
                         │    speaking      │
                         └──────────────────┘

┌────────────────────┐                      ┌────────────────────┐
│  Evaluative stage:  │                     │ Introduce grammar/ │
│   individual or     │                     │  lexical/cultural  │
│    interactive      │                     │      concept       │
└────────────────────┘                      └────────────────────┘

┌────────────────┐                          ┌────────────────────┐
│   Revise for   │                          │ Guided/controlled  │
│    accuracy    │                          │     practices      │
└────────────────┘                          └────────────────────┘

                     ┌──────────────────┐
                     │    Effective     │
                     │ writing assignment│
                     └──────────────────┘

┌────────────────────┐                      ┌────────────────────┐
│ Organize thoughts  │                      │    Paired and      │
│ to express meaning │                      │  group activities  │
└────────────────────┘                      └────────────────────┘

┌────────────────────┐                      ┌────────────────────┐
│    Authentic       │                      │    Authentic       │
│ writing situations │                      │ listening materials│
└────────────────────┘                      └────────────────────┘

                     ┌──────────────────┐
                     │    Authentic     │
                     │ reading materials│
                     └──────────────────┘
```

Design for Testing Writing as Part of an Exit Exam

The design for the writing phase of the exit exam asks students to perform two short tasks, one in the present tense and the other in the past tenses. In this section of the test, students must demonstrate a required performance level in both morphosyntactic and lexical accuracy. Control of the use of the present and the past tenses is a performance goal that each student must be able to demonstrate. (See Table 11.)

Because of the emphasis placed on lexical and grammatical accuracy in this section of the test, a system of analytical evaluation has been adopted that scores each student's performance according to morphosyntaxis (40%), lexical usage (40%), content/organization and development (5%), and mechanics (10%). Performance levels have been identified that range from excellent to very good to very weak. Additionally, the course coordinator has written descriptions of each category in order to establish a higher degree of uniformity in the grading process.

Conclusion

In a recent survey of Spanish placement testing in 1990, Wherritt and Cleary (1990, p. 163) concluded that our evaluation procedures need to encompass "the exit from undergraduate language requirements, language majors, and teacher certification." Many language programs also report the problematic transition from introductory to intermediate courses. Students often feel that they are doing something different in the second year than they were in the first. Language assessment through an exit exam seems especially appropriate because it pinpoints where students are when they finish one level of study and facilitates the establishment of a smoother transition to the next level. More important, with a proficiency basis for classroom teaching and a global evaluation of the four skills of listening, speaking, reading, and writing, what language learners can do and how well they can do it are clearly identified.

During the first two years of exit exam testing in Spanish at the University of South Carolina, the results have proved positive and encouraging. (Comparative Table 12 shows the failure rate for each skill area.) The results indicate that the failure rate for listening has decreased noticeably in year 2, during which a textbook with a strong listening program was adopted. An even more important trend is that students are accepting the responsibility for their own improvement in the one

Table 11
Writing Present and Past Tenses

1) You have a new penpal in Quito, Ecuador, who has just written to you for the first time. He or she asks you to describe yourself, your family, the city where you go to school, and your daily routine during the school year. Write your response in the form of a 75-word letter in Spanish.

2) Choose either *a* or *b* and write a narration in the past tenses in the space provided at the bottom of this page (50 words minimum).

   a) The Spanish Club to which you belong is offering a free, four-week trip to Spain for the coming summer. The club is looking for persons who have had a variety of experiences and past activities. Whoever writes the best essay about his or her previous summer will win. Write a composition in Spanish (using the past tense) that you would submit in the hope of winning this contest.

   b) Using the past tense, tell what happened last week to the people represented in the drawing below. You must create an ending.

---

or two skill areas in which they fail the test(s). Accountability for one's own improvement in language study is perhaps the most positive outcome of the Exit Exam testing. Both the language instructor and the students now have a way of tracking strengths and weaknesses in each language modality.

Several messages are evident in the application of an exit requirement:

1) Effective placement and exit mechanisms can be established.

2) The ability to use the language at an acceptable performance level in all of the modalities of language acquisition (speaking, listening, reading, and writing) is enhanced.

3) Articulation is an area that may be addressed in part through adequate placement and exit instruments (from high school to college, from introductory to intermediate, and from a classroom-tailored language orientation to an emphasis on literary topics).

4) Students should be able to apply the use of the language in context.

5) Needing to be established for exit testing are testing modes that indicate an adequate level of performance in each language modality.

6) Accountability is an ongoing concern. The level of accountability in both the instructor and the students is enhanced through the solid integration of effective placement and exit testing.

Though much progress has been made, even better procedures for achievement, placement, and exit exams need to be found. Much time is

Table 12

Spanish 122 (Semester 3) Exit Exam Comparative Results: Retake and End of Semester Percentages

Fall Semester, 1988
Descriptive oral evaluation: 6% retakes
Narrative oral evaluation: 3% retakes
Situation-based oral evaluation: 10% retakes
Listening: 10% retakes
Reading: 2% retakes
Writing (present and past): 14% retakes
End of semester failure rate: 4.6%

Spring Semester, 1989
Descriptive oral evaluation: 9% retakes
Narrative/situation-based oral evaluation: 17% retakes
Listening: 10% retakes
Reading: 14% retakes
Writing (present and past): 13% retakes
End of semester failure rate: 2.8%

Fall Semester, 1989
Descriptive oral evaluation: 8% retakes
Topic card oral evaluation/present tense: 13% retakes
Topic card oral evaluation/past tenses: 32% retakes
Listening: 5.5% retakes
Reading: 10% retakes
Writing present: 3.5% retakes
Writing past: 8.5% retakes
End of semester failure rate: 2.6%

Spring Semester, 1990
Descriptive oral evaluation: 14% retakes
Topic card oral evaluation: 17% retakes
Listening: 7% retakes
Reading: 11% retakes
Writing present: 6% retakes
Writing past: 11% retakes
End of semester failure rate: 4.5%

currently devoted to developing instruments that allow us to articulate more effectively the sequence of instruction. As we continue through the decade, language departments are increasingly confronted with the need to measure students' progress at different points in their instruction. The rationale and the formats for exit testing at the end of the required sequence of language learning that are presented in this study will serve, we hope, as a stimulus for continued work in this area.

Works Cited

ACTFL. *ACTFL Proficiency Guidelines*. Yonkers, NY: ACTFL Materials Center, 1986.

Barnett, Marva A. "Teaching Reading Strategies: How Methodology Affects Language Course Articulation." *Foreign Language Annals* 21 (1988): 109-19.

Campbell, Christine. "The Practical Alternative: Testing the Reading Comprehension of Large Numbers of Students with a Multiple-Choice Proficiency Test." *Realizing the Potential of Foreign Language Instruction*. Ed. Gerald L. Ervin. Lincolnwood, IL: National Textbook Company, 1990: 86-99.

Chamot, Anna Uhl & Lisa Kupper. "Learning Strategies in Foreign Language Instruction." *Foreign Language Annals* 22 (1989): 13-24.

"Excursiones." *El Mundo* (9 de septiembre 1990): 54.

Harlow, Linda L. & Rosario Caminero. "Oral Testing of Beginning Language Students at Large Universities: Is It Worth the Trouble?" *Foreign Language Annals* 23 (1990): 489-501.

Heilenman, Laura K. & Isabelle Kaplan. "Proficiency in Practice: The Foreign Language Curriculum." *Foreign Language Proficiency in the Classroom and Beyond*. Ed. Charles J. James. Lincolnwood, IL: National Textbook Company, 1986: 55-78.

Larson, Jerry W. & Randall L. Jones. "Proficiency Testing for the Other Language Modalities." *Teaching for Proficiency, the Organizing Principle*. Lincolnwood, IL: National Textbook Company, 1986: 113-38.

Long, Donna Reseigh. "Second Language Listening Comprehension: A Schema-Theoretic Perspective." *Modern Language Journal* 73 (1989): 32-40.

Magnan, Sally Sieloff. "From Achievement toward Proficiency through Multi-Sequence Evaluation." *Foreign Language Proficiency in the Classroom and Beyond*. Ed. Charles J. James. Lincolnwood, IL: National Textbook Company, 1986: 117-45.

Omaggio, Alice C. *Teaching Language in Context*. Boston: Heinle & Heinle Publishers, 1986.

Rogers, Carmen Villegas & Frank W. Medley, Jr. "Language with a Purpose: Using Authentic Materials in the Foreign Language Classroom." *Foreign Language Annals* 21 (1988): 467-78.

Underhill, Nic. *Testing Spoken Spanish*. Cambridge: Cambridge University Press, 1987.

Valdés, Guadalupe, Enrique Lessa, María Paz Echeverriarza & Cecilia Pino. "The Development of a Listening Skills Comprehension-based Program: What Levels of Proficiency Can Learners Reach?" *Modern Language Journal* 72 (1988): 415-25.

Wherritt, Irene & Anne T. Cleary. "A National Survey of Spanish Language Testing for Placement or Outcome Assessment at B.A.-granting Institutions in the United States." *Foreign Language Annals* 23 (1990): 157-65.

Just Do It: Directing TAs toward Task-based and Process-oriented Testing

Sally Sieloff Magnan
University of Wisconsin-Madison

Few would deny that, in our grade-oriented educational system, classroom tests supply implicit, if not explicit, goals for student learning. This is precisely what Barnes, Klee, and Wakefield (1991) observed at the University of Minnesota: when proficiency exit tests were implemented, students began to work to attain not only good grades but the functional language ability necessary to pass the proficiency exam. Course objectives stated by the language program director (LPD) and conveyed to students by teaching assistants (TAs) are likely to be forgotten, as the content and format of the tests become the short-term and, by extension, the long-term goals for the courses.

TAs, as well as students, may be influenced by this backwash effect of tests on the curriculum. Research discussed by Shohamy (1991) shows how tests can narrow the scope of education when instructors teach primarily for the tests and neglect other content. It may be hard for TAs to resist teaching toward course tests, especially when a direct focus on the test helps students feel secure, encouraging a positive and trusting class atmosphere – one of the few tenets of good teaching advocated by different methodologies over the years (Grittner, 1990). Indeed, the American tradition of test fairness tells us that our tests must have instructional validity. In the case of *Debra P.* v *Turlington*

(1979), this tradition of educational fairness was supported by an appellate court ruling that a high school graduation test was "fundamentally unfair in that it *may* have covered matters not taught in the schools of the state" (Madaus, 1983, p. 22). We must test *what* we teach in a way that we make accessible through *how* we teach.

For about 20 years now, we have purported to teach for communicative competence, for ability to use a variety of linguistic and sociolinguistic skills to interact appropriately with members of another culture. Yet for the sake of expediency, many programs still test mainly isolated components of these skills or the knowledge on which they are based, as witnessed in decontextualized, discrete-point grammar tests. By allowing discrete-point testing to transfer from grammar-based into communication-oriented classrooms, we may reinforce teaching traditions of spending most of the class period on grammar (Grittner, 1987; Long, 1986; Nerenz, 1979) and lead students to believe that grammar is the primary focus of language study. Research suggests that students' beliefs about foreign language study, even if inaccurate, influence their success in foreign language classes (Horwitz, 1990), and that these perceptions are shaped in large part by what happens in their first foreign language classes (Duff & Polio, 1990). It may be ineffective to tell TAs and students to concentrate on integrating skills for communicative purposes if our tests are limited to the additive and analytic features of language study.

This is not to say that discrete-point grammar testing has no place at all in a communicative curriculum, but it is to advise that our testing practices must evolve to reduce the potentially serious discrepancy between how and for what purpose foreign language is taught and how it is tested. In 1981, Wesche stated the problem clearly:

> Language testing which does not take into account propositional and illocutionary development beyond the sentence level, as well as the interaction between language behavior and real-world phenomena, is at best getting at only a part of communicative competence (p. 552).

Our lack of discourse-driven testing for functional language use may stem from three main factors: (1) students or teachers may prefer more familiar discrete-point testing (Bacon & Finneman, 1990), as it may seem more straightforward and hence more accessible and objective; (2) teachers may find it difficult and time-consuming to design and grade discourse-based and functional tests; and (3) the profession has not yet developed a widely accepted, practical model of what communicative testing should entail.

Just as communicative language teaching encompasses a range of methodologies and language acquisition theories that underlie them

(Schulz, 1991), suggestions for classroom-based communicative testing are becoming more diverse and at times contradictory. Should we test skills separately so that measurement of ability in one skill is not compromised by ability in another? Or should we measure ability to use skills together, concentrating on integrating the many linguistic and sociolinguistic components of language learning? Should we embed grammar items in paragraph-length stories in order to provide a discourse framework through which we can grade meaning as well as form? Or are such paragraph story items to be rejected as artificial in favor of personalized or situational formats?

All these questions relate to testing the *product* of learning. They differ only in how that product is defined and thus how it is evoked from the student. When we speak about making language tests more communicative, we should seek to measure not only *products*, or stages in learning, but also *processes* of acquisition. Research today uses the term *process* quite broadly to include learning strategies and styles, communicative strategies and techniques for conversational management, and curriculum design features, such as writing as a process. It is in this very broad sense that *process* will be discussed in this article – the many and complex ways a learner attempts to acquire a foreign language and use it to interact with target language speakers, to negotiate meaning by calling on different skills as appropriate to the task and the situation. Clearly, all these processes are highly individual, and thereby seem to defy objective assessment. Yet for our testing to reflect what goes on in our classrooms, we must seek out ways to reward students for their attempts to process language as they direct their own learning.

Shohamy (1991) suggests that it is time to broaden our definition of what constitutes assessment, to include, in addition to tests, self-evaluation, peer-assessment, and collections of student work in portfolios, diaries, and observations. I will suggest how to broaden the tests themselves, to spiral test exercises from rather isolated discrete-point items through more global exercises to interactive and communicative activities wherein process is considered as well as language product.

This article, then, examines the tension between the profession's desire to make classroom testing more communicative and the situational constraints imposed by the nature of multisection, TA-taught programs. It will explore the following areas: our evolving view of what constitutes a good foreign language test; ways to direct TAs to create tests that are more communicative; ideas for making tests more process-oriented and task-based; and strategies for spiraling different test formats through the curriculum. For all language programs, the effects of the testing program are far-reaching. In TA programs, backwash effects have an additional dimension: not only do tests direct how undergraduates learn; they also serve as models that influence how TAs teach throughout their professional careers.

Evolving View of Classroom Testing: Considerations for TAs

From the beginnings of communicative methodologies in the 1970s, innovations in testing have lagged behind innovations in teaching. Tests in the 1970s still consisted mostly of grammar, with occasional reading passages, essays, and dictations. These grammar items usually asked students to give morphological forms without a context or to fill in the blanks in unrelated sentences. Grammatical accuracy made up a disproportionate part of the grade and was taken into consideration in all areas, especially in the grammar sections, where meaning was often not involved. Such discrete-point testing was considered efficient; context was superfluous.

Although Valette (1977) suggested ways to test each of the four skills, culture, and literature, relatively few teachers put these suggestions into practice. Speaking, in particular, was considered too labor-intensive to test. The testing of culture fell out of favor over the years because of difficulties in defining what constituted culture. Both speaking and culture were often considered too subjective to grade easily: students complained, TAs were hesitant, and LPDs wondered if assessment of these "skills" could not just be included in class performance.

In the early 1980s, the movement for integrated communicative testing was encouraged by the ACTFL proficiency interview and guidelines. Despite research showing no statistical difference between discrete-point and integrative tests (Farhady, 1979) and the recognition that integrative tests may have less diagnostic and remedial guidance value (Henning, 1987), the profession now actively sought more integrative and communicative types of classroom testing.

Grading Communication of Meaning

An early and essential innovation toward creating more communicative tests was a change in what was graded. Savignon (1982), examining what students must consider when doing a dictation, proposed a three-part grading system to represent the complexity of this task, with one point for conveying the meaning, one point for capturing the sound, and one point for using the exact word, including its spelling. Even if

Savignon's system appeared cumbersome for regular classroom use, especially in TA-taught programs, it had an important impact on the thinking of test developers. Points should be awarded for understanding meaning as well as for reproducing exact language; points should be awarded for approximating what was heard, that is, for showing evidence of the hypothesis-testing process of language learning.

A similar message is seen in the grading of early speaking tests, such as the recorded Indiana University Communicative Ability Test (Valdman & Moody, 1979) in which points are awarded for appropriateness of speech as well as for grammatical form and for accuracy and fluency of pronunciation. Language was thus evaluated not only for adherence to grammatical norms but also for respect for semantic and sociolinguistic notions and for attempts to use communicative strategies.

Testing Each Skill Separately versus Testing Skills Together

Such innovation in testing paved the way for fairly wide acceptance, if not practice, of more communicative testing in each of the four skills. Patterned after the ACTFL guidelines in which each skill has its own description, tests emerged for evaluating speaking, listening, reading, and writing independently of one another. To test listening or reading comprehension, ACTFL-type proficiency tests often use multiple-choice and true-false questions in the students' native language in order to avoid confusing students' ability to handle the test passage with their ability to understand the questions. Although multiple-choice or true-false questions can be designed to provide insights into students' attempts to process meaning (e.g., by focusing on guessing, summarizing, getting the gist, rephrasing, or inferencing), many of these items concentrate primarily on product (choice of the correct grammatical form or vocabulary word or recall of specific details).

An alternative method for testing the receptive skills – now used mainly in research – is the recall format. After hearing or reading a passage, students write down in their native language all they can remember. Recalls may provide unique opportunities for considering students' attempts to process language, since students are freer to show individual interaction with language in recalls than when responding to specific questions made by test developers. Unfortunately, in classroom testing the potential of the recall format is not often realized, perhaps because grading appears more time-consuming and more subjective.

Consideration of process might fit more naturally into activities that integrate rather than segregate skills. Important questions are raised. Is it unnatural or artificial to separate skills in an approach aimed at building communicative competence? If we are to test, and teach, skills together, is there a most natural or most effective pairing? Instead of the traditional association of listening and speaking and reading and writing, Swaffar (1991) prefers the division of recursive tasks (reading and writing) and immediacy tasks (listening and speaking). Coupling reading and writing, for instance, would allow us to consider the cognitive processes used with the written mode, processes that are different from those required by speech and listening. For example, students could skim reading material to make lists of important points. They could note areas of redundancy in reading and summarize the reading material in telegraphic style. They could keep track of sections where they needed to reread, diagraming logical connectors, noting details, or listing and defining difficult terms. With listening and speaking, students could practice and ultimately be evaluated on turn taking, on the ability to identify main points and to return to them later in the conversation, and on how they indicate to their conversation partners that they are listening attentively.

Such tasks demand several types of interaction–between skills, between persons, and between learner and the oral or written input. Systematic consideration of these interactions could provide insights into what processes students use as they negotiate and convey meaning to others. Of course, since students process language in different ways, evaluation cannot be overly prescriptive. Rather, it should be descriptive, looking at the quantity of processing attempts as much as at the quality of these attempts as judged by the instructor. Quality judgments could still be made in terms of efforts to use strategies practiced in class and whether strategies lead to successful communication. But especially given the uncertain state of research, we must be careful not to assess negatively a processing strategy that may be successful for a particular student although not for others. As Stevick (1990, p. 146) reminds us, teaching students to use strategies requires the instructor to "perceive and work with what is available within each individual learner." Such individual consideration must certainly also be true of assessment–perhaps even more so.

A dynamic, task-based, and process-oriented approach to testing may exert a more positive influence on the curriculum than separate-skill, product-based testing can. In teaching to task-based and process-oriented evaluations, we move our programs farther along the communicative continuum and take into account the purposes and individual natures of language learning.

Testing Cultural Notions

Testing cultural notions has always been problematic, no doubt because many languages are associated with more than one culture and because we have not yet arrived at a suitable definition of what "culture" is. Problems in defining culture work against our creating separate tests for culture, but they should not discourage us from incorporating cultural aspects into our other testing: passages for testing listening and reading should be authentic and often contain cultural content; tests of writing ability should demonstrate the depth of students' progress in attaining cultural goals for the course; tests for speaking should re-create, as much as possible, authentic purposes for communication and the conditions under which it occurs in the target country.

In fact, understanding cultural differences is basic to all communication. Processing language for interpersonal interaction means, of necessity, respecting and responding to cultural difference. Cultural notions should thus be fundamental to all types of testing in the communicative curriculum, not segregated from them.

Testing Reading and Listening with Authentic Materials

The notion of separating skills is consistent with Heilenman and Kaplan's (1985) argument that foreign language curricula should take into account how different skills are acquired at different rates and with different degrees of control. Typically, the ability to understand exceeds the ability to produce a foreign language. The realization that teaching receptive and productive skills should not march in tandem encourages instructors to use authentic texts in class, often combined with product-oriented, multiple-choice, or true-false questions.

Bacon and Finneman (1990) review the literature on using authentic reading materials to conclude that learners can cope with authentic materials and seem to be motivated by them, provided that they are *willing* to let go of certain beliefs (e.g., that beginners need simplified language) and try material written for a native audience. Of key importance is the authors' note that "if students suspect that the input is not directly related to their evaluation in the course, they may be less willing to interact with it" (p. 467). Once again, the link between testing and teaching becomes critical.

Anxiety related to dealing with the unfamiliar may well be the greatest obstacle to the use of authentic listening and reading texts, particularly for testing. Research by Horwitz, Horwitz, and Cope (1986) indicates that both the unfamiliarity inherent to authentic texts and the testing situation increase anxiety for some students. Testing with authentic texts may also increase anxiety for those TAs who, having themselves learned the target language in a situation in which input was controlled, perceive it as overly difficult or unfair to ask students in a testing situation to cope with what might be seen as extraneous variables.

One way of dealing with this anxiety would be to test the process of reading as well as the product, as suggested by Swaffar, Arens, and Byrnes (1991). How did students approach the text? Did they use guessing strategies? If so, were those guessing strategies effective? When computer-adaptive testing becomes available, students can check on definitions and uses of words and instructors can receive a printout of their inquiries, providing insights into how students go about extracting meaning from the text. Partial or extra credit could be awarded for demonstrated attempts to use processing strategies, even if the product (final answer, interpretation, or communicative attempt) is faulty. Just as math students often recapture points by "showing their work," foreign language students should be rewarded for the interlanguage gains they can demonstrate by revealing their communicative and learning processes.

Authentic material has also become important for testing listening. Because of situational constraints, the instructor must often reproduce the oral input or play it from a tape, making "simulation of nonclassroom discourse . . . necessarily imperfect, incomplete, and artificial" (Herschensohn, 1990, p. 455). In the case of language that was not originally intended to be presented through recording, an instructor's re-creation can restore the immediacy of the original and allow students to benefit from seeing the mouth of the speaker. It can also greatly reduce anxiety: the familiarity of the instructor's voice helps to counteract the unfamiliarity of the input. One thing is essential if the teacher chooses to re-create the listening material or devise his or her own: the listening text must be given to students with its redundancies, repetitions, and even false starts, which research has shown to impact strongly on comprehension (Chaudron, 1988).

Another primary consideration for testing listening is the question of which norm to follow: orthoepic, popular, or slang. Indeed, this question remains open for both teaching and testing (Joseph, 1988). Whatever language we consider suitable and useful for teaching, that language should also be used in testing. Although prewritten, concise passages in normative language may be appealing for standardizing the multisection course, such creations may become a hindrance to students' ability to understand. Furthermore, limiting testing of such passages to product-based questions, be they in multiple-choice, true-false, or more open formats, restricts learners from fully demonstrating their evolving communicative ability and endangers communicative teaching goals. Ultimately, it is not the format of tests – or of learning activities – that makes the distinction between product and process; rather, it is how that format is used. As we consider process in testing as well as in teaching, we will find a greater resemblance between the two: a good way to teach something becomes a good way to assess that it has been learned.

Testing Extended Writing

Reviewing studies on both writing and reading, Bernhardt (1991) shows that recent research has not yet provided clear answers on how to test – or teach – these skills. Most analyses of how to evaluate writing offer mainly descriptions of what has worked in specific programs, focusing on writing as a process and on composition grading (Gaudiani, 1981; Semke, 1984; & Terry, 1989). Suggestions for teaching the process of writing could well be converted into assessment techniques, including webbing activities, making notes, listing pros and cons, categorizing and outlining information, and doing partial composition, such as creating titles or finishing incomplete stories. Such skeletal writing activities would probably be quicker to grade – an important consideration for TAs – allowing us to include them more regularly on our tests. They would also lend themselves to evaluating meaning, organization, and logic, in that grammar would tend to be telegraphic. By considering such test items, TAs would gain experience in focusing on elements of communication as well as, or in preference to, elements of form.

For grading extended writing, Terry (1989) gives examples of both holistic and analytic techniques. Calming the fear that holistic grading is too subjective, research by Kaczmarek (1980) shows substantial reliability in teachers' subjective judgments, which correlate strongly both with similar judgments by independent raters and with scores obtained through an objective technique centering on efficiency, accuracy, and linguistic appropriateness of expression. This research offers two important messages for LPDs and TAs: (1) that TAs can probably do holistic grading in a consistent manner, if they are properly prepared, and (2) that even "objective" grading need not focus on grammar and spelling. Workshops are needed to help groups of TAs gain consistency in grading writing tasks with an emphasis on communication and on the unique characteristics of extended written discourse. In such workshops, TAs and the LPD could independently rank-order and then grade the same compositions, discuss the expectations on which they based their evaluations, and eventually articulate a group consensus of what it means to test and grade writing as a communicative skill.

Analytic scoring breaks subjective grading into categories in an attempt to make the procedure more objective. Although perhaps more time-consuming than holistic grading, analytic scoring can offer useful information to students or be an effective development technique for TAs. Most suggestions for analytic scoring still focus predominately on linguistic elements as products: grammar, vocabulary, mechanics, fluency, appropriateness (Heaton, 1975, cited in Terry, 1989). To encourage also expression of meaning and the processes underlying it, the categories might be arranged differently: attempts to address the audience appropriately; markers revealing logic and coherence of argument; use of circumlocution and other communicative strategies; expression of key points; and fluency and accuracy of writing. Again, workshops offer a useful forum for LPDs and TAs to articulate categories and work toward consistency in their use.

Testing Grammar

Of the many linguistic elements used in communication, grammar is, rightly or wrongly, still the one most widely tested and the one with the greatest emphasis on accuracy of product. Although discrete-point, form-based grammar testing in isolated words or single sentences is still very common, and at times useful, it is being replaced by contextualized testing, including a range of convergent to divergent activities in discourse frames. According to Omaggio (1986), contextualized testing has several advantages over discrete-point items in isolated sentences: it puts linguistic features into naturalistic contexts; it allows grading for meaning as well as for form; and it motivates students because it resembles authentic language use while providing targeted feedback for teachers and students. Of the diverse formats found along the continuum of contextualized item types, the following three appear to be the most commonly used for testing grammar:

1) Use of *paragraph frames* that embed grammatical items in a meaningful chunk of language, either giving cultural information or telling a story, often with imaginary characters.
2) Preference for *personalized responses*, wherein the grammatical item is evoked through questions about students' lives and ideas.
3) A move toward eliciting personalized responses through *situations* that invite students to use specific linguistic functions and even grammar items.

These three tests formats are outgrowths of the popularity of similar activities in teaching and in textbooks. Of them, the first, the use of paragraph frames, especially for creating stories with fictious characters, is probably the most controversial.

Paragraph Frames

The embedding of grammar items into paragraph-length stories can be limited to individual test sections, or the same story line can be woven throughout a single test or even throughout the tests of an entire semester. For example, Myton (1989) prepared a contextualized exam telling about someone's reaction to a chain letter. Each section converted a standard testing technique on typical grammatical material into an episode in a story. (See Table 1.)

Fox (1987) wrote a series of quizzes and exams that over an entire semester continued the story of two students meeting, falling in love, getting married, and traveling abroad. Such extended contextualization aims to maintain students' interest and to help their comprehension through understanding the characters and anticipating the plot.

It may be, however, that the testing situation and the emotions associated with it overpower the appeal of a story line. Walz (1989) suggests that when doing textbook activities, students may not pay attention to the contexts in which discrete grammar tasks are embedded,

---

Table 1
Sequence of Activities in a Contextualized Grammar Test

Test title: *La lettre de chaîne.*

Test introduction: Describes Marcel, a reasonable but superstitious student who receives a chain letter.

Section 1: *Le contenu de la lettre.* (Dictation.)

Section 2: *Chez le receveur des postes.* (Students assume the role of Marcel, who complains to the postmaster, and write answers to the postmaster's questions.)

Section 3: *Chez le psychologue.* (A fill-in dialogue telling what happens when Marcel goes to the psychiatrist for advice. Students write commands that the doctor gives to Marcel.)

Section 4: *Dans le Restau-U.* (A fill-in conversation between Marcel and his friends. Students complete the dialogue in the past tense and learn that one of Marcel's friends sent the chain letter as a joke.)

Section 5: *Au tour de Marcel!* Students create another chain letter for Marcel to send to his friend in order to get even.)

---

especially if they can perform the task without understanding the surrounding context. VanPatten's (1990) research on grammar and listening alerts us to a potentially more basic problem: early-stage learners may not always be capable of processing input for both meaning and grammar simultaneously. Does the context, then, become a burden, simply making the exercise harder and longer for students to do and more difficult for TAs to write? Especially in testing, embedding discrete grammar items in paragraph frames would then be inefficient and perhaps discouraging. It would also be limiting in that it reduces the variety of forms tested within each exercise.

Especially in testing, embedding discrete grammar items in paragraph frames would then be inefficient and perhaps discouraging. It would also be limiting in that it reduces the variety of forms tested within each exercise. Walz (1989) and VanPatten (1991) also lead us to question the theoretical value of creating story lines for the purpose of discrete grammar testing. Is imposing a false reality through carefully devised tales about imaginary people consistent with the notion of authentic communication? Are we not just masking discrete-point structural tests and tricking ourselves into believing that we are testing communication, when we should be searching for more truly integrative and communicative techniques? Are we not still focusing nearly exclusively on product – on correctly selecting and forming the targeted grammatical forms – and neglecting the crucial role of process?

These are serious questions, yet they may not be cause to abandon entirely the notion of embedding grammar items in paragraph frames. Walz (1989) summarizes research attesting to the value of context for understanding reading and listening texts and for learning vocabulary. If, as in Myton's chain letter, students must understand a story line in order to successfully complete the test, we are in effect testing how reading comprehension interacts with the other skills being tested. If within each activity the context is crucial to making the right choices on the tests, we may be, as Omaggio (1986) hopes, directing students to focus on the purpose of language as well as its form? In acknowledgment of students' varied learning styles, interests, and motivations, we should not dismiss too quickly the positive effect that such discourse frames might have for some students, while annoying others. As Henning (1990) advises, research on the value of contextualized testing should be a high priority in the 1990s – research in terms of the narrow definition of contextualization as paragraph frames and, in Omaggio's (1986) broader sense, including, among other formats, the personalized and situational activities that are discussed below.

Paragraph Frames Leading to Personalization

Concerns for lack of naturalness and authenticity might be alleviated by talking about the students themselves instead of imaginary characters. For example, the activity in Table 2 begins as a paragraph-framed test of question formation, at times discrete-point and at times more open-ended, and ends with related personalized questions.

This exercise exhibits many features already noted for paragraph-framed discrete-point items. Half the items in part A (1, 3) are discrete-point, having only one response. The others (2, 4) are more open-ended for form but still fairly restricted for content. Part B is personal but does not make the link between answering these written questions on the test and the possibility of answering similar questions in real life (see Galloway & Labarca, 1990, pp. 138-39, on personal authenticity). Although such test items may be useful – even necessary – for diagnosing specific learner weaknesses and for measuring and rewarding the ability to monitor language for careful style, if they are not balanced by more open-ended testing they could distract students from working toward communicative goals.

Table 2

Linking Paragraph-framed Grammar Items to Personalized Expression

1) *Conversation au restaurant universitaire*. Ecrivez les questions d'André.
   Modèle:
   André: Salut, Martine. Ça va?
   Martine: Oui, *ça va*.
   a) André: _____ est-ce que Suzanne et Marie ne sont pas ici?
   Martine: *Parce qu'*elles étudient.
   b) André: _____ ?
   Martine: A la bibliothèque. Elles préparent un examen.
   c) André: _____ est leur examen?
   Martine: Demain. Elles sont très agitées.
   André: C'est pour quel cours?
   Martine: Leur cours d'allemand.
   d) André: _____ ?
   Martine: Moi, non! Pas l'allemand! J'étudie le français.
2) *Et vous?*
   a) D'habitude, où préférez-vous étudier?
   b) Quand avez-vous votre prochain examen? Dans quel cours est-ce?
   c) Qu'est-ce que vous faites quand vous n'étudiez pas?

Note: Created by a group of TAs at University of Wisconsin-Madison, 1989.

The exercise in Table 2 goes beyond simple paragraph-framed discrete-point grammar testing in several ways that are advantageous for the communicative curriculum. It requires students to understand the dialogue in order to fill in most of the blanks. It introduces students to a topic about which they then comment freely in relation to their own lives. And it offers instructors the opportunity to use both objective and subjective grading, weighted toward items that require more expanded production and expression of personal meaning.

Personalization in Situation

More direct forms of personalized testing often ask students to envision themselves in a typical situation in the target culture and to react appropriately. For example, the task in Table 3 aims to test whether students can make a polite refusal.

In all these examples, cultural appropriateness is at issue. Would wine be offered at a party in the target culture and if so, would a guest refuse it? Do students study at the library? Are chain letters part of the target culture? Would people send them as jokes? As with any interaction, students must be made aware of when they are using the foreign language to express their own background and values and when they are learning to understand or assume those of another culture.

Although paragraph-framed stories and personalized and situational exercises could provide opportunities to assess processes of communication and language learning, this is unfortunately not often done. To date, the profession has focused primarily on preparing items, leaving the evaluation of students' incomplete or imperfect attempts to communicate at the rudimentary level of giving a point for appropriate meaning (often word choice or basic communication) and a point for correct grammatical form.

Directing TAs to Create Communicative Tests

For the TA-taught program, the most crucial consideration in choosing among test types may be how well TAs can create them. Of the techniques discussed, paragraph-framed grammar items and extended listening comprehension items are probably the hardest for TAs to write. For personalized and situational grammar items and for most writing exercises, TAs offer a stimulus from which students generate language. For paragraph-framed grammar activities and for most global listening and some reading comprehension items, TAs need to produce the language, anticipate the student response, and shape the test accordingly.

Table 3
Personalized Task in a Situation

At a dinner party, you are offered wine that you do not like. You wish to refuse the wine but do not want to hurt the host's feelings. You say: _____.

Some TAs may lack the materials and the linguistic and cultural sophistication needed to write authentic-like passages. Beginning TAs in particular do not yet know the textbook or their students well enough to understand the long-term course goals established by the LPD. As part of an instructional team, TAs are asked to respect the wishes of their peers in creating tests when these wishes may not be clear to them, and to grade consistently with colleagues whose graded tests they may rarely see. Considering their inexperience and the teaching situation, it is not surprising that many TAs find test writing time-consuming and anxiety-provoking.

To assist TAs in test preparation, LPDs usually devise a system whereby work is shared: the LPD creates the tests, TAs work in rotating teams, or TAs prepare tests in committee meetings. There are, of course, variations on these basic procedures, such as whether TAs do the actual writing of test sections independently at home or during meetings with the course supervisor or LPD present (Lee, 1989). The common – and troublesome – element is that beginning and experienced TAs usually share the writing task equally.

As an alternative approach, beginning TAs could be excused from creating tests during the first few weeks or the first semester and instead be asked to examine and analyze tests written by experienced TAs or the LPD. To direct their critiques, TAs could be given a list of questions such as those offered in the Appendix. Their critiques could be shared among the TAs and used by the LPD to create the final version of the test.

Responding to the notion that attention to input should precede demand for output, this approach has several advantages. Beginning TAs are involved in the test-writing process without spending large amounts of time. As they analyze the work of more experienced colleagues, they prepare themselves to write tests in the future. Examining the efforts of others, they see more objectively the potential problems with certain test items. By sharing critiques, they learn to understand and respect what TA colleagues and the LPD feel is important in a multi-section test and how to work as an instructional team. Moreover, the final test is no doubt improved, at least in terms of its acceptability to all instructors.

Understanding the Problem: Paper-and-Pencil Tests

Still, regardless of the basic differences among the testing techniques discussed so far and their important implications and limitations for TA-taught programs, these testing models all share a feature that greatly limits their potential as measures of communicative competence: they rely on paper-and-pencil formats. Written tests are traditionally efforts of the individual, while linguistic interaction customarily involves two or more persons. Written tests typically measure static products of instruction, while interaction is dependent more on the dynamic processes of communication that interact with individual processes of acquisition. As Galloway and Labarca (1990) point out, measuring language *products* may tell us little about the *process* that leads students to, and beyond, those products. If we are to teach for interactional competence, as suggested by Kramsch (1986), we must supplement traditional paper-and-pencil tests with task-based activities that offer us insights into communication and acquisition processes.

A First Step toward Diversity in Testing: Adding a Speaking Test

We have already taken a first, tentative step away from paper-and-pencil testing by initiating speaking tests. In their 1988 survey of French, German, and Spanish beginning language programs at large TA institutions, Harlow and Caminero (1990) found that 57% give, at least once a term, a speaking test that contributes substantially to the final course grade – most commonly 10%. In the various test designs reported we can still note a certain product orientation, reminiscent of oral testing models of the 1970s (Linder, 1977; Valette, 1977) and of parts of the ACTFL Oral Proficiency Interview. These include, in order of popularity, individual or paired interviews, role-plays, descriptions of pictures, and combinations of these with a section on pronunciation. (For examples of these and other oral testing strategies, see Gutiérrez, 1987; Magnan, 1985; Omaggio, 1983, 1986; Pino, 1989; Swain, 1984; Terry, 1986). Emphasis on product is noted more in grading than in test format. Grading was mostly global (60%) with consideration of both content and form. There was no mention, however, of specific components of grading that attempted to look at process.

To focus on the process of interactive discourse, we might assign some points for the following features, several of which are suggested by Kramsch (1986): asking for clarification; following or making a change in topic; taking turns and managing the conversation; holding the floor and gaining time with rhetorical questions; understanding and reacting to the tone of the conversation; and recognizing the viewpoints of the conversation partner and using this knowledge to make persuasive arguments. To elicit the type of interaction that would allow us to evaluate these features, we would need to emphasize interaction through such techniques as role-plays, which attempt to reduce the imbalance of power between instructor and student, and activities in which there is an opportunity for group interactions.

To facilitate testing speaking in the TA-taught program, Harlow and Caminero (1990) make a number of useful suggestions. To save time, TAs can test on tape, in class, or in pairs or groups of students. Or the LPD can lighten the syllabus and use a few teaching days for oral testing, with the added benefit of having classrooms available for giving the tests. Testing guidelines and grading procedures can be prepared either by the LPD or by teams of TAs and supported by workshops at which TAs can listen to or watch taped tests, participate in microtesting sessions with real students, rate tests independently, and discuss evaluations.

Toward Process-oriented, Task-based Testing

Innovation away from the typical paper-and-pencil test does not need to be limited to the evaluation of speaking. Given that we often use more than one skill in communicative interactions, competence in all skills can – and should – be assessed in a task-based testing model. Process-oriented testing that integrates skills can extend assessment from a static demonstration of knowledge to a more dynamic and individual notion of using language for communicative purposes.

For this discussion, a task-based test activity is defined as one in which students *use* language in a natural way to accomplish a task they might realistically need to perform in the target culture. Task-based tests should involve several types of interaction, which, as Kramsch (1986) points out, are essentially relative, variable, and unpredictable: interaction between student and language input (oral and/or written); between student and others (classmates, instructors, native speakers); between student and the conventions, values, and beliefs of the target society; and between student and his or her developing interlanguage system.

We can add a process dimension to a task-based test by asking learners to make evident the learning and communicative strategies they use to accomplish the tasks. Our response to their processes must be directive in its evaluation, yet flexible. We must reward students for expanding processes that lead them effectively toward communicative goals, without using grades to dictate the use of certain processes exclusively.

Testing activities, much like teaching activities, could be based on interactive situations that learners might experience in the target country. For example:

1) *Task: Getting information from a loudspeaker about plane departures.* In an airport in Paris, you hear an announcement over the loudspeaker. Write down what information you hope and expect to hear. Then take notes on the information you actually hear and talk with another student to determine whether you heard the information correctly. You will be evaluated on how well you organize your listening, whether you use guessing strategies where needed, how you use language to interact with your partner, and on whether you understand the information given.

   Considerations in grading, in addition to fluency and accuracy:
   a) Predicting information, with consideration for breadth and guessing as needed.
   b) Taking notes, with consideration for queries or guessing possible meanings.
   c) Discussing with a classmate, with consideration for initiating and managing the conversation and communicative strategies used.

2) *Task: Selecting and summarizing written information for someone else.* You are looking for information about a preselected topic. Look over these three short texts and decide which contains the information you need. Show how you interact with the text in order to make your decision (underline what you read, make notes, or comments, etc.). After you find the text containing the information, read it in more detail and write notes to summarize it for a classmate. Record any aids you use in reading the text (dictionary, classmate, grammar reference). Finally, tell your summary to a classmate, so that he or she can in turn give this information accurately to the class. You will be graded on the accuracy of information conveyed and on how you use language to find the information and convey it to others.

   Considerations in grading, in addition to fluency and accuracy:
   a) Selecting the text, with consideration for the number and appropriateness of strategies revealed.
   b) Noting the main features of the text, with consideration for queries or guesses and using aids where needed.

c) Summarizing for a classmate, with consideration for organizing the summary and verifying partner's comprehension.

d) Conveying information to the class, with consideration for organization and speculation about meaning if needed.

3) *Task: Solving a problem collaboratively.* You will work in a group of three to arrange an event. Discuss all relevant options. Select three resource materials to help plan the event and write down how you will use each resource. Find useful information in one of these resources and take it down in note form. Write messages or invitations to announce the event. Turn in one set of work for the group. You will be graded on the group product and on how you individually use language to interact with your group and plan this event.

Considerations in grading, in addition to fluency and accuracy:

a) Selecting relevant resource materials and noting their use, with consideration for strategies used.

b) Taking notes from one resource material, with consideration for queries and guesses where needed.

c) Writing messages or invitations according to social conventions, with consideration for use of appropriate aids during preparation.

d) Interacting with the group throughout the planning, with consideration for responding to others' remarks, taking turns, introducing and building topics, holding the floor, and other strategies for communication and conversation management.

Selected areas for evaluation would, of course, vary according to the linguistic level of the students and the extensiveness of the task. Grading grids, such as in Table 4, could be designed to help instructors make a global evaluation of how task interacts with process.

Table 4
Possible Grading Grid for Task and Process

Evidence of Process	Accomplishment of Task			
	Highly Successful	Basically Successful	Partly Successful	Not Successful
Strong	A+	A	B	C-
Some	A	A-	B-	D+
Little	A-	B+	C+	D
No	B+	B	C	F

For example, in task 3 above, a student who is "basically success-ful" in writing invitations for an event would receive between an A and a B for that task, depending on the quantity and/or effectiveness of demonstrated processing strategies (including, perhaps, making an organizational list, outline, or sketch; looking up needed vocabulary, insightful questioning, using paraphrases; editing; and rewriting). This system would "require" students to pay attention to process, under the assumption that learners can always continue to expand their linguistic flexibility. In the case of a student who is "not successful" in writing the invitation, a minimally passing grade of C- could still be earned if the student showed "strong" attempts to process language – a reward for interlanguage progress too often neglected in solely product-oriented grading. By grading process, we would encourage students to make their processing strategies evident; the backwash effect would promote teaching and learning of diverse ways of interacting with language.

To supply input for using the grid, students could be observers and record processes used by their classmates. Or the students involved in the activity could subsequently participate in a debriefing wherein they articulate the processes they used to accomplish the task and speculate on the appropriateness of those processes for the target-language envi-ronment. By having students focus on the processes they and their classmates are using, the test becomes a stronger teaching tool, helping students diagnose their own strengths and weaknesses and identify ways to improve their own abilities. Student involvement in assessment should also help instructors respect individual processing styles, to move, where needed, from prescription for grading to description for learning and motivation.

Several advantages of task-based and process-oriented testing are appealing. Patterned after testing through work samples common in other disciplines (Allen & Rueter, 1990), task-based testing simulates real-world language use more closely than commonly used paper-and-pencil and even speaking test formats. In its greater naturalness, it offers students – and instructors – more compelling reasons to adhere to sociocultural norms and to include them more centrally in assessment. A process orientation calls for interaction – among skills, persons, and situations. It allows for differences between receptive and productive skills and for natural variance in individual approaches to learning. It offers a bridge between paper-and-pencil testing and evaluation of port-folios and other collections of student work done outside a traditional testing situation, thus adding to our broadening definition of assess-ment. For TAs, such task-based activities should focus the curriculum and be easier to create than paragraph-framed grammar or global comprehension items, since instructors supply only the situation as stimulus. The content is dynamic: it is created by the students according to the task and according to the processes they apply to it.

Spiraling Test Formats through the Curriculum

Given the complex notions involved in teaching and testing intercultural communication, the uncertainty of the profession as to how language learning occurs in a classroom setting, and concern for individual learning and teaching styles, it is not surprising that suggestions for improving testing programs emphasize diversification. Omaggio (1986) recommends "hybrid" tests that include some convergent and divergent items, some open-ended naturalistic expressions items, and some global comprehension items. Elsewhere I have advocated "multi-sequence evaluation": varying testing formats from test to test throughout the course in a progression that respects short-term goals for both receptive and productive language use while working toward long-term goals of communication and cultural understanding (Magnan, 1985).

Typically, tests in the same course tend to resemble one another in format. The content changes from lesson to lesson and the length increases from quizzes to cumulative exams, but the activity types are repeated. Students have grown accustomed to this procedure and find it fair: by taking quizzes, they learn what to expect on more important tests. TAs also find security in this system: from previous models, they learn to create future tests and how to prepare their students for them. But this procedure limits us in terms of the variety of formats and the types of skills we can measure. Perhaps most important, it discourages integrative testing and encourages a focus on individual linguistic features, usually grammatical ones. Although it may seem logical to begin by testing small pieces of language (grammar, vocabulary, sounds), it may then be difficult to shift to more integrative and communicative testing. And yet as long as we remain with discrete, additive tests, we continue to emphasize product and we fail to realize our intent of spiraling our curriculum toward more dynamic communicative goals.

If we vary formats among quizzes and especially from quizzes to major, cumulative exams, we can integrate different skills on different tests and in different ways, taking advantage of the complexity of the relationships among them. In fact, most programs have already begun to diversify their testing programs by adding speaking tests to the traditional written quiz/exam sequence. To diversify our testing further, we might consider a cyclic or spiraled sequence that confines heavily product-oriented testing to early stages of each lesson, and then moves through various modes of paper-and-pencil communicative testing toward more task-based and process-oriented testing on major, cumulative exams. Collections could, if desired, be added at summative points of the grading period. (See Table 5.)

Of course, as the notion of spiraling suggests, these formats would be interwoven throughout the course and could at times be combined on the same test to avoid what could otherwise be seen as an unfortunate and artificial distinction between "grammar tests" and "language use tests." What is important is that we spiral out from limited use of forms (and the discrete-point and single-skill formats that test them) to the use of language for communication and to task-based tests that reveal the developing communicative processes of students.

Diversifying test formats may also help ease beginning TAs into test writing. TAs could work in teams to create specific types of sections based on their backgrounds and abilities (Lee, 1989) and on how well they responded to particular sections on the critiques. Gaining experience with one format before moving on to another, TAs could eventually participate on different teams and learn to create all types of test sections.

Conclusion

Testing in any foreign language course is complex. In the multisection, TA-taught course, this complexity is magnified by the number of people involved and by the inexperience and time limitations of much of the teaching staff. Perhaps because of this complexity, we might be tempted to let innovation in testing take a back seat to innovation in teaching. The imperative "Just Do It" in the title of this paper assumes a dual meaning.

From a theoretical perspective, we need to focus testing, as well as teaching, on having students *do* things through the target language, so as to use language for natural communicative purposes. Our testing programs must lead beyond a focus on product (be it a paper-and-pencil demonstration or one that shows accomplishment of a task) to linking product with process. The dynamic relationship between how language is used and the result it obtains is the essence of interpersonal interaction in its unpredictability and sensitivity to the sociocultural variables unique to each situation and to each group of interlocutors.

From a practical viewpoint, "Just Do It" is an imperative to the profession to begin a serious search for innovative techniques for communicative language testing. By spiraling test types through our curriculum, we can move from an additive focus on product to an integrative focus

Table 5
Diversifying Test Format for a Cyclic Curriculum

Type of Material Tested	Type of Test	Format
Rote learning of vocabulary	Short checks	Discrete items
Sound/meaning discrimination		Single-skill items
Basic cultural facts		
Structured use of vocabulary and grammar	Quizzes	Contextualized items, including paragraph-frame, personalized, and situational format
Basic self-expression		Multiskill, global items
Basic focused comprehension		
Basic cultural notions		
Functional use of skills necessitating cultural awareness or understanding	Major exams	Task-based and process-oriented items
	Collections	Portfolios, interviews, and self-assessments

on process. Responding to the diverse needs of our students, we can direct them toward their ultimate communicative goals. The purpose of classroom testing is more far-reaching than student assessment. It serves to reshape the curriculum, and, in TA-taught programs, it is the experience that shapes the professional development of the TAs who will become the future leaders of our profession. We cannot afford to neglect these opportunities.

Works Cited

ACTFL. *ACTFL Proficiency Guidelines*. Yonkers, NY: ACTFL Materials Center, 1986.

Allen, R. R. & Theodore Rueter. *Teaching Assistant Strategies: An Introduction to College Teaching*. Dubuque, IA: Kendall/Hunt Publishing Company, 1990.

Bacon, Susan M. & Michael D. Finneman. "A Study of the Attitudes, Motives, and Strategies of University Foreign-Language Students and Their Disposition to Authentic Oral and Written Input." *Modern Language Journal* 74 (1990): 459-73.

Barnes, Betsy K., Carol A. Klee & Ray M. Wakefield. "Reconsidering the FL Requirement: From Seat-Time to Proficiency in the Minnesota Experience." *Challenges in the 1990s for College Foreign Language Programs.* Ed. Sally Sieloff Magnan. Issues in Language Program Direction. Boston, MA: Heinle & Heinle Publishers, 1991.

Bernhardt, Elizabeth B. "Developments in Second Language Literacy Research: Retrospective and Prospective Views for the Classroom." *Foreign Language Acquisition Research and the Classroom.* Ed. Barbara F. Freed. Foreign Language Acquisition Research and Instruction. Boston: D.C. Heath & Company, 1991: 221-51.

Chaudron, Craig. *Second Language Classrooms: Research on Teaching and Learning.* Cambridge Applied Linguistics Series. New York: Cambridge University Press, 1988.

Duff, Patricia & Charlene Polio. "How Much Foreign Language Is There in the Foreign Language Classroom?" *Modern Language Journal* 74 (1990): 154-66.

Farhady, Hossein. "The Disjunctive Fallacy between Discrete-Point and Integrative Tests." *TESOL Quarterly* 13 (1979): 347-57.

Fox, Cynthia. Personal communication concerning tests prepared at Indiana University-Bloomington, 1987.

Galloway, Vicki & Angela Labarca. "From Student to Learner: Style, Process, and Strategy." *New Perspectives and New Directions in Foreign Language Education.* Ed. Diane W. Birckbichler. ACTFL Foreign Language Education Series. Lincolnwood, IL: National Textbook Company, 1990: 111-58.

Gaudiani, Claire. *Teaching Writing in the Foreign Language Classroom.* Language in Education, Theory, and Practice, Vol. 43. Washington, DC: Center for Applied Linguistics, 1981.

Grittner, Frank. M. *A Three-Year Evaluation of the NEH German Summer Institute Program Conducted at the University of Wisconsin-Stevens Point.* Unpublished report. Madison, WI: Department of Public Instruction, 1987.

_____. "Bandwagons Revisited: A Perspective on Movements in Foreign Language Education." *New Perspectives and New Directions in Foreign Language Education.* Ed. Diane W. Birckbichler. ACTFL Foreign Language Education Series. Lincolnwood, IL: National Textbook Company, 1990: 9-43.

Gutiérrez, John R. "Oral Testing in the High School Classroom: Some Suggestions." *Hispania* 70 (1987): 915-18.

Harlow, Linda L. & Rosario Caminero. "Oral Testing of Beginning Language Students at Large Universities: Is It Worth the Trouble?" *Foreign Language Annals* 23 (1990): 489-501.

Heaton, J. B. *Writing English Language Tests.* London: Longman, 1975.

Heilenman, Laura K. & Isabelle Kaplan. "Proficiency in Practice: The Foreign Language Curriculum." *Foreign Language Proficiency in the Classroom and Beyond.* Ed. Charles J. James. ACTFL Foreign Language Education Series. Lincolnwood, IL: National Textbook Company, 1985: 55-78.

Henning, Grant. *A Guide to Language Testing: Development, Evaluation, Research.* New York: Newbury House, 1987.

_____. "Priority Issues in the Assessment of Communicative Language Abilities." *Foreign Language Annals* 23 (1990): 379-84.

Herschensohn, Julia. "Toward a Theoretical Basis for Current Language Pedagogy." *Modern Language Journal* 74 (1990): 451-58.

Horwitz, Elaine K. "Attending to the Affective Domain in the Foreign Language Classroom." *Shifting the Instructional Focus to the Learner.* Ed. Sally Sieloff Magnan. Report of the Northeast Conference on the Teaching of Foreign Languages. Middlebury, VT: Northeast Conferences, 1990: 15-33.

_____, Michael B. Horwitz & Joann Cope. "Foreign Language Classroom Anxiety." *Modern Language Journal* 70 (1986): 125-32.

Joseph, John E. "New French: A Pedagogical Crisis in the Making." *Modern Language Journal* 72 (1988): 31-36.

Kaczmarek, Celeste M. "Scoring and Rating Essay Tasks." *Research in Language Testing.* Ed. John W. Oller Jr. & Kyle Perkins. Rowley, MA: Newbury House, 1980: 151-59.

Kramsch, Claire. "From Language Proficiency to Interactional Competence." *Modern Language Journal* 70 (1986): 366-72.

Lee, James F. *A Manual and Practical Guide to Directing Foreign Language Programs and Training Graduate Teaching Assistants.* New York: Random House, 1989.

Linder, Cathy. *Oral Communication Testing: A Handbook for the Foreign Language Teacher.* Lincolnwood, IL: National Textbook Company, 1977.

Long, Donna R. "What's Really Going on in the Classroom?" *Second Language Acquisition: Preparing for Tomorrow.* Ed. Barbara Snyder. Proceedings of the Central States Conference on the Teaching of Foreign Language. Lincolnwood, IL: National Textbook Company, 1986: 28-37.

Madaus, G. "Minimum Competence Testing for Certification: The Evolution and Evaluation of Test Validity." *The Courts, Validity, and Minimum Competence Testing.* Ed. G. Madaus. Boston: Kluwer-Nijhoff Publishing, 1983: 21-61.

Magnan, Sally Sieloff. "From Achievement toward Proficiency through Multi-Sequence Evaluation." *Foreign Language Proficiency in the Classroom and Beyond.* Ed. Charles J. James. ACTFL Foreign Language Education Series. Lincolnwood, IL: National Textbook Company, 1985: 117-45.

Myton, Rebekah. Test prepared as a TA and student in a graduate methodology course at the University of Wisconsin-Madison, 1989.

Nerenz, Anne. "Utilizing Class Time in Foreign Language Instruction." *Teaching the Basics in the Foreign Language Classroom: Options and Strategies.* Ed. David P. Benseler. Proceedings of the Central States Conference on the Teaching of Foreign Languages. Lincolnwood, IL: National Textbook Company, 1979: 78-98.

Omaggio, Alice C. *Proficiency-oriented Classroom Testing.* Language in Education 52. Washington, DC: Center for Applied Linguistics/Harcourt Brace, 1983.

_____. *Teaching Language in Context*. Boston: Heinle & Heinle Publishers, 1986.

Pino, Barbara Gonzalez. "Prochievement Testing of Speaking." *Foreign Language Annals* 22 (1989): 487-96.

Savignon, Sandra J. "Dictation as a Measure of Communicative Competence in French as a Second Language." *Language Learning* 32 (1982): 33-51.

Schulz, Renate. "Second Language Acquisition Theories and Teaching Practice: How Do They Fit?" *Modern Language Journal* 75 (1991): 17-26.

Semke, Harriet D. "Effects of the Red Pen." *Foreign Language Annals* 17 (1984): 195-202.

Shohamy, Elana. "Connecting Testing and Learning in the Classroom and on the Program Level." *Building Bridges and Making Connections*. Ed. June K. Phillips. Report of the Northeast Conference on the Teaching of Foreign Languages. Middlebury, VT: Northeast Conference, 1991: 154-78.

Stevick, Earl W. "Research on What? Some Terminology." *Modern Language Journal* 74 (1990): 143-53.

Swaffar, Janet K. "Language Learning Is More than Learning Language: Rethinking Reading and Writing Tasks in Textbooks for Beginning Language Study." *Foreign Language Acquisition Research and the Classroom*. Ed. Barbara F. Freed. Foreign Language Acquisition Research and Instruction. Boston: D.C. Heath & Company, 1991: 252-79.

_____, Katherine M. Arens & Heidi Byrnes. *Reading for Meaning: An Integrated Approach to Language Learning*. Englewood Cliffs, NJ: Prentice Hall, 1991.

Swain, Merrill. "Large-Scale Communicative Language Testing." *Initiatives in Communicative Language Teaching: A Book of Readings*. Ed. Margie S. Berns. Reading, MA: Addison-Wesley, 1984: 185-201.

Terry, Robert M. "Testing the Productive Skills: A Creative Focus for Hybrid Achievement Tests." *Foreign Language Annals* 19 (1986): 521-28.

_____. "Teaching and Evaluating Writing as a Communicative Skill." *Foreign Language Annals* 22 (1989): 43-54.

Valdman, Albert & Marvin Moody. "Testing Communicative Ability." *French Review* 52 (1979): 552-61.

Valette, Rebecca. *Modern Language Testing*. 2d ed. New York: Harcourt Brace Jovanovich, 1977.

VanPatten, Bill. "Attending to Form and Content in the Input: An Experiment in Consciousness." *Studies in Second Language Acquisition* 12 (1990): 287-301.

_____. "The Foreign Language Classroom as a Place to Communicate." *Foreign Language Acquisition Research and the Classroom*. Ed. Barbara F. Freed. Foreign Language Acquisition Research and Instruction. Boston: D.C. Heath & Company, 1991: 45-73.

Walz, Joel. "Context and Contextualized Language Practice in Foreign Language Teaching." *Modern Language Journal* 73 (1989): 161-68.

Wesche, M. "Communicative Testing in a Second Language." *Canadian Modern Language Review* 37 (1981): 551-71.

Appendix
Questions to Guide TAs in Critiquing Paper-and-Pencil Tests

In that these questions would be offered only as ideas for consideration, TAs could comment on any aspect of the test. To further encourage freedom of analysis and to facilitate consolidating critiques, TAs should be asked to write their comments directly on the test draft.

Considerations for the Test as a Whole

1) Does the test format allow us to test learning goals that are appropriate for this point in the curriculum? In a spiral program, are the formats used appropriate to the type of test? Do they proceed naturally from formats used previously and lead to formats planned for future tests?

2) Is the test balanced appropriately in items covered and in skills tested?

3) Does the grading reflect this balance? How many points are there for communication? for form?

4) Does the layout make the test clear to students and easy to grade?

5) How long is it likely to take students to complete the test?

Considerations for Individual Sections

1) What type of exercise is this – isolated discrete-point, paragraph-framed grammar, situational, global, task-based, process-oriented? What is the exercise testing? For a test at this point in the curriculum, is this the best match between format and testing objective?

2) Are the directions and examples clear? Can students do what they are being asked to do, ideally in more than one way?

3) Is the target language used naturally and correctly, yet in a way that students can understand it? Does the discourse hold together and sound natural?

4) Are cultural references correct and accessible to students? Are there any troublesome stereotypes that should be avoided?

5) Does grading correspond to what students have to do? Is there an appropriate allotment of points for communication, both receptive and productive, and of points for form?

7) How long is it likely to take students to complete this section?

9) Will students enjoy doing this section? What will they learn from it?

10) What will instructors learn from this exercise to help guide students in their continuing acquisition process?

A Survey and Analysis of Tests Accompanying Elementary French Textbooks

Joel Walz
University of Georgia

Without doubt, one of the past decade's major changes in materials designed for the teaching of foreign languages at the college level has been the availability of a wide variety of new ancillaries to accompany first-year textbooks. Adopters now receive a package that goes far beyond the annotated teacher's edition/workbook-lab manual/ tapescript of a decade ago to include overhead transparencies, realia, videotapes, computer programs, slides, answer keys, and a cassette for students. Of particular interest is the possibility of receiving a package of tests that were written with this very textbook in mind. After all (or so the logic goes), who should know better than the textbook's authors how to test for the goals that the text and its ancillaries established?

On the other hand, motivation to produce such a package must be low. Authors and publishers cannot receive direct royalties from writing the tests, since the packages are always free to adopters. The actual quality of the tests probably does not help with sales, since very often the testing component is not published at the same time as the text-book, or potential adopters may not automatically receive that compo-nent. Further, it is unlikely that a serious analysis of individual tests would carry much importance in the adoption process; course directors have simply too many other factors and too many other textbooks to consider for this part of the program to be a deciding factor. In brief, tests are a short-term drain on profits, since someone is paid to write them, and in many cases only the fact of their existence, rather than their quality, helps in sales, at least in the first year or two.

Be that as it may, the idea of commercially prepared tests has considerable appeal. Many teachers of today's undergraduates have little free time to create imaginative tests: teaching assistants (TAs) have their own studies to worry about, university faculty have publishing pressures, and college teachers frequently have heavy teaching loads. With a new focus on proficiency, language tests go far beyond the fill-in-the-blanks items traditionally seen in classrooms. Writing sections may have interesting contexts or problems to solve. Reading can involve authentic documents that must be read for content rather than form or for a general overview rather than for discrete items. Listening comprehension may have realistic recordings of native speakers of different ages from various areas of the world in widely differing situations. All of these components, which reflect current emphases in language teaching, take an enormous amount of time to develop, or may be impossible to create in many circumstances, yet textbook publishers provide them for free. Indeed, in multisection courses taught by TAs, well-written tests can have a "backwash effect," that is, can influence the type of teaching that is provided (Hughes, 1989, pp. 1-2). By preparing students for certain types of tests, TAs may actually improve their own teaching. Commercial tests may also create the impression of a national standard since most textbooks are sold across the United States. I use the term *impression* because no one ever gathers the results of these tests to evaluate them. The tests can prove useful even if not given as part of the regular testing program, especially since it is unwise to administer the same test more than once. Teachers can save them for makeup tests, as a written assignment to prepare students for an examination, or as a model to follow in making their own. Commercial tests can also serve as a model for discussion in pedagogy classes or TA meetings. Thus, commercial language tests have a potential value for the teaching profession.

A major problem with commercial tests – as with all tests – is one of validity: do they reflect instructional goals?[1] Ensuring that tests are consonant with goals is hard enough when one person teaches and constructs the tests; having an outsider create tests compounds the problem. The situation becomes quite complicated. Test writers (who often are not the same as the authors of the book) must attempt to match testing procedures to the professed goals of the book, while teachers try to adopt a book that will allow them to achieve the goals they themselves have in mind. We thus have many variables, and while textbooks allow for a certain amount of variation in the way they are taught, tests on a printed page are much less adaptable.

A second and equally important problem is how to test undergraduates in today's foreign language classroom. Since most textbooks state language proficiency as their goal (see below), validity would require proficiency tests. Teachers, however, use tests to assign course grades to students, and only achievement tests are appropriate in this case, for as Dandonoli (1987), Higgs (1987), Magnan (1985), and Schulz (1986) point out, proficiency tests must inevitably cover some aspects of language and culture that have not been or cannot be taught. In addition, proficiency develops very slowly; many learners would not show a measurable increase in proficiency from the beginning to the end of a course even while their achievement was progressing from day to day. According to Heaton (1990), the progress measured by classroom tests encourages students because they see that they are improving, but such would not be the case with frequent proficiency tests. A related morale factor is that college classrooms often cannot avoid true and false beginners at the first-year level. Tests of proficiency give an advantage to students with high school preparation who are starting over (often to get a good grade), in comparison with students who may spend more time studying the language with the book and tapes, but feel intimidated by *faux débutants* (Hill & Mosher, 1989; Loughrin-Sacco, 1991). Many teachers are bothered when hardworking students score lower than those who have more experience, but less interest. Ignoring this problem has the potential for destroying student and TA confidence in the testing program.

It would seem, then, that tests of specific textbook material would not be valid for measuring the ultimate goal of proficiency, and that tests of proficiency would not provide the weekly feedback needed by students and required by universities. Fortunately, scholars have addressed this problem. Omaggio (1983) presents the idea of the "hybrid" test, one that has the characteristics of a proficiency test (a realistic context, paragraph- rather than sentence-level tasks, etc.) but assesses specific structures and vocabulary students have learned. Magnan (1985) proposes a "multi-sequence" approach that uses achievement tests for short-term goals, moving toward proficiency at key stages. One way of judging the validity of commercial tests would be to compare them with a standard, an "ideal" test. Such a test and such a comparison would imply, however, that all language programs and teachers have identical goals *and* that we are sure we know how to test those goals. Even given this improbable situation, one can delineate certain characteristics to look for in good language tests.

One should expect a balance of five skills, taking into account the possibility of combining them (e.g., writing + culture, listening + reading); Chastain (1980) recommends selecting two skills for each test without telling students in advance which two will be tested. Listening comprehension should test a basic understanding of realistic texts rather than linguistic elements or contrived passages. Writing tasks may include discrete items to satisfy the requirement for achievement testing, but the items should appear in a meaningful context rather than allow students to memorize forms. Tests should include writing sections that stress meaning over form, so that students demonstrate their ability to convey messages. Individual teachers must decide the proportion of discrete versus integrative sections, but the latter sections should be more frequent as the course progresses and in comprehensive examinations as opposed to chapter tests.

Reading tests should resemble listening comprehension tests by involving only realistic texts and seeking a basic understanding of the message. The "achievement" nature of the test can be increased by constructing sections that relate to the themes of the textbook chapters being tested. Thus, students reading the new passage will be familiar with the vocabulary and the ideas it contains. Reading tests often relate closely to the study of the target culture through the information they contain. Other ways to test culture involve writing, but it is preferable to focus on functioning in a country where the language is spoken as opposed to asking students to repeat isolated facts. The same is true of speaking tests, which must elicit personal information within the limits of reasonable expectations of student proficiency levels.

These brief guidelines have been designed to help us answer the question that lies at the heart of this paper, Do commercial testing programs accurately assess the language proficiency of beginning French students in America's colleges and universities?

Survey of Commercial Tests

To answer the question, I examined 12 testing programs of the 15 college-level textbooks of elementary French that were published or re-edited between 1988 and 1990 and that advertise the availability of testing material. Two testing programs had not yet been published by the time this analysis was finished, and the editor of one other declined to participate.[2] To convince publishers to send me this highly confidential material, I promised not to identify the specific sources; it is unlikely the publishers would have agreed otherwise. In a larger sense, the purpose of this analysis is not to identify the "best" or "worst" tests, and not identifying specific testing programs, textbooks, or the source of my examples does not detract from the goal of evaluating trends. I would also like to point out that the conclusions do not describe any single program that teachers can use; rather, the remarks are offered only to characterize the current state of commercial language testing.

All paper tests are printed on 8½-by-11-inch paper, but the similarities end there. They vary in length from 49 to 358 pages. Most are ready for reproduction; of the three that are not, one provides only test suggestions and the other two have tests that are too long for a class period, in order to allow for teacher selection. Most programs provide tests[3] for each chapter; two test only paired chapters. Since two chapters may be as much as one-seventh of a year's study, the latter arrangement might prove too infrequent for some teachers. Three of the programs offer a quiz format (i.e., less than 50 minutes) by providing only test suggestions, by furnishing separate vocabulary quizzes, or by separating the four skills. Eight offer answer keys in addition to the script of the oral part, and seven provide suggested point values for each test section.

Seven programs combine more than two chapters to offer hour exams, midterms, and finals. Three of those divide chapters equally according to the semester system and four for both semesters and quarters. Some of the authors who provide tests but not comprehensive exams point out that books are not always divided mathematically. In other words, a teacher on the semester system may not divide a 14-chapter book as 1-7 and 8-14. In such a situation, it is possible to add material to a cumulative test but very difficult to remove it. Ironically, the better the tests (i.e., the more they integrate the various linguistic features of the textbook to provide realistic communicative tasks), the less flexible they become in adapting them for different chapters. Achievement-oriented tests, because they cover specific items students have learned, suffer less in this way than proficiency-oriented tests do.

Three packages offer two versions of each test, while another offers substitution items. One package has three versions of each test and exam and another a generous four. Seven programs also provide suggestions for oral examinations, through personalized questions, situations for role playing, or both. Seven use art or realia in the tests; of those, two are minimal uses and one extensive. Providing artwork with tests is a definite advantage in that many teachers cannot produce it themselves. Art is extremely useful in language testing because students must write a specific message without having verbal cues. Verbal cues have the disadvantages of providing necessary vocabulary if they are in the target language and of encouraging translating if they are in English.

Unfortunately, the reproduction of some of the realia has small print or is of marginal quality and would not allow for thermofaxing.

I will base my analysis primarily on chapter tests since that is the only type common to all 12 programs. As described below, the examinations do not differ radically from chapter tests except in length. Five student copies of the tests have directions written in French more or less along the lines of the language of the grammar explanations of the accompanying textbook. Although it is commendable that the tests reflect a philosophy requiring exclusive use of the target language, the French may get too complicated for a testing situation:

> Logique. *Votre ami français, lui, a réponse à tout. Son défaut c'est qu'il est beaucoup trop catégorique et emploie le futur là où les conséquences de ses hypothèses sont incertaines. Nuancez ses prognostics en mettant les verbes en italique au conditionnel et à la forme affirmative et ou négative selon vos convictions. Commencez vos phrases par des expressions d'opinion et ajoutez aussi des adverbes.*[4]

This section requires three separate grammatical manipulations as well as a communicative task. One of the grammar changes (*expression d'opinion*) could make another (future to conditional) impossible by requiring the subjunctive. These directions place too much emphasis on the reading skill in a context that is not useful in real life: grammatical analysis.

The tests show a certain amount of variation in the balance of the five skills tested, although not as much as one might think. Since speaking tests are separate and only three packages give questions or situations for all chapters, I will compare the relative importance of the four other skills. Listening comprehension accounts for 15 to 25% of chapter tests, except in four programs that do not test all four skills. In those, the range is 25 to 35%, with one package reaching 50% on occasion. Writing, which combines grammar and the skill of writing, is usually 50 to 60% of each test. Those percentages are lower in two and higher in three, with a maximum of 80% in only one program. Tests that address only two skills are more likely to have a heavier writing component. Reading accounts for 10 to 25% when it is tested separately, with only one program going as high as 35%. Culture is tested separately in only four programs, at 10 to 15% of each test. Additionally, three programs test vocabulary, one at 25%, another at 10%, and the third with supplementary tests. The predictable conclusion concerning the balance of skills is that writing predominates. The type of writing required will be discussed below.

Analysis

Instructions for Testing

All of the testing programs give hints or instructions on testing a foreign language, supplying this information in the teacher's edition of the textbook, in the test manual itself, or in both places. Most are explanations of how to use the tests provided, but six discuss language testing in more general terms. The latter is essential if authors are to show how the objectives of the textbook are to be met. Such ideas can be useful to TAs who are just beginning their careers and to faculty who have not been able to keep up with changes outside their fields of specialization. The latter problem is especially true with the group of testing programs studied here. Nine of the twelve accompanying textbooks claim proficiency as a goal, two communication, and one a functional use of French. Many college teachers received no training in pedagogy, or received it before any of these emphases became popular.

On the other hand, the more the authors of a textbook and testing program develop a specific philosophy, the more likely they are to make statements with which a course director disagrees, thereby creating conflicts for TAs. For example, one textbook discourages the use of dictation on tests because it involves so many tasks. Another encourages the use of unknown words in dictations even though many teachers prefer to control vocabulary with that type of test. In programs in which course directors maintain consistency in teaching and testing, the directors will have to study these sections carefully and discuss disagreements with instructors.

Testing advice is but one area that can cause problems of compatibility between tests written for a nationally distributed textbook and tests used at a specific college or university. The major problems in adapting tests in a multisection program with classes taught by TAs (other than the quality of the tests themselves, to be discussed later) can be summarized as follows:

1) The printed advice contradicts what the course director or department believes, as discussed above. *Solution:* meetings to discuss differences.
2) The printed format, ready for photocopying, makes a change in the balance of tasks or skills difficult. *Solution:* cut and paste.
3) The point values of each section printed on students' copies also make the balance of skills difficult to change. *Solution:* correction fluid or tape and a separate answer key with new point values.

4) Grouping chapters for examinations in a different way from what is done in the course is not a question of goals, but it does present a virtually insurmountable problem.

It is only fair to note that the features of some testing programs actually reduce problems of compatibility by way of the following:

1) Separating the skills into different tests (only one package does this), or at least into different sections
2) Offering more sections than needed, to allow for deletions
3) Having two versions of each test with different emphases (grammar vs. communication; only one program does this)
4) Printing point values on the answer key rather than on the student's copy
5) Providing data diskettes so that teachers can change and delete items with a word processor without having to type and proofread

In conclusion, it is important to note that in some situations program directors and TAs may not be able to make the tests compatible with course goals, although the analysis that follows will show that this is not often the case.

Listening Comprehension

All testing programs include a listening comprehension (LC) component on all tests. The most surprising feature is the almost-total lack of dictation as a testing technique. While dictation has enjoyed varying degrees of popularity over the years (Stansfield, 1985), it is generally considered a good test of overall language proficiency (Oller & Streiff, 1975) and has been adapted to a wide variety of formats (Davis & Rinvolucri, 1988). Only four programs include dictations systematically: two as a paragraph, one having sentences with a context, and one without. Fortunately for teachers who like dictations, they are among the easier test formats to construct.

Two to three LC sections seem to be the norm for chapter tests. Only three of the programs rely heavily on discrete-item formats, the validity of which has been called into question (Farhady, 1983). Tasks of this type include listening for a certain grammatical feature (gender of the person mentioned, contrasting verb tenses), writing out a number heard in a sentence, making an either-or choice based on a grammatical feature, and circling a word heard in a sentence from a list of three or four. An example of a discrete item with LC is as follows:

[Students hear:] *Je n'ai pas assez d'argent.*

[Students see on test copy:] / *assez – a ses – à ces* /

The ability to pick out individual words in an utterance does not necessarily demonstrate the ability to understand the entire message. In a needlessly complicated task in another test, students are presented with a long list of verbs; while the teacher reads a paragraph, the students must number the verbs in the order in which they appear. The teacher would have to read the passage with unnatural pauses, making the mechanics more difficult than the skill being tested. While not dealing adequately with the comprehension of messages, discrete-item tests do have the advantages of diagnostic possibilities (Madsen & Jones, 1981). In other words, if students cannot pick out the numbers they hear in sentences, the teacher may conclude that students need more practice listening to numbers. But if students cannot get the gist of a passage, diagnosing a specific problem and remedy is much more difficult.

Numerous sections test LC in a more global situation, where an entire message (sentence, paragraph, dialogue) must be understood. Formats of "pure" LC (i.e., where no other skills are involved) include sentences that are either logical or illogical based on internal content; the similar true-false decision is based on the vocabulary used in the sentence; and the fill-ins seek specific information students hear in a passage. Some tests misuse the term *logical-illogical* to refer to grammatical correctness:

8) *Pourquoi n'y a-t-il pas de pain?*
– *C'est parce que je suis pas allé à la boucherie.*

12) *Où vos parents habitaient-ils?*
– *Ils habitent près de la Nouvelle-Orléans.*

The answer key lists both as illogical, but the first is based on meaning and the second on grammar (change of verb tenses). Asking students to switch from grammar to content can be an unnatural task. Another problem with isolated sentences is that one finds statements that would tax students' knowledge of the world, requiring information unrelated to the study of French:

[true-false:] *Il n'y a pas de lait dans la moutarde.*

Avec du bleu plus du rouge, on a cette nouvelle couleur.

[multiple-choice answers:] *orange jaune violet*

Of course, the logical-illogical, true-false, and multiple-choice formats are also applied to the content of passages that students hear. To allow for pure LC, the tests do not shy away from the use of English in such formats as multiple-choice, taking notes, and answering questions. For example:

You will hear a radio weather report. Based on the report, answer the questions below in English. You need not use complete sentences. You will hear the report twice.

1) What time was the report given?
2) What will the weather be like in Paris this afternoon?
3) What will the weather be like in the Alps?

The short paragraph and questions provide the context and proper schema to help students understand the passage. The use of English allows the testing of LC without the interference of other skills, but many teachers object to the intrusion of the native language. In virtually all cases of multiple-choice, the possible answers are printed on the student's copy. Only one test uses the frequently recommended format of situating an overheard conversation, a test that would seem to correspond nicely to the tenets of the proficiency movement because it requires understanding the gist of a message in a specific context the learner is likely to encounter in the target culture.

Many LC sections do add other skills, primarily writing. Students must write down the essential points of a paragraph they hear; give advice, an opinion, or a reaction to an oral statement; or answer a question based on either an oral text or their own lives, that is, personalized questions. The latter may be the testing technique with which the students are most familiar owing to classroom practice:

La musique et vous. You will hear some questions about music and the arts. Answer each question as it applies to you.

[Student hears:] *Jouez-vous d'un instrument? Si oui, duquel?*

Pensez-vous que le gouvernement doive subventionner les arts?

The problem is that a student error is more difficult to diagnose; it may be a listening or a writing problem.

On occasion, this exercise is too tightly controlled:

Parlez-vous anglais dans la classe de français? (tout le monde)

Other formats suffer occasionally from the same problem:

Answer the following questions in complete sentences in French. Use an appropriate direct-object, indirect-object, or disjunctive pronoun in each answer.

Since all 12 textbooks are communicative, functional, or proficiency-oriented, these limitations on student answers are unwarranted.

Another problem with personalized questions is that often they are not contextualized or, when they are, the context is artificial, as in an "interview" situation followed by any five questions the test author could devise. In fact, only half of the test programs systematically contextualize the LC component. When they do, the context unifies the sentences, but it never affects the outcome. Chastain (1987) and Walz (1989) have already pointed out that a context is authentic only if it influences or determines the answer, as in real life. One item that does so is the following:

> **Quel prix?** *Anne choisit toujours les vêtements les plus chers* (the most expensive). *Ecoutez la vendeuse et écrivez les vêtements qu'elle choisit.*

The problem with contexts/test directions that determine correct answers is that students tend not to read them (Cohen, 1980, p. 44). The example above is an oral test, which would allow the teacher to emphasize the context. With written tests, to be discussed below, the potential for disaster is great.

One last feature of oral testing is available with only one package: a professional recording of all the oral sections. The advantages of this component are enormous: native speakers using a fast, natural rendition with authentic intonation for emotions; multipart dialogues with different voices; and increased authenticity, such as a slight Quebec accent for a person from Quebec and a child's voice. Thus, students hear authentic speech as they would encounter it in a target culture, rather than speech watered down to promote better grades. Walz (1981) presents anecdotal evidence to show that TAs vary widely in the way they read LC passages, including their rate of speech, the number of times they repeat a text, and, in the case of dictations, the number of pauses they insert in sentences. Having all students hear the same version is a solution to this lack of reliability in test administration.

To conclude, these commercial tests offer a sufficient number of LC sections that are both "pure" and combined with other skills. Variety is substantial enough in most to maintain student and teacher interest. Teachers who are unhappy with the balance can delete sections and change the point values. Negatives are artificial restrictions to open-ended questions, discrete items, and unnatural tasks; however, these are all fairly few in number.

Written Language

In general, these tests of written language cover the skill of writing as well as a knowledge of grammar. Given the suggestions of Omaggio (1983) and Magnan (1985) mentioned above, one would expect grammar sections to "blend" into open-ended writing on each test, as tests progress through the book, and as students move from tests to exams. Whether and how tests progress from grammar to writing (i.e., from discrete to integrative) and from grammar to communicative provide a good basis for analyzing them, given the need both to verify achievement and to check on progress toward proficiency. While all textbooks in this survey are based on a grammatical syllabus, all stress the development of the ability to communicate as a goal, hence the apparent dichotomy. Since validity is a major consideration in the construction of tests, the writing skill in particular brings up the problem of reliability, especially in scoring. The more open-ended a test becomes, the more likely a teacher is to be inconsistent in grading a set of exams. In departments with numerous TAs in charge of several sections of the same course, interjudge reliability is a problem, with lack of experience a contributing factor. Walz (1981) describes TAs' giving wildly varying scores on a single test copy, even though the test had fairly controlled answers. The more discrete the test questions, the more scorer reliability is increased, but validity suffers.

The balance of grammar versus writing varies considerably. Of the 12 test packages, three rely heavily on discrete-item tests. One of these is the program that tests all skills receptively, having only multiple-choice fill-ins for testing grammar (especially morphology). An item is "integrative" when it requires more than one grammatical feature (Oller, 1979, p. 37) and the structures tested are not announced. In this sense, four programs are primarily integrative. An integrative skills test is one that requires the use of more than one skill at a time to complete the task.

It is essential to distinguish between integrative skills tests and integrative features tests. Though the latter require comprehension and an ability to put structural features together, they primarily test grammar, whereas an integrative skills test demands higher-level processing but is not an achievement test, which makes grading difficult. Of the four packages that have integrative tests, two involve skills and two grammatical features. Of the five remaining programs, three move from discrete to integrative as the course progresses, one has separate versions of each test for this purpose (although the difference is not always clear), and the other mixes the two throughout.

Before dismissing discrete-item tests, it is important to remember that they can be either mechanical or meaningful (Paulston & Bruder, 1975). A mechanical item does not require understanding:

connaître: Paul et Marie ne _____ pas ce roman.

A meaningful item does require understanding to obtain the right answer:

sortir ou partir: . . . je _____ pour mes cours à huit heures . . .

Meaningful items are preferable because they demand lexical as well as grammatical facility and do outnumber mechanical items by far. Given the necessity of ensuring students' grasp of a wide variety of structures rather than allowing them to reuse a limited number over and over, meaningful discrete-item tests are an acceptable part of commercial tests.

Another feature that many teachers have come to expect is a context for all test items. Only six of the programs contextualize their written tests, more or less along the same lines as they do with their LC tests. While no one has demonstrated that contextualization leads to greater proficiency, the six programs that lack this feature do advertise contextualized exercises for the accompanying textbook. One would expect more consistency between textbook activities and test items.

The last feature I analyzed, and perhaps the most important one, is whether the written sections test grammar or the ability to communicate. The distinction is not always easy to draw, as Terrell (1990) points out. Some grammatical features lend themselves directly to communication, such as the future tense:

> *Faites cinq phrases pour expliquer comment vous préparerez et réaliserez votre (prochain) voyage en France.*

What is implicit in this item is that students should use the *futur simple* and not the *futur proche*, an artificial limitation made necessary by the testing situation.

Other features, such as relative pronouns or a group of morphologically similar but semantically diverse verbs, require considerable gymnastics to test communicatively. One way tests can get around this problem is to divide the task into separate sentences:

> D) *Tout est relatif.* Complete each sentence according to your own situation or preferences. Pay attention to what kind of clause must follow *qui* or *que.*
>
> 1) *J'ai des cours qui*
> 2) *J'aime bien les profs qui*
> 3) *J'ai vu un film que*

While not as integrative as the example above using the future tense, this section does successfully convert a discrete item into a test involving communication.

Five programs limit written tests primarily to grammatical features (i.e., 80% or more of written exercises based on specific, often announced grammatical structures). One is the receptive test mentioned above, and another has tests long enough to delete a grammar section in order to increase the percentage of communication. The same grammatical feature may receive very different treatment in different testing programs. To take descriptive adjectives as an example, one finds tightly controlled exercises like this one:

> *Mlle Brunot: Hier/il/faire/beau,/donc/je/aller/parc./Dans/ parc/je /voir/fille/petit./Elle/être/malheureux/parce que/elle/vouloir/ limonade/mais/elle/ne . . . pas/avoir/assez/argent. /Je/donner/lui/ 2/francs/et/elle/dire/me/merci./Moi aussi,/je/avoir/soif,/donc/je/ prendre/Coca-Cola.*

Another program includes adjectives in this section:

> *Donnez une description physique précise de votre ami(e).*
> *Il a les bras musclés.*
> *Elle a les mains fines.*

While both items are integrative (the former more in features and the latter more in skills), the latter would be chosen by most teachers as a better test of the ability to use French because it reflects a task that might occur in real life.

Often tests attempt something open-ended but then narrow it down with stipulations that reduce the communicative value, as seen above with LC tests and with this extreme example:

> Let's try to combine some subjunctive forms, some interrogative pronouns, and some interrogative adjectives and come out with a paragraph or dialogue that "holds together" on some topic touching on the media and the arts. For example (don't copy it), you might start out this way:
>
> A) –*Qu'est-ce que tu as fait le weekend dernier?*
> B) –*Je suis allé voir la nouvelle pièce à l'Odéon. Il faut que tu la voies. C'est épatant.*
>
> You should write about ten lines total and we expect at least two *natural* subjunctives (*vouloir que, afin que, il est temps que,* . . . are just some expressions you might use) and two interrogative pronouns or adjectives.

Few test items are as complicated as this one, either in what they ask for or in how they are written.

Techniques for testing the written language are too numerous to list completely but include answering questions and rewriting sentences with and without cues or global commands, dehydrated sentences, fill-ins, and finishing sentences with specific words or narrow contexts. Only two programs make a consistent use of translation, that is, one section on almost every test.

Five testing programs achieve a blend of grammar and communication, with the latter accounting for a quarter to a third of the written exercises. While one communicative exercise in four might not seem like a lot, this group of tests is highly integrative, having grammar tests that resemble true acts of writing more closely than the discrete-item format does. Techniques involve answering questions, finishing sentences, or writing sentences and occasionally a paragraph within a specific context. The other two programs are heavily communicative, with half or more of written test sections allowing for original responses. Any of these seven programs seems to offer a good compromise between the desire to test what has been taught in a consistent manner and the desire to test students' ability to use the language in the most natural ways possible.

Reading Tests

LC and writing are the only two skills tested in all 12 programs; only seven have reading tests. To test the skill of reading, a test must present an original passage. Asking students questions about a passage read previously in the textbook or elsewhere places too much emphasis on memory to assess reading ability accurately. The only sections or test items of this type are labeled culture, not reading tests. Further, some testing techniques may require another skill – usually writing – to such an extent that the scorer could not be sure of the source of student errors. Only one of the seven programs adds enough writing to dilute the test. An example is a restaurant menu followed by a dialogue to complete in which the test copy provides the waiter's questions (*Et comme légume?/Et qu'est-ce que vous buvez?*) and the student writes in the diner's order. The section stresses vocabulary and production of syntax much more than a traditional reading passage does, but the task is a very realistic. Other examples would not even be called reading tests by many teachers – for instance, a chart of pluses and minuses for activities done or not done that students must convert into prose. This program is also the only one to test reading at the sentence in addition to the paragraph level, although one other has very short paragraphs. An example is two lists of sentences for matching advice with problems:

c) *Détends-toi un peu!*

5) *Je suis nerveux, anxieux et déprimé.*

Isolated sentences emphasize vocabulary and structure over a text-processing approach of longer passages.

The other six programs rely almost exclusively on "pure" reading tests, much like the LC tests mentioned above. Production is reduced or eliminated through true-false, multiple-choice, fill-in, and matching formats as well as answering questions in English. Writing in French is occasionally necessary with supplying short answers to questions, completing sentences, and writing a one-sentence summary, but these occurences are much less frequent than in the "pure" tests.

It should be pointed out that there is no absolute need for "pure" tests. The idea of testing one skill at a time comes no doubt from the audiolingual movement, when it was thought that teachers had to (and would be able to) diagnose sources of learning errors in order to eliminate them. Since we now know that it is not possible to eliminate learner errors or desirable to teach in a way that does not permit them, one-skill tests seem less important than they once did. Reading is a skill that combines easily with tests of LC (the answers on the student's copy), grammar/writing (directions to the sections as well as the sentences within each section), and culture. In fact, of the five programs that do not test reading separately, only three have little or no reading, that is, test only sentences themselves. On the other hand, given the call for the testing of language in many contexts in proficiency-oriented instruction (Omaggio, 1986), longer passages seem necessary because an authentic cultural context takes time to develop.

All seven programs with reading tests have the additional benefit of using texts that are thematically related to the textbook chapters they cover. This feature is critical if the tests are to bridge the gap between achievement and proficiency tests. Students should already have the context and some vocabulary in mind. Four programs have passages written specifically for the tests; one has articles adapted from authentic texts, with new words translated; and the other two have totally authentic documents, down to the photocopy reproduction. In the last, no unknown words are translated or explained. Techniques for testing authentic documents include multiple-choice word definitions and text meaning, true-false statements about content, and drawing general conclusions. One useful approach is to have fill-ins that use words different from those in the passage:

[Text:] *Visa. C'est la plus diffusée . . .*
[Test:] *La carte la plus populaire est . . .*

[Text:] *American Express. Apparue en France en 1961 . . .*
[Test:] *La carte American Express est sortie en France en . . .*

These items test discrete meanings rather than global understanding, but they do require scanning, a useful skill. It would seem, then, that only two programs follow the proficiency movement to the letter by reducing the level of comprehension required rather than the difficulty of the passage (Grellet, 1981, pp. 7-8). Nonetheless, all the reading tests are effective assessments of that skill in that they present a written text and ask the student to demonstrate an understanding of the message. Given the work involved in finding a passage at the right level for unit tests and the difficulty in writing them, these seven programs provide an important service by testing this skill.

Speaking

Seven programs furnish tests of the speaking skill. The reduced number is not surprising, since conversation is so personal and since necessary follow-up questions cannot be predicted. Two programs provide material for major exams, and four have much shorter sections for each chapter. One testing program consists of situation cards not available for review. The seven programs use only two techniques, though more than two dozen have been identified in commercial tests (Madsen & Jones, 1981). Four have groups of personal questions; all but one package group these thematically. A thematic group is illustrated by the following example:

> *En voyage*
> *Aimez-vous voyager? Pourquoi?*
> *Qu'est-ce que vous aimez faire en vacances?*
> *Où préférez-vous aller?*
> *Comment préférez-vous voyager?*

All questions are based on structures taught in the chapters the test covers, which produces an achievement test, but the thematic relationship (travel) introduces elements of a natural conversation, a proficiency orientation.

Five testing programs have situations similar to those in the ACTFL Oral Proficiency Interview. The situations are at a "novice" to "intermediate" level, which is appropriate to a first-year class (Magnan, 1986), with the exception of one program that suggests debates between pairs of students. Since the topic is related to the chapter, an acceptable "debate" might take the form of declarative statements of opinion by students who do not agree with each other.

The best oral tests are the only two that provide both questions and situations. They are also the two that combine chapters to make oral testing a major event, a more realistic approach than the weekly or biweekly format. Publishers should consider adding more information about oral testing, such as asking follow-up questions and indicating how to score student responses, even though most university programs have training in this area.

Culture

Since all French textbooks published in recent memory place substantial importance on the teaching of culture, not only French but in most cases of the French-speaking world, it would be logical to expect culture tests too. In fact, only five packets include regular culture tests as a separate skill, with one other testing culture occasionally. Two do not have separate test sections but do embed cultural contexts in tests of other skills; in another, cultural readings appear infrequently. Three are culturally neutral, in that if test sections are contextualized (and most are not), the situation created is not specific to a French-speaking culture.

The type of culture tested closely follows what is presented in the textbooks: almost exclusively the daily life of natives of France. Francophone culture is present but not frequent. Virtually no questions on what is called "big C" culture are to be found; the closest are two short readings on Quebec history and two on French. Nothing from arts and letters is tested.

The six programs that do test culture separately use only four elicitation techniques: true-false statements, multiple-choice fill-ins, a short answer, and a paragraph to write. These are all pure memory items since the answers come from statements in the textbooks. For example, in the true-false format is this:

In France, the government owns all the television stations.

Flic is a slang term for movie in French.

Items such as these may test cultural notes or students' ability to remember the content of reading passages.

Techniques involving writing are obviously more open-ended and also allow for personalization by asking students what they think is important or striking or how they would function in a specific situation:

B) *Différences culturelles.* During the last few weeks, you have been introduced to some cultural differences. Which one struck you the most?

Comment faites-vous pour changer un chèque de voyage en France?

The former item would be "free points" for students, since they could hardly write an incorrect answer, but the teacher might make interesting discoveries. The latter is a combination of culture and writing and would be best scored purely on how well meaning was conveyed.

Of course, the tests that use authentic documents for reading passages and LC also add a cultural component even if all the required knowledge is furnished. One test section first presents the results of a poll on what counts most for young French people (studies, friends, family, etc., with percentages of respondents) and then presents sentence-completion items such as these:

2) *A mon avis, il vaut mieux . . .*

4) *Il est peu probable que le sondage . . .*

The section is highly integrative in both skills (reading, writing, and culture) and grammatical features. What the section really tests would be determined by the way in which the answer is scored: anything from the ability to communicate opinions and cultural sensitivity to a discrete test of subjunctive verb forms. This is but another example of the importance of training TAs in multisection courses if interjudge reliability is to be maintained.

The tests of other skills that rely on a cultural context are of particular interest. Unlike the example above, the context usually adds nothing, since a situation in the student's native culture may be substituted for the names of people and places in the ubiquitous party, home, café, or telephone call that appear in contextualized tests. Some cultural contexts, however, are important to the exercise: a dialogue to complete of a discussion of Africa, oral questions on the French post office requiring written answers, another LC passage on preparing bouillabaisse and a passage identifying the French store where one buys each item from a list. Certainly these tasks are a more realistic use of culture than exercises such as this one:

Compare in English the French and American educational systems.

When students learn that culture is an integral part of listening, speaking, reading, and writing, the pedagogical materials have succeeded.

Examinations

Given the notion of moving from achievement- to proficiency-oriented testing by using different chapter tests or sections of the same test for different purposes as cited above, one would hope that those examinations which combine several chapters would be more open-ended and communicative than chapter tests. For many students, the final exam will be their last opportunity to use the target language to communicate messages. Of the seven programs that provide examinations in addition to chapter tests, none shows a marked difference between the two types. Five of the seven have longer exams than tests by a factor of two to three, but both types are similar. Two have slightly more open-ended tasks with exams, particularly for the writing skill, while another adds a

culture section. Most, however, have only length as distinguishing feature. This similarity does not present a problem to teachers who are
satisfied with the mechanical/communicative, discrete/integrative,
achievement/proficiency mix to begin with, but in general it would
seem that many publishers missed an opportunity to reinforce the
stated goals of their textbooks by either not providing comprehensive
examinations or not developing less achievement-oriented test sections
for them.

Recommendations

The analysis of these testing programs leads naturally to recommendations for improving the current situation.

1) Textbook publishers should make a concerted effort to issue testing
   programs at the same time as they do textbooks. Teachers need
   them when changing books because they do not have any tests of
   their own at that point; a year or two later, they do. Tests also provide an additional way in which adopters can evaluate the goals of
   the textbook. Some of the tests are so good that they could encourage adoptions.
2) Publishers should try to include as many features as possible from
   the present description, including examinations, oral tests, and
   tapes of the LC component. If doing so is not feasible, they should
   concentrate on LC and reading tests, as these are the most difficult
   for TAs to construct owing to the amount of time involved and the
   native-level proficiency required.
3) When constructing tests, authors should carefully examine the balance of achievement- and proficiency-oriented tasks, as many tests
   are deficient in the latter. No program offers a test that combines *all*
   the chapters of the textbook. Perhaps such a test could be oriented
   toward global, communicative tasks, leaving discrete grammar for
   chapter tests. It should test all five skills with more sections than are
   needed so that individual course directors could choose the balance of skills they seek.

Conclusion

Even for teachers who feel they must create their own tests, commercial
tests provide an important service to the profession. Unfortunately,
teachers cannot choose the textbook of one publisher and the tests of
another in order to get what they consider the best of each. The tests of
LC and reading examined for this study are good, with minor excep-

tions, because they test for global meaning of passages with frequently encountered contexts or true cultural insights. With writing sections, teachers will have to study the mix of discrete-point/integrative, controlled/open-ended, meaningful/communicative exercises the tests provide to see if they reflect instructional goals. The tests vary from total achievement to a good mix of achievement/proficiency-oriented tasks and are markedly better than the tests examined by Rea (1985), which were predominantly grammar tests. Many tests are more imaginative than teachers have time to be. They may even promote the backwash effect.

As far as testing programs' reflecting the goals of the textbooks they accompany, the programs are moderately successful. My conclusion is that six of the twelve are valid tests of their described goals, with two others coming close. The problem, however, is as much with the goals as with the tests. We must test achievement to inform students of their progress and assign them grades, whereas prefaces to textbooks shy away from this fact, preferring instead to concentrate on goals that may be unreachable. To answer the original question, Do commercial testing programs accurately assess the language proficiency of beginning French students in America's colleges and universities? the answer is a qualified yes. Eight of the twelve have a mix of achievement- and proficiency-oriented tasks that, with some work, can serve to evaluate student and teacher progress.

Notes

1. For a discussion of the various types of validity, see Hughes (1989, chap. 4), or Underhill (1987, pp. 104-6).

2. I chose the years 1988-90 to keep the number of tests to a manageable level while using only the most recent ones. I would like to thank the editors of the various publishing houses who provided the test packages, thereby making this research possible. The tests I examined accompany the following textbooks:

Ariew, Robert & Anne Nerenz. *C'est A Dire. Premiers Echanges.* Boston: Heinle & Heinle Publishers, 1989.

Dinneen, David & Madeleine Kernan. *Chapeau! First-Year French.* New York: John Wiley, 1989.

Hagiwara, M. Peter & Françoise de Rocher. *Thème et Variations: An Introduction to French Language and Culture.* 4th ed. New York: John Wiley, 1989.

Jarvis, Gilbert A., Thérèse M. Bonin & Diane W. Birckbichler. *Invitation: Contextes, culture et communication.* 3d ed. New York: Holt, Rinehart & Winston, 1988.

Jian, Gérard & Ralph Hester, with Gail Wade. *Découverte et Création: Les Bases du Français Moderne.* 5th ed. Boston: Houghton Mifflin Company, 1990.

Muyskens, Judith A., Alice Omaggio Hadley & Claudine Convert-Chalmers. *Rendez-vous: An Invitation to French.* 3d ed. New York: McGraw-Hill, 1990.

Phillips, June K., Francine Marie-Victoire Klein & Renée Nicolet Liscinsky. *Quoi de Neuf? French in Action: A Beginning Course.* New York: Random House, 1988.

St. Onge, Susan & Robert Terry. *Vous Y Etes! French for Proficiency.* 2d ed. Boston: Heinle & Heinle Publishers, 1990.

Siskin, H. Jay & Jo Ann M. Recker. *Situations et Contextes.* Fort Worth: Holt, Rinehart & Winston, 1990.

Terrell, Tracy D., Claudine Convert-Chalmers, Marie-Hélène Bugnion, Michèle Sarner & Elizabeth M. Guthrie. *Deux Mondes. A Communicative Approach.* New York: Random House, 1988.

Valette, Jean-Paul & Rebecca M. Valette. *Contacts: Langue et Culture Françaises.* 4th ed. Boston: Houghton-Mifflin Company, 1989.

Walz, Joel & Jean-Pierre Piriou. *Rapports: Language, Culture, Communication.* Second edition. Lexington, MA: D.C. Heath & Company, 1990.

3. I will use the following terms in this analysis:

quiz: test of less material than is taught in a textbook chapter

test: test of one or two chapters

exam(ination): test combining three or more chapters forming a midterm or a final

item: one test question

section: all items grouped together under one set of directions

4. All examples are quoted verbatim from the testing packages. No attempt has been made to reproduce the original physical appearance of the examples, such as typeface, spacing, or lines for student answers.

Works Cited

Chastain, Kenneth. *Toward a Philosophy of Second-Language Learning and Teaching.* Boston: Heinle & Heinle Publishers, 1980.

_____. "Examining the Role of Grammar Explanations, Drills, and Exercises in the Development of Communication Skills." *Hispania* 70 (1987): 160-66.

Cohen, Andrew D. *Testing Language Ability in the Classroom.* Rowley, MA: Newbury House, 1980.

Dandonoli, Patricia. "ACTFL's Current Research in Proficiency Testing." *Defining and Developing Proficiency: Guidelines, Implementations, and Concepts.* ACTFL Foreign Language Education Series. Lincolnwood, IL: National Textbook Company, 1987: 75-96.

Davis, Paul & Mario Rinvolucri. *Dictation: New Methods, New Possibilities.* Cambridge: Cambridge University Press, 1988.

Farhady, Hossein. "New Directions for ESL Proficiency Testing." *Issues in Language Testing Research.* Ed. John W. Oller, Jr. Rowley, MA: Newbury House, 1983: 253-69.

Grellet, Françoise. *Developing Reading Skills: A Practical Guide to Reading Comprehension Exercises.* Cambridge: Cambridge University Press, 1981.

Heaton, J. B. *Classroom Testing*. London: Longman, 1990.

Higgs, Theodore V. "Oral Proficiency Testing and Its Significance for Practice." *Theory into Practice* 26 (1987): 282-87.

Hill, David & Art Mosher. "The Articulation of Curriculum through a Standardized Proficiency-based Diagnostic/Placement Test: The USC Experience." *Language in Action: Theory and Practice. Dimension: Languages '88*. Ed. T. Bruce Fryer & Frank W. Medley, Jr. Columbia, SC: SCOLT, 1989: 101-11.

Hughes, Arthur. *Testing for Language Teachers*. Cambridge: Cambridge University Press, 1989.

Loughrin-Sacco, Steven J. "On Apples and Oranges: The Effects of Integrating Beginners and False Beginners in Elementary French Classes." *Challenges in the 1990s for College Language Programs*. Ed. Sally Sieloff Magnan. Issues in Language Program Direction. Boston: Heinle & Heinle Publishers, 1991: 89-112.

Madsen, H. S. & R. L. Jones. "Classification of Oral Proficiency Tests." *The Construct Validation of Tests of Communicative Competence*. Ed. A. S. Palmer, P. J. M. Groot & G. A. Trosper. Washington, DC: TESOL, 1981: 15-30. ERIC ED 223 103.

Magnan, Sally Sieloff. "From Achievement toward Proficiency Through Multi-Sequence Evaluation." *Foreign Language Proficiency in the Classroom and Beyond*. ACTFL Foreign Language Education Series. Ed. Charles J. James. Lincolnwood, IL: National Textbook Company, 1985: 117-45.

_____. "Assessing Speaking Proficiency in the Undergraduate Curriculum: Data from French." *Foreign Language Annals* (1986): 429-38.

Oller, John W., Jr. *Language Tests at School: A Pragmatic Approach*. London: Longman, 1979.

_____ & Virginia Streiff. "Dictation: A Test of Grammar Based Expectancies." *Testing Language Proficiency*. Ed. Randall L. Jones & Bernard Spolsky. Arlington, VA: Center for Applied Linguistics, 1975: 71-82.

Omaggio, Alice C. *Proficiency-oriented Classroom Testing*. Language in Education: Theory and Practice, 52. Washington, DC: Center for Applied Linguistics, 1983.

_____. *Teaching Language in Context: Proficiency-oriented Instruction*. Boston: Heinle & Heinle Publishers, 1986.

Paulston, Christina Bratt & Mary Newton Bruder. *From Substitution to Substance: A Handbook of Structural Pattern Drills*. Rowley, MA: Newbury House, 1975.

Rea, Pauline M. "Language Testing and the Communicative Language Teaching Curriculum." *New Directions in Language Testing: Papers Presented at the International Symposium on Language Testing, Hong Kong*. Ed. Y. P. Lee, Angela C. Y. Y. Foh, Robert Lord & Graham Low. Oxford: Pergamon Press, 1985: 15-32.

Schulz, Renate A. "From Achievement to Proficiency through Classroom Instruction: Some Caveats." *Modern Language Journal* 70 (1986): 373-79.

Stansfield, Charles W. "A History of Dictation in Foreign Language Teaching and Testing." *Modern Language Journal* 69 (1985): 121-28.

Terrell, Tracy David. "Trends in the Teaching of Grammar in Spanish Language Textbooks." *Hispania* 73 (1990): 201-11.

Underhill, Nic. *Testing Spoken Language. A Handbook of Oral Testing Techniques.* Cambridge: Cambridge University Press, 1987.

Walz, Joel. "Grading Foreign Language Tests." *Canadian Modern Language Review* 38 (1981): 58-67.

_____. "Context and Contextualized Language Practice in Foreign Language Teaching." *Modern Language Journal* 73 (1989): 160-68.

On the Dual Nature of the Second Language Reading Proficiency of Beginning Language Learners

James F. Lee
University of Illinois at Urbana/Champaign

To evaluate the foreign language proficiency of our undergraduate students entails understanding the phenomenon to be evaluated. To gain such an understanding is not always easy. Matters of language learning, both first (L1) and second (L2), involve memory and cognition and are therefore complex. Let's take reading as one such manifestation of language that involves complex cognitive activity. Huey (1968, p. 8) once stated that "to completely analyze what we do when we read would almost be the acme of a psychologist's dream for it would be to describe very many of the most intricate workings of the human mind, as well as to unravel the tangled story of the most remarkable specific performance that civilization has learned in all its history."[1] In this paper, I hope to shed light on a limited very aspect of the intricate workings of the human mind and to unravel a small piece of the tangled story of foreign language reading proficiency.

An examination of the research reveals that what has been classified as "reading" comes in four guises, more appropriately referred to as research paradigms. First, there is oral reading, or rendering written language into oral language. In this paradigm, the researcher is concerned with categorizing and classifying the errors (termed "miscues") produced during reading. Second, there is reading of cloze passages. A cloze passage is a text from which words have been deleted (referred to as a mutilated text by some cloze researchers). There are various methods for deciding which words to delete and these will be seen below. The readers' task is to demonstrate their understanding of the passage by filling in the blanks with the appropriate words. The researcher's task is to determine what information was used or not used by the readers to accomplish the task. Third, there is verbalization (commonly referred to as think-aloud protocols). In this paradigm, the readers verbalize their thought processes as they read a passage (introspection) or after they have read one (retrospection). The researcher classifies and categorizes how the readers have extracted meaning from what they have read. Finally, there is silent reading, the way one typically reads outside of experimental settings. Silent reading is the broadest of paradigms, since the researcher's purpose varies widely, as will be seen below.

To shed light on a very limited aspect of the intricate workings of the human mind, a subset of the research that falls under each of the four research paradigms will be examined. What subset? Foreign language proficiency is a developmental phenomenon. That is, we know that learners become increasingly fluent as their foreign language linguistic systems become increasingly sophisticated; that is, they pass through stages of development. Proficiency, then, is not a static phenomenon but a dynamic and evolving one. To gain insights into the developmental aspects of foreign language reading proficiency, the review of research carried out here will focus only on those studies which have empirically examined learners representing different stages of language development. To narrow the corpus further, only those studies which have compared the reading performance of beginning language learners with that of more advanced learners and/or with native readers will be examined.[2] While the focus might seem too narrow, these studies offer the most direct information about developmental aspects of L2 reading.

To draw together the work of researchers who are each pursuing their own agenda is difficult. Many problems present themselves, not the least of which is how to render an across-the-board classification of the subjects on whom data have been gathered. For example, in foreign language circles many refer to the second year of language instruction (the third and fourth semesters) as the intermediate level. In English as a Second Language (ESL), the language proficiency of students who are termed intermediate level is beyond that of intermediate foreign language students. How does one begin to differentiate one level from another, theoretically and empirically? The first source that could be consulted is the previous research on L2 reading, which indeed is the source for the present work. Extremely few studies have categorized subjects according to levels of proficiency, and those which do have utilized their own methods for determining proficiency. On the other hand, 80% of existing research categorizes subjects by language experience, a quantification of the subjects' exposure to the second or foreign language. Admittedly, language experience is not equivalent to language proficiency, yet if the starting point for the present work is the previous research, we must work with the research as it is. Therefore, for the purposes of carrying out the present review of L2 reading research, the subjects on whom data have been gathered will be categorized based on the scheme in Table 1 (derived from Lee, 1988, 1990). The time line is used in this paper as a way to derive a comparable classification of the subjects across the various studies reviewed. Any problems in interpretation are noted.

The preliminary attempt to unravel a small piece of the tangled story of L2 reading led to the separation of the research into the four paradigms described above. The subsequent examination of the findings

Table 1

Categorization of Subjects of Previous Research into Stages

Stage	Language Experience	Rationale
Beginning	0-300 hours	Roughly corresponds to basic language instruction in foreign languages taught in the United States and the beginner level of instruction in English as a second/foreign language
Intermediate	301-600 hours	Roughly corresponds to the hours foreign language majors and minors experience and the intermediate level of instruction in English as a second/foreign language
Advanced	601+ hours	Roughly corresponds to the experience of students pursuing graduate degrees in foreign languages and the advanced level of instruction in English as a second/foreign language

of the research led to classifying the findings into one of two categories. First, the research reveals that across stages of development there are common performance patterns. That is, the learners are performing the same way. Not that there are no significant differences based on stage of development; these differences do exist but are quantitative, not qualitative, in nature. Second, the research reveals that particular to a stage of development there are characteristic performance patterns. The findings show language learners at one stage perform in a way that is qualitatively different from how learners perform at another stage. Foreign language reading proficiency can therefore be characterized as having at least a dual nature.

What follows is a review of the research that has compared the reading performance of beginning-stage language learners with the reading performance of more advanced language learners and/or native readers. It is important to bear in mind that the beginning *language learners* examined to date are *not* beginning *readers*. The subject pool comprises mostly university-age language learners, with some adolescents represented. All interpretation of the data must be done in light of the fact that we are not discussing beginning readers. The nature of foreign language reading proficiency for undergraduates cannot be discussed without acknowledging their sophistication as readers in their native language.[3]

Review of the Literature

Common Performance Patterns across Stages

Since learners are performing similarly from stage to stage (or level to level), we are unable to classify their reading behaviors as belonging to one level or another; the reading behaviors overlap. That beginning language learners perform similarly to the way more advanced language learners and native readers do is noteworthy. While language ability as a factor in nonnative reading performance cannot be dismissed, the review of empirical comparisons reveals some fundamental similarities between the reading performance of beginning language learners and that of more advanced learners and native readers. Thus, while the beginners may not have been as successful as the comparison group(s), their performance paralleled that of the comparison group(s).

Oral Reading/Miscue Analysis

Clarke (1980) compared the L1 and L2 oral reading performance of a good L1 and a poor L1 reader. He analyzed the errors, or miscues, produced when they read aloud. Clarke found that the good reader produced fewer miscues than the poor reader in both L1 and L2 reading. The good reader's miscues showed a greater degree of syntactic and semantic acceptability than the poor reader's. For each comparison, however, the difference between the good and the poor reader diminished considerably from the L1 to the L2. Clarke concluded that the good L1 reader was also the good L2 reader but that only certain L1 reading skills were transferred to L2 reading. Moreover, limited control over the L2 caused what he termed a "short circuit" in the good reader's system.

McLeod and McLaughlin (1986) examined the oral reading errors of 20 adult native speakers of English and 44 adult ESL students. The latter were divided into two equal groups of 22, beginning and advanced, based on their scores on a university placement test. Subjects were given two passages to read aloud. Two categories of errors were scored, meaningful (syntactically and semantically acceptable) and nonmeaningful (graphemically based but not syntactically and semantically acceptable).

McLeod and McLaughlin found that in oral reading, beginning and advanced language learners made significantly fewer syntactically and semantically acceptable errors than native readers did. The difference between the native and nonnative readers was significant; the difference between the two nonnative groups was not. Beginning language learners, however, exhibited the same pattern of error types as advanced learners, even though beginners made significantly more errors. Yet compared with native readers, the oral reading errors of language learners were largely graphemically based and not syntactically and semantically acceptable. McLeod and McLaughlin concluded that neither beginning nor advanced language learners made use of syntactic and semantic information during oral reading.

Cloze Test Performance

Chihara et al. (1977) examined the cloze test performance of 41 native speakers of English and of 71 beginning-, 66 intermediate-, and 64 advanced-level learners studying English as a foreign language in Japan. They presented the subjects with two traditional cloze passages in which every sixth or seventh word had been deleted. The content of the passages appeared in sequential and scrambled orders. The results showed significant interactions between passage and level of language learner and between order and level of language learner. An analysis of the significant interactions demonstrated qualitative differences between native and non-native readers. Native readers showed no differences in performance across the two passages whereas the nonnative readers did. The native readers' performance was, however, affected by the sequential versus scrambled versions of the passages, whereas the nonnatives' was not. Chihara et al. concluded that nonnative readers were more sensitive to passage itself than native readers were but that native readers were more sensitive to discourse constraints across sentences than nonnative readers were.

Markham (1985) examined the cloze test performance of 61 beginning and 20 advanced learners.[4] He presented the subjects with two rational deletion cloze passages in which only content words had been deleted. The content of the passages was presented in either sequential or scrambled order. He then compared performance utilizing two scoring procedures, exact word and semantic and syntactic acceptability. Markham's results echo those of Chihara et al. (1977). He found that there were no differences for sequential-versus-scrambled order for either scoring procedure. He did find significant differences for passage and for level of language learner in the expected direction but no significant interactions. Markham concluded that across all levels of language learners, readers attended only to the immediate environment of the blank and not to intersentential relationships, since scrambling the order of information had no effect on performance.

Nunan (1985) examined the cloze test performance of two groups of ninth-grade nonnative speakers of English. The two groups of 50 subjects each were distinguished by length of exposure to the language. One group's exposure to English began prior to the start of formal schooling (advanced learners), whereas the other's exposure began after this time (beginning learners).[5] Subjects took two rational deletion cloze tests, one on a familiar topic, the other on an unfamiliar topic. All deleted items were the second end of a cohesively marked logical, referential, or lexical relationship. Responses were scored on the basis of syntactic and semantic acceptability. Nunan found significant differences for level of language learner and for passage content but no significant interactions. Both beginning and advanced language learners performed better on familiar-topic cloze tests than they did on unfamiliar ones. Nunan concluded that content familiarity was an important factor affecting cloze performance across all levels of language development.

Clarke (1980) administered cloze tests to 21 beginning language learners in their L1 and L2. The subjects were classified as good and poor readers in their native-language based on their performance on the native language cloze test. The unacceptable cloze responses of these two groups were analyzed for their syntactic and semantic acceptability. Clarke found that in their native language, the good readers relied on semantic rather than syntactic cues. The poor readers relied on syntactic rather than semantic cues. In the second language, the use of syntactic cues was equal for both good and poor readers and their use of semantic cues was very nearly equal. Clarke concluded that reading in a second language reduced the distinction between good and poor readers. Somehow, a good reader's system was "short-circuited" by limited control over the L2.

Silent Reading

Perkins (1983) examined whether L2 readers use their knowledge of the world to contribute to information found in a text (what he termed "semantic constructivity"). He examined a total of 43 adult subjects representing beginning, intermediate, and advanced levels of language development.[6] Subjects read 10 three-sentence paragraphs in which locative and spatial relationships were expressed. Subsequently, subjects were given four types of statements related to each paragraph and asked to indicate whether they had read the statement or not. The four statement types were a true statement, a false statement, a true inference, and a false inference. Performance was scored for the number of misrecognized statements and inferences. Of primary interest to Perkins were the inferences. If subjects indicated they had indeed read a true inferential statement in the paragraphs when in fact they had not, then that would be evidence they were contributing their knowledge to the text.

Perkins found no significant difference between the total number of misrecognitions made by beginning and intermediate learners, but both beginning and intermediate learners made significantly more misrecognitions than advanced learners did. Perkins concluded that the L2 readers clearly constructed meaning by making inferences across the sentences of a text.

Bernhardt (1986) carried out an eye-movement analysis of beginning, advanced, and native readers of German. Subjects read three texts three times and after each reading wrote what they remembered from the text. The texts were classified as an easy pedagogical text, a difficult pedagogical text, and a natural text. (Pedagogical texts are written expressly for a nonnative speaking audience.) The data were analyzed for fixation frequency, fixation duration, regressive fixations, and reading speed.

Bernhardt found that beginning learners, advanced learners, and native readers were sensitive to certain kinds of textual factors in reading. All groups' reading speed increased proportionately for an easy pedagogical text, a difficult pedagogical text, and a natural text, respectively. She also found that beginning and advanced language learners ignored the same kinds of elements when reading, in that neither systematically fixated on punctuation. The regressive fixations of all groups were nearly the same (about one-third of all fixations were regressive).

Hudson (1982) carried out a study in which a total of 93 beginning-, intermediate-, and advanced-level learners were exposed to three different treatments to determine the effects of inducing appropriate schemata on reading comprehension.[7] Each subject read three passages graded for proficiency level; a different treatment accompanied each passage. The treatments were: (1) topically oriented visuals and questions; (2) a list of essential lexical items and a discussion of the lexical items; and (3) a read-test, then reread and retest treatment. Across all stages of language development, nonnative readers comprehended more from texts when provided with some kind of treatment to activate their knowledge. For both beginning and intermediate learners, the most beneficial treatment was topically oriented visuals that activated content schemata.

Introspection/Retrospection Procedures

Sarig (1987) utilized introspective data elicitation procedures to examine how readers analyze main ideas and synthesize overall content when reading in their first and second languages. Ten high school seniors served as subjects. They read two passages, one in their native language (Hebrew) and the other in the L2 (English).[8] The introspections were analyzed for the types of strategies used by readers in their native and nonnative languages to perform the two tasks.[9]

Sarig found that subjects used four strategies to analyze main ideas and synthesize overall message in both native and nonnative reading and that these strategies contributed to success and failure in carrying out the tasks in almost identical ways in both languages. The strategies employed were (1) technical-aid strategies, such as skimming, scanning, marking a text, and skipping parts; (2) clarification and simplification strategies, such as utterance substitutions, circumlocutions, and paraphrase; (3) coherence-detecting strategies, such as use of background knowledge and identifying people in the text and their actions; and (4) monitoring strategies, such as any conscious and controlled change of planning. Sarig also carried out an analysis of individuals' reading strategies in the two languages. He found that each reader utilized her own characteristic combination of strategies. Sarig concluded that the same processes underlie the performance of high-level reading tasks in L1 and L2 to almost the same extent. Moreover, how a reader carried out a task was highly individualized. Last, the individualized combinations of strategies used called into question the classical dichotomy of good-versus-poor reader that has been based on classifying reading strategies as good if good readers use them and poor if poor readers use them.

Characteristic Beginning-Level Reading Performance

That learners who have experienced fewer than 300 hours of language instruction perform in ways particular to them is not surprising and indeed expected. The qualitative differences between the reading performance of beginning language learners and that of more advanced learners and native readers are rather limited in scope. Presented below is a summary of the findings of the research that allows us to characterize the performance patterns "unique" to beginning language learners. That is, the performance of the beginning language learners not only might be quantitatively different but is definitely qualitatively different from that of the comparison group.

Cloze Test Performance

In addition to the research on oral reading errors described above, McLeod and McLaughlin (1986) examined the extent to which beginning learners, advanced learners, and native readers were sensitive to syntactic constraints on an oral cloze test. Subjects were read two or three lines and then guessed at a missing word. Their performance was scored for the syntactic plausibility of the word they provided.

McLeod and McLaughlin found that each group was significantly different from the other two. The native readers averaged an almost-perfect score, demonstrating their sensitivity to syntactic constraints on cloze test responses. The scores for the advanced language learners were closer to those of the native readers than they were to those of the beginning learners, showing that advanced learners were sensitive to syntactic constraints but that beginners were not. McLeod and McLaughlin concluded that only native readers were completely able to make use of syntactic and semantic constraints in oral reading or on an oral cloze; the beginning language learners, not at all; and, inexplicably, the advanced learners only sometimes.

Silent Reading

Hudson (1982) carried out a study in which a total of 93 beginning-, intermediate-, and advanced-level learners were exposed to three different treatments to determine the effects of inducing appropriate schemata on reading comprehension; this study is described more fully above. Hudson found that beginners exhibited a different pattern from intermediate and advanced learners in the utility of the various treatments. Beginners were benefited to a greater degree by topically oriented prereading visuals than by either lexically oriented activities or a rereading of a text. Intermediate learners were most benefited first by topically oriented visuals, then by rereading, and last by vocabulary activities. Advanced learners demonstrated a completely different pattern, in that all three activities were equally effective; their performance was the same no matter what the reading treatment.

Bernhardt (1986) carried out an eye-movement analysis of beginning, advanced, and native readers of German; this study is described more fully above. Bernhardt found that beginners exhibited a particular pattern to their fixation frequency and reading speed on successive readings of texts. Beginners, unlike advanced language learners and native readers, did not increase either their eye-fixation frequency or their speed when they reread. The words that beginning language learners fixated on were different from those that advanced learners and native readers fixated on. Beginners fixated primarily on content words, ignoring function words. Advanced learners and native readers fixated not only on content words but also on function words.

Bernhardt concluded that since advanced language learners fixated on the same textual elements as natives but beginning language learners did not, reading behaviors were not generic from language to language but were specific to a particular language, and that language-specific reading behaviors appeared to develop as language proficiency developed. She also concluded that reading speed was the most telling variable in her study and that it might be an indicator of L2 reading proficiency.

Omaggio (1979) compared the effect of a number of pictorial contexts on the comprehension of beginning language learners of French as a foreign language with that of native readers of English. Subjects included 233 beginning language learners, who were assigned to one of six pictorial contexts, and 431 native readers, half of whom read the English translation of the French passage and were assigned to one of six pictorial contexts. (The other half acted as a control group of sorts, receiving no text, only the pictorial contexts.) The six pictorial contexts examined were (1) no picture; (2) a picture depicting a single object related to the theme of the passage; (3) a picture depicting a scene from the beginning of the passage; (4) a picture depicting a scene from the main portion of the passage; (5) a picture depicting a scene from the end of the passage; and (6) a series of three pictures, depicting scenes from the beginning, middle, and end of the passage. Subjects read a 650-word story that was edited for difficulty by glossing lexical items and structures in the margin. After reading, the subjects wrote a summary of the passage and then completed a 20-item test composed of 10 multiple choice and 10 true-false questions. Subjects who had no text, only visuals, wrote a story suggested by the picture(s) and then completed the 20-item test. Subjects' performance was analyzed for (1) total number of facts recalled and correct inferences made; (2) total number of correct responses on the recognition test; and (3) total amount of incorrect information recalled.

Omaggio found no significant differences between the various comprehension scores of subjects who received only a pictorial context and no text. For subjects who actually read a text, qualitative differences emerged between the native and nonnative readers. There were no significant differences between the native readers on all three measures among the pictorial contexts. In essence, their reading performance was the same no matter which pictorial context they were given (or not given, since "no picture" was one of the contexts). Pictorial context was, however, a differentiating factor in nonnative reading performance. On both recall and recognition measures, having some kind of picture improved subjects' performance. The pictorial context that most enhanced performance was the picture depicting a scene from the beginning of the story; the contexts that contributed least to performance were the "no picture" context and the picture depicting a single object related to the theme of the passage. Indeed, the beginning language learners' errors in recall were highest for these last two contexts. Omaggio concluded that in L1 and L2 reading, pictures did not act independently of textual content but with it. Not all pictures were equally effective in enhancing L2 comprehension. Pictorial aids might have been superfluous for native readers because the passage was a relatively easy one.

Perkins (1983) examined whether L2 readers use their knowledge of the world to contribute to information found in a text (what he termed "semantic constructivity"); this study is described more fully above. Perkins carried out detailed analyses on four sentence types for each level of language learner. Whereas beginning, intermediate, and advanced language learners contributed information to text comprehension, their patterns of performance on specific statement types varied from level to level. All learners recognized false inferences to a higher degree of accuracy than with other sentence types. There is no differentiation among true inferences, true statements, and false statements for beginning learners, and none among true inferences and true statements for intermediate learners. Advanced learners, on the other hand, differentiated among all four statement types.

Introspection/Retrospection Procedures

Carrell (1989) related the performance of beginning and advanced language learners reading in their first and second languages to their responses on a questionnaire concerning their metacognitive awareness of the reading process. The subjects were 45 native speakers of Spanish who were advanced learners of ESL and 75 native speakers of English who were beginning-level learners of Spanish as a foreign language. Each subject read two texts in their L2 and then answered 10 multiple-choice questions. The procedure was then repeated for their native language. Subsequently, they filled out a 36-item questionnaire in which they judged their use of silent-reading strategies in four categories: (1) confidence strategies, or ability to read in a language; (2) repair strategies, or what they did when they did not understand; (3) effective strategies, or what they focused on in order to understand more; and (4) causes of difficulty, or things that made reading in a language difficult. It should be noted that the variable of level of language learner is crossed with or confounded by the differences in native and second languages; any discussion of whether the findings are related to level of language learner or to language itself must be tentative.

For L1 reading, Carrell found that (1) no confidence items or repair strategies were significantly related to reading performance; (2) disagreement that sound-letter information or grammatical structure (bottom-up strategies) made reading difficult correlated positively with reading performance; and (3) awareness of top-down strategies (e.g., gist, background knowledge, and text organization) was not significantly related to reading performance, since almost all readers agreed that top-down strategies were effective. For L2 reading, Carrell found that many items were language-specific, but that across languages, the more subjects agreed that not giving up while reading was important, the better they performed in L2 reading. The items that were language-specific did not fall into neat categories of either top-down or bottom-up factors. For reading in Spanish as a foreign language (the beginning language learners), the more subjects agreed with the statement that they were able to question the significance or truthfulness of what the author said and that word meaning and syntax caused reading difficulty, the higher their reading performance. For reading in ESL (the advanced language learners), the more subjects agreed that differentiating main points from supporting details, the more they disagreed that sound-letter correspondences were important, and the more they disagreed that difficulties arise by relating the content of the text to background knowledge, the higher their reading performance. Carrell concluded that beginning language learners were more bottom-up in their orientation and that advanced language learners were more top down in theirs. Since only a few items out of a total of 36 designed to assess metacognitive awareness in L1 and L2 reading were significantly related to reading performance, only tentative conclusions can be reached. The case for the advanced language learners' being more top-down in their orientation is stronger than the case for beginning language learners' being more bottom-up in theirs. For the beginners, only 2 of the 36 items correlated significantly with performance; one was a bottom-up item and the other a top-down one.

Discussion

The Orientation of Beginning Language Learners

Clarke's (1980) short-circuit hypothesis has been the dominant framework for describing and discussing the reading performance of beginning-stage language learners. The hypothesis states that limited control over the language "short-circuits" the good reader's system, causing him or her to revert to poor reader strategies when confronted with a difficult or confusing task in the second language. In other words, readers shift from engaging in top-down processing to engaging in bottom-up processing as they shift from L1 to L2 reading, a qualitative shift in the way they perform in L2 from the way they perform in L1. As Carrell's (1989) results show, beginning language learners are aware of their limited language ability; they perceive that bottom-up factors affect their performance.

It is important to note, however, that the short-circuit hypothesis gains most of its credence from the findings of two research paradigms, oral reading and cloze test performance. With two exceptions (Bernhardt's [1986] finding that beginners do not increase their reading speed on subsequent readings of the same text and Carrell's [1989] finding that beginners' performance is correlated with their perception that syntax causes difficulties), the findings from research on silent reading and verbalizations do not support the notion that the good L1 reader's system is short-circuited by the L2.

The evidence from studies in all four paradigms reveals that beginning language learners engage in top down processing during L2 reading. Beginners are sensitive to different passages (Bernhardt, 1986; Chihara et al., 1977; Markham, 1985) and different topics (Nunan, 1985). They make inferences (Perkins, 1983). Their comprehension can be increased through activating content schemata (Hudson, 1982; Omaggio, 1979). And finally, the reading performance of beginners is related to their perception that it is important to be able to assess the truth value of an author's message. While Clarke's short-circuit hypothesis remains an important way to conceptualize the reading performance of beginning language learners, its domain seems restricted to particular tasks, such as oral reading and cloze testing, that require language-based processing. The reading performance of beginning language learners is best accounted for by an interactive model of reading in which top-down processes come into play simultaneously with bottom up ones. Beginning language learners who are sophisticated L1 readers are oriented neither from the bottom up nor from the top down; they are bi-oriented.

Assessing Foreign Language Reading Proficiency

The review of research from the four paradigms reveals both common performance patterns across stages and characteristic beginning-level performance patterns. Can this information be put to practical use? What can we do to assess the foreign language reading proficiency of our undergraduate students? Those tasks utilized in the research which yielded characteristic beginning-level performance patterns offer us some possibilities for gathering information on the reading proficiency of our students. These possibilities, however, are not necessarily assessments of reading proficiency itself but, rather, are indicators or correlates of proficiency. The same caveat is given by those who have correlated cloze test performance with oral proficiency. That is, one could gain an indication of oral proficiency through a cloze test even though cloze tests are not tests of oral proficiency. Presented in the next paragraph are ways to gain knowledge about learners' foreign language reading proficiency.

The research suggests that we might gain an indication of beginning-level reading proficiency in one of four ways. First, assess reading speed across subsequent readings of a passage; beginners will not increase their speed on subsequent readings (Bernhardt, 1986). Second, determine the pattern of responses to true-false statements/inferences; beginners will perform the same on true and false statements and true inferences (Perkins, 1983). Third, gauge the syntactic plausability of responses to an oral cloze test; only 33% of beginners' responses are syntactically plausable (McLeod & McLaughlin, 1986). And fourth, assess the relative utility of various treatments designed to enhance comprehension; beginners should be most benefitted by topically-oriented visuals (Hudson, 1982) that depict scenes from the beginning of the passage (Omaggio, 1979).

Summary

In this paper, I hope to have shed light on a very limited aspect of the intricate workings of the human mind and to have unraveled a small piece of the tangled story of foreign language reading proficiency. The research has been reviewed from four pradigms: (1) oral reading/miscue analysis; (2) cloze test performance; (3) silent reading; and

(4) verbalizations. While both the readers' and the researchers' tasks vary from paradigm to paradigm, the paradigms represent the whole of reading performance. Since foreign language proficiency is a developmental phenomenon, the review concentrated on those studies which have compared empirically the reading performance of beginning language learners with that of more advanced learners and/or with native readers. The findings were presented in two categories, common performance patterns across stages and characteristic performance patterns of beginning language learners, demonstrating that foreign language reading proficiency can be characterized as having at least a dual nature. It was proposed that assessing the reading proficiency of beginning language learners in classroom settings could be done as it was done in the research that yielded characteristic performance patterns of beginning-level learners. Doing so provides a sound empirical base to classroom testing.

Notes

1. Anderson and Pearson (1984) start their chapter with this same quote from Huey. As I began writing this paper, I wanted to impress on the reader that to discuss reading proficiency is to discuss a very complex issue; Huey's words capture that complexity as well as give me a line to follow throughout the paper.

2. There is research in which the reading performance of intermediate language learners is compared with that of advanced learners and/or native readers. Likewise, there is research that compares advanced learners with native readers. A preliminary review of that research is available in Lee (1990). To include the research in these three categories in the present paper would require many, many more pages than are allowed here or than are necessary to make my point. I am currently preparing a work that demonstrates there are two types of findings: common performance patterns across levels and characteristic performance patterns within levels (Lee, in progress). These two types of findings form the basis for the present paper, which focuses on beginning language learners.

3. I am grateful to Barry McLaughlin for emphasizing (at the second conference on Research Perspectives on Adult Language Learning and Acquisition, Columbus, Ohio, October 1990) that these beginning language learners were not beginning readers. Originally I had deferred making the point until the conclusion of the work but see that it colors the interpretation of the data. I have previously acknowledged the sophisitication of our undergraduate students as readers in their native language (Lee, 1988). In that paper, I proposed the Cognitive Maturity Assumption as a framework for examining the teaching and testing of foreign language reading.

4. Markham (1985) included three levels of subjects in his analyses: beginners, enrolled in first-year German; intermediates, enrolled in second- or third-year German; and advanced, who were either graduate students in German or

native speakers of German. His groupings of subjects does not match the divisions being used in the present work. Utilizing the time line explained previously, Markham's beginning and intermediate subjects were easily recategorized as beginning language learners. A more specific numerical breakdown of his advanced subjects is not given; that is, it is not known how many native speakers were in the group. For the purposes of the present study, I decided to classify his third group as advanced language learners rather than native speakers since the group did include advanced learners.

5. Nunan (1985) provided little information about the subjects, and categorizing them was therefore a guess on my part. He states only that "Group A consisted of long-term 'second-phase' learners who had arrived in Australia before the start of formal schooling. I therefore interpreted this group to be advanced language learners. Group B consisted of learners who arrived in Australia after the start of formal schooling" (p. 46). No other information is provided on group B, and so I categorized them as beginners.

6. Perkins (1983) classified subjects according to the reading class they were enrolled in – beginning, intermediate, or advanced. Just as with Hudson (1982), the assumption was made that the subjects' reading-class level was equivalent to their level of language development. In his discussion of the data, Perkins himself made the statement that the reading-class levels were associated with different levels of language proficiency (p. 25).

7. Hudson (1982) classified subjects according to level of reading proficiency as determined by the intensive English class in which they were enrolled. There is an indication in the article that the reading-class level matched subjects' stage of language development. That is, the research questions were phrased in terms of "levels of L2 language proficiency" (p. 10).

8. Sarig's (1987) subjects had studied English as a foreign language an average of eight years, four or five hours per week. Sarig's description of them stated that based on teacher evaluations and an English-language proficiency test, subjects had high, intermediate, and low English proficiency. He did not indicate, however, the proficiency level of any specific subject. For the purposes of the present work, Sarig's subjects are all classified as beginning language learners for two reasons. First, at no point in Sarig's research is language proficiency analyzed as a factor. Second, the time line presented in the present work is based on university-level instruction, which is more intensive than that at the high school level. Adjusting for university-versus-high-school instruction, it would seem that Sarig's subjects would at best be intermediate-stage language learners; however, given the information that the group of 10 subjects varied in proficiency level from low to high, it was decided to classify them as beginning language learners.

9. The unit of analysis utilized was the reading move, defined by Sarig as "each separate move the reader took while processing the text" (p. 110). Most researchers define reading strategy the same way, and since "reading strategy" is the more common phrase, it is used here instead of "reading move." Indeed, the examples Sarig provided of reading moves are compatible with what others call strategies.

Works Cited

Anderson, Richard & P. David Pearson. "A Schema-Theoretic View of Basic Processes in Comprehension." *Handbook of Reading Research*. Ed. P. D. Pearson. New York: Longman, 1984: 255-91.

Bernhardt, Elizabeth B. "Cognitive Processes in L2: An Examination of Reading Behaviors." *Delaware Symposium on Language Studies: Research on Second Language Acquisition in the Classroom Setting*. Ed. J. Lantolf & A. LaBarca. Norwood, NJ: Ablex, 1986.

Carrell, Patricia L. "Metacognitive Awareness and Second Language Reading." *Modern Language Journal* 73 (1989): 121-34.

Chihara, Tetsuro, John Oller, Kelly Weaver & Mary Anne Chavez-Oller. "Are Cloze Items Sensitive to Constraints across Sentences?" *Language Learning* 21 (1977): 63-73.

Clarke, Mark. "The Short Circuit Hypothesis of ESL Reading – or When Language Competence Interferes with Reading Performance." *Modern Language Journal* 64 (1980): 203-9.

Hudson, Thom. "The Effects of Induced Schemata on the 'Short Circuit' in L2 Reading: Non-decoding Factors in L2 Reading Performance." *Language Learning* 32 (1982): 1-31.

Huey, E. *The Psychology and Pedagogy of Reading*. Cambridge, MA: MIT Press, 1968. (Originally published by Macmillan 1908.)

Lee, James F. "Toward a Modification of the 'Proficiency' Construct for Reading in a Foreign Language." *Hispania* 71 (1988): 941-63.

_____. "A Review of Empirical Comparisons of Nonnative Reading Behaviors across Stages of Language Development." *Variability in Second Language Acquisition*. Ed. H. Burmeister & P. Rounds. Eugene, OR: University of Oregon, 1990: 453-72.

_____. *L2 Reading: A Developmental Perspective*. In progress.

McLeod, Beverly & Barry McLaughlin. "Restructuring or Automaticity: Reading in a Second Language." *Language Learning* 36 (1986): 109-23.

Markham, Paul. "The Rational Deletion Cloze and Global Comprehension in German." *Language Learning* 35 (1985): 423-31.

Nunan, David. "Content Familiarity and the Perception of Textual Relationships in Second Language Reading." *RELC Journal* 16 (1985): 43-50.

Omaggio, Alice. "Pictures and Second Language Comprehension: Do They Help?" *Foreign Language Annals* 12 (1979): 107-16.

Perkins, Kyle. Semantic Constructivity in ESL Reading Comprehension. *TESOL Quarterly* 17 (1983): 19-27.

Sarig, Gissi. "High-Level Reading in the First and in the Foreign Language: Some Comparative Process Data." *Research in Reading in English as a Second Language*. Ed. J. Devine, P. L. Carrell & D. E. Eskey. Washington, DC: TESOL, 1987.

Assessing Foreign Language Listening: Processes, Strategies, and Comprehension

Susan M. Bacon
University of Cincinnati

Does the tree falling in the forest make any noise if no one is present to hear it? Philosophically, the answer is no. To extend the metaphor to all experience, hearing requires two participants: one to send the message, the other to interpret it. Once labeled a "passive activity," listening is now recognized to be a dynamic process whereby individuals construct meaning from a stream of noise based on their prior experience, perceptual style, and comprehension strategies. But for second language (L2) listeners, the forest is not in their immediate experience; the words, like the trees, may seem thick and impenetrable.

Even within the forest, where not all trees fall with the same resonance, not all listening tasks are equal. Some tasks require local, analytic strategies; others, global, synthetic ones. Some command listeners to extract specific, key information; others expect only that listeners understand the intent of the message. For the L2 curriculum, this diversity mandates including as great a variety of authentic or near-authentic texts and tasks as possible. For learners, the goal is not only to hear the tree fall in the forest but also to know the forest's location, perhaps the species of the tree, and most important, whether or not they should move out of the way.

Moving from the forest to the classroom, this paper will discuss three aspects of L2 listening: (1) purposes of listening in general; (2) the process and strategies involved with listening, and (3) activities and tasks for beginning- and intermediate-level L2 classes. The guiding principle throughout this discussion is that students must learn to control their listening process in order to become proficient L2 listeners.

Purposes of Listening and Language Authenticity

Listeners are motivated by one or more of three principles: to understand in order to act, to learn new information, and/or to participate in discourse. First, simple comprehension often satisfies an immediate need for further action. For example, when listeners hear "yes" to the question, "Is dinner ready yet?" they sit down to eat. When they hear the number of their flight announced, they take out their ticket and move toward the gate. These listening tasks often require a physical rather than a verbal response.

Second, listeners may incorporate new information into their knowledge structure. This may include knowledge in the form of discrete facts, such as who won the Rose Bowl, or more complex world knowledge, such as events leading to changes in the political organization of Eastern Europe. In terms of the linguistic system, new knowledge may include formal aspects of language, such as morphological, phonological, prosodic, lexical, or discourse features. Lexical items are probably the most salient because they often have a concrete referent (e.g., car, baseball, hair dryer). They are attended to idiosyncratically, however, because the individual decides whether or not they are important enough to remember.

In the third instance – listening to participate in discourse – nonverbal input is often as important a contributor to understanding the message as is verbal input. Facial expression, for example, may indicate whether or not a response is expected. The stance of the speaker suggests anger, frustration, intimacy, and so forth. The context of the exchange (hotel, train station, restaurant) helps the listener anticipate the message.

In the classroom, the teacher is the primary source of listening input. Breen (1985) suggests, however, that pedagogical language tends to distort reality. L2 classroom listening may in fact contradict real-world listening. When teachers rarely go beyond listening for minimal pairs of phonemes, verb or noun morphology, or even display questions (e.g.,

"What color is your shirt?"), learners will not become proficient listeners. Indeed, providing learners with input that is both authentic[1] and accessible for further processing may be the greatest challenge facing teachers today. The classroom must therefore provide a continuum of simple learning tasks, authentic learning/communication tasks and authentic communication texts. Authentic and near-authentic texts allow listeners direct access to language conventions that permit them to apply prior knowledge of norms of communication (Breen, 1985, p. 69).

Listening Processes

Cognitive psychology identifies three recursive and interrelated stages of comprehension (Anderson, 1985). In the first stage, *perception*, listeners rapidly attend to whether the sound is potentially meaningful (i.e., language) or is simply noise. As soon as the sound is recognized as language, the hearer assumes coherence: the input will be meaningful, not random.[2] Listeners work to segment the sound into meaningful units by focusing on key words, phrases, intonation, pausing, and so forth, in order to construct underlying propositions. The sounds of an aural text are represented in echoic memory, which, with its extremely limited capacity, replaces old information with new almost immediately.

In the *parsing* stage, listeners begin to construct meaningful representations, though the verbatim speech is lost after each clause boundary. The size of the "chunk" is a factor of the listener's language proficiency and background knowledge as these interact with how the information is presented. Listeners tend to focus on semantic, rather than syntactic, information.[3]

In the final stage, *utilization*, listeners relate the input to background knowledge and schemata.[4] Faerch and Kasper (1986) would say that comprehension occurs as the interaction between the input and the background knowledge. Since each stage is recursive, however, listeners may then backtrack and revise an earlier hypothesis or inference. Because the working memory can hold only a limited number of chunks, the larger and more complex each chunk (as a factor of background linguistic or world knowledge), the richer the potential for comprehension and learning (Miller, 1956).

Second language Listening Factors

L2 listeners must deal with a variety of factors that may impede comprehension. Although some of these factors are true for L1 listening as well, they tend to be exaggerated in L2 listening.

First, the learners' echoic memory in L2 is even more limited than that for their native language. The principles of primacy and recency may limit them to hearing the beginning or ends of phrases, but not the middle. The limitation of the L2 learner's working-knowledge capacity also confounds the listening process: listeners may believe they have understood something only to immediately forget it, or find they can not relate a detail to the larger idea. They may pause too long on what seems to be a key word and then have difficulty catching up again and reestablishing the context of the passage. This delay may cause them to lose focus. Learners often complain, moreover, that the rate of speech is too fast. This processing shortcoming may lead to an affective response in which the learner feels emotionally unable to hear. When listeners perceive the task as one in which they have little or no control, they work at an emotional disadvantage (Horwitz, Horwitz & Cope, 1986).

Second, the learner's background knowledge may be culturally quite different from the background knowledge presupposed by the L2. In reading (Bernhardt, 1984) and listening (Markham & Latham, 1987), research has shown that the cultural knowledge of the learner interacts with the text in such a way that learners not only comprehend differently but also infer meaning that is not included explicitly in the text. Novices, especially, tend to apply their own cultural reality to whatever input they hear.

The motivation and attitude of the listener are important listening variables as well. When the listener reacts positively or negatively to the tone of voice, accent, or anticipated content, the level of comprehension and/or interpretation may be affected. Listeners will attend differently to a sports broadcast from the way they do to a movie review depending on their interest in the topic. Individuals listen to details, such as numbers, not only depending on how they perceive that the information will aid their understanding of the message but also depending on their affective response to that kind of information in general.

Linguistic or discourse schemata may transfer from L1 to L2 listening and can work to the learner's benefit. A listener may use knowledge of syntax to anticipate actors and objects, for example. Awareness of discourse, such as the format of a commercial, will help listeners anticipate details that may be included: price, size, color, advantages, and the like. As they listen, they will match their expectations to the information they hear.

External factors, such as the quality and origin of the message, affect comprehension as well. The rate of natural speech differs among native speakers; the rate of classroom speech tends to be artificially reduced, at times even distorted. Some recent research suggests, moreover, that listeners attend differently to male versus female voices: Markham (1988) hypothesized that male voices are perceived to be more "expert" than female voices, which causes listeners to pay more attention to men than to women. In addition, listeners may feel they lose control when they cannot face the speaker, such as occurs when listening to the radio or a tape or when talking on the telephone.

In summary, listeners not only must deal with comprehending the message but also must interpret, respond, react, learn, or otherwise process it further in order to benefit from it both cognitively and affectively. The listening process is a complex interaction of factors both internal and external to the learner. Instruction and assessment of listening must help coordinate these factors to the benefit of each individual.

Listening Tasks and Strategies

O'Malley and Chamot (1990, p. 1) define learning strategies as conscious or unconscious plans or behaviors for comprehending, learning, or retaining information. Those most obviously involved with listening are metacognitive, cognitive, and (to a lesser degree) social and affective.

Strategies are independent of language ability but must be consonant with an individual's perceptual style. A person who tends to be analytical in style, for example, may have difficulty adopting a set of global strategies.

The point of examining strategies (as well as listening skills) is that doing so focuses the discussion on the *process* of listening rather than simply the product. Often listeners are not aware of which strategies help them and which do not during each stage of listening. Often teachers are unable to help students improve because they do not know how their students listen. Several studies suggest that strategies can be taught; they are most effective when integrated with the class and when taught explicitly (Oxford & Crookall, 1989).

Metacognitive Strategies

Metacognitive strategies include planning for the task and monitoring comprehension and the effectiveness of strategies. Effective listeners use context, the expectations of the task, and monitoring to their advantage. For example, a traveler enters a bank with the intention of finding out where to change money and what the current rate is. As the individual listens, she checks her comprehension and her plan to judge its effectiveness. In L1, metacognitive strategies are fairly automatic and unconscious. They may not transfer easily to L2 contexts, however. In fact, research has shown that learners are less aware of using metacognitive than cognitive strategies (Chamot & Kupper, 1989). In-class listening, moreover, may either deprive students of context, or fail to encourage listeners to use metacognitive strategies.

Cognitive Strategies

Listeners use cognitive strategies to manipulate and reorganize the incoming message so as to make it comprehensible. Referring back to the introductory metaphor, not all trees make the same noise when they fall; not all listening tasks are equal. Listeners must learn to recognize the kind of task they are facing in order to know which cognitive strategies to employ. Again, context is essential to help determine what combination of analytical and global strategies is required. Analytical, or local, strategies focus on discrete information in order to deduce meaning. For example:

1) A listener in a restaurant in France wishes to order something that she recognizes. Her strategy is to listen for the dishes that match her lexicon. Unless she is feeling courageous, she ignores the ones that do not match.
2) At a used-car lot, the buyer arrives with a series of mental questions that she hopes to have answered: price, number of kilometers, name and telephone number of the previous owner.
3) When the listener turns on the radio expecting to hear the weather, she listens for the details that will allow her to know what to wear that day.

These are all examples of analytical tasks wherein listeners expect specific information and must respond accordingly.

Global tasks differ from analytical ones in that they require the listener to "get the gist" or to synthesize information. The details are supportive to the entire picture but may not be as important to remember verbatim. Here are situations in which global strategies work well:

> In a restaurant, you overhear a heated discussion between the owner and a patron. Depending on who appears to be angrier, you may infer that either the meal was substandard or the patron is unable to pay the tab.

In this example, the listener's curiosity will influence whether or not she decides to listen for details and confirm an initial hypothesis.

> You are talking to a friend at a party. Although the friend's words are unintelligible, you guess that you are being invited to dance.

In a social context such as a party, the quality of the signal may be distorted, again forcing the listener to try to get the gist or to infer meaning from gestures. The question, "Want to dance?" is understood by the context and a gesture rather than from words.

More complex examples of global listening occur in any number of contexts wherein the listener summarizes and reorganizes information, as in the following instance:

> A salesman is describing the advantages of one computer over another. One is more expensive, operates faster, and has more storage space and a higher-resolution monitor.

After the salesman's pitch, most listeners would have to refer to the printed material in order to restate the actual size of the processor, the megabytes on the hard drive, and the number of pixels on the monitor. The detail is reorganized by the listener into larger, more elaborate chunks of information.

Another key cognitive strategy is elaboration, or relating what one hears to what one already knows. Efficient listeners are constantly thinking of ways in which to relate new information to existing knowledge. This elaboration may be visual or linguistic. When listeners hear the word *house*, for example, they first build a mental representation of what the word means to them and then either hypothesize or infer what the passage may be about. Obviously, the mental representation is always affected by the listener's experience. The word *liberal*, for example, may evoke a positive or a negative image depending on the listener's point of view.

Effective listeners therefore combine analytical and global strategies depending on the kind of task that faces them. Moreover, they constantly try to relate what they hear to what they already know.

Social and Affective Strategies

Social strategies, such as appealing for assistance or asking for clarification, are helpful when the listener has an interlocutor. Affective strategies are internal to the listener: a self-assurance that "everything is OK," or that "you can do it." Affective strategies may be especially important before the listening task in order to instill a feeling of calm and purpose.

In summary, everyone uses strategies, but to different degrees during any particular task. Often strategies do not effectively transfer from L1 to L2. Unless learners are conscious of how strategies can be used in different tasks and know how to plan, monitor, and evaluate, they may try to apply a uniform strategy across tasks. Listening should include both practicing and evaluating strategies, as well as assessing comprehension. The remainder of this paper will focus on strategy development and the evaluation of listening comprehension.

Strategies and Assessment

This section will present a series of activities to encourage awareness and to practice listening strategies. They are presented in English with the understanding that the actual passages would be in the target language. Recommended sources are radio broadcasts or semi-scripted conversations.[5]

1) Developing Metacognitive Awareness

Example: The listening plan
You are about to hear two people talking on the bus. You cannot see them, but they are right in front of you and so you can hear them quite well. What is your plan? Write down on a sheet of paper what you will do.

In this task, the listener has very little information except the context of the bus. The purpose of the writing activity is to have students think about what they may hear and to formulate questions or hypotheses before they begin to listen. Some students will write down specific details, such as where the people are going or what in particular they are talking about. Others may want to know if they are male or female, acquaintances or strangers, making small talk or being serious. Two lists can be compiled on the blackboard, one more global, the other more local. Then students should brainstorm exactly what they should listen for to understand the gist: intonation, level and tone of voice, and key words that will help them hypothesize. For example, if they hear weather or sports terms, they might guess that the two people are making small talk. If they hear political terms, they might guess that the people are talking about current political events.

Example: Did the plan work?
Now listen to the conversation. Afterward, write everything you remember hearing in the conversation.[6] Give both specific information and guesses about what may be going on. All guesses must be supported by something that you heard.

This activity makes the task explicit and helps listeners evaluate whether or not their listening plan worked for them. For example, one may write that the speakers are close friends because they use first names and a familiar form of address. Another may say that the speakers' intonation suggests a serious discussion. Perhaps the parents are involved because the student heard the word *father*. Again, a list of ideas can be compiled and the class should arrive at a consensus regarding which of the ideas are feasible. Finally, all students should be asked to think about how their plan worked for this particular activity and how they might refine the plan for subsequent occasions.

Metacognitive awareness is generally taken for granted in L1 because listeners are accustomed to using context to their greatest advantage. In L2 listening, however, the context is usually less clear, either because of cultural differences or because of classroom artificiality. By explicitly practicing metacognitive strategies, students will become more proficient listeners.

2) Listening for the Gist

In almost any listening activity, there is occasion to listen both for the gist and for detail. By separating the two kinds of strategies, however, listeners can discover each one's value and place.

Example: Discourse clues

Listen to the following short radio announcements. Then identify the intent of each. Some possibilities include selling something, reporting a news item or other event, introducing the next segment, or presenting one side of an argument, as in a debate. Now explain the discourse or other clues that helped you arrive at that conclusion.

Example: Prosodic clues

You pick up your telephone and hear two men talking. From their tone of voice, decide which of the following contexts is probable: a father to his adult son; a salesman to a client; a teacher to a child. What intonation or other clues led you to that conclusion?

3) Listening for Detail

When the context makes the task obvious, listeners focus on key information. Often the task requires the listener to attend to numbers as an important element of information.

Example: Matching expectations

You are on your way to the airport when you decide to check the weather forecast. What lets you know whether your flight may be canceled?

In this example, listeners simply match their expectations with what they hear. If they hear "clear skies," they have little reason to process the message further.

Example: Matching expectations

You are in the train station in Madrid. You know your friend is due to arrive from another Spanish city at 5:00 P.M. Which announcement may be for her train?

a) Train number 5 on track 7 arriving from Paris at 17.00 hours

b) Train number 15 on track 5 arriving from Sevilla at 16.00 hours

c) Train number 10 on track 4 arriving from Barcelona at 17.00 hours

In this example, the listener processes only the announcement that matches expectations of time and city.

4) Combining Local and Global Strategies

In extended listening, students must integrate local and global strategies in order to extract both the intent and the important information.

Example: Intonation and detail

You will hear descriptions of two items. First, from the tone of voice, decide whether the person is interested in buying or selling the items. Second, record all the information you can about each item, and then decide which is the better buy. Support your decision with information from the passage.

In this task, the listener must focus both on the intent of the message and on the supporting detail and must then reorganize the message based on background knowledge.

Example: Detail and analysis

You will hear a radio spot describing an event. First decide whether or not the event has already taken place; then record as much information about it as possible. Based on what you hear, give reasons that you would or would not be interested in attending this event.

Here listeners search for key information to judge time: last week, tomorrow, and so on. They formulate hypotheses that can be tested, such as whether the event involves sports, music, or art. Then they reorganize the information to determine whether or not they are interested in attending.

5) Deciding When to Listen to Numbers

Numbers present a complicated task for listeners. Unless the prelistening instructions specifically require listeners to focus on numbers, there will be little uniformity as to whether or not they are heard. Since numbers are used to identify (gate 1, table 3, etc.) and to quantify (100 kilometers, 25° celsius, etc.), listeners must decide immediately whether to listen to them as an exact number, as a concept, or as a piece of supporting information that does not require further processing.

Example: Numbers as identity

You are in the bus station. When you hear the bus for Mexico City announced, make note of the platform where it will board and the time it will leave.

Example: Numbers as concept

The travel agency will give you minimum and maximum temperatures for three European cities. Which one offers the most temperate climate?

Example: Numbers as supporting information

You will hear a description of a product that will allow you to convert the voltage of appliances. Find out when it would be necessary to have this device.

In the first example, numbers are key to allow the listener to act. In the second example, the concept of temperature being hot, cold, or mild is more important than hearing the exact number of degrees. In the third example, the passage most certainly will include references to 110, 220, and other voltages. The listener does not have to remember which country uses which voltage in order to understand that electric systems are not uniform throughout the world. Since not every listener will attend to numbers in an equal fashion, however, listeners must practice deciding in advance whether or not the numbers are key to comprehension.

In summary, listening strategies can and should be part of listening assessment in foreign language. Simply instructing listeners not to translate or to listen for key words will not suffice. The listeners must also have a plan and must practice evaluating how their plan worked.

Assessing Listening Comprehension in the Classroom

In the purest sense, listening comprehension is assessed without mixing in other receptive or productive skills. Evidence of comprehension is manifested by some sort of physical response (raising a hand, drawing a picture) or by responding or reporting in the listener's native language. In reality, however, listening is often closely connected to other language skills. As stated earlier, listening activities should mirror reality as closely as possible. Since the goal of listening instruction is to lead students to interact with speakers of the target culture, authentic or near-authentic sources should be used as often as is feasible.

The final section of this paper suggests other activities that help promote and assess proficiency in L2 listening. The procedure is to build from pure comprehension to an integration of comprehension and production so as to approach reality as closely as possible within the constraints of the classroom.

Example: Nonverbal response

You are in a physician's office. Nod your head if you hear an activity or symptom that relates to your stomachache.

Assessment

Out of 10 activities and symptoms, 5 relate to the stomach. The remainder relate to other ailments. Eight out of 10 correct responses are required.

Example: Response with L1 reading

Listen to your friend's shopping list. Write the number of the item beside its category in English. For example, if you hear "First, apples," write "1" beside "fruit." You may put more than one number beside a category.

Assessment

Out of 20 items, students must correctly categorize 18.

Example: Response with L1 writing

After you hear the news report, write in English everything that deals with the German-speaking world.

Assessment

Out of news items, students must correctly identify three.

Example: Response with L2 reading

Listen to the telephone instructions on how to walk from the train station to the Hotel de la Place. Trace the route on the map of Paris.

Assessment

Only one correct route.

Example: Response with L2 dictation

Your friend invites you to have coffee this afternoon. Write down the time and directions on how to get to the café.

Assessment

Both time and directions must be exact. No penalty for spelling and grammar errors.

Example: Response with L2 reading and cloze

You are helping an elderly person fill out his insurance form. In the spaces provided on the form, write the information he gives you.

Assessment

Nine out of 10 responses, including correct spelling, required.

Example: Response with L2 written summary

You will hear a radio report about a natural disaster. Summarize what you hear for a local newspaper.

Assessment

Five out of seven required. Students may use other resources to correct spelling and grammar.

Example: Response with L2 written opinion

You will hear two sides of an issue. Take one side and support your opinion with details that you hear presented. State also why the other side is unfounded.

Assessment

Opinion must be supported by two out of three stated reasons. The other side must be rejected for one reason. Students may use other resources to correct spelling and grammar.

Example: Response oral L2, short answers

Respond to a survey about members of your class (how many students there are, etc.)

Assessment

Five out of five questions must be answered in a logical way. Responses may be a word or a phrase.

Example: Response Oral L2, Supported Answers

Respond to the credit manager's questions about your financial history. You must convince him that you can pay back the loan you have applied for.

Assessment

Students must respond with correct grammar to four out of five questions. They must also supply two coherent reasons for the loan application. The reasons must be intelligible, although they may not be entirely correct grammatically.

These examples progress from pure reception to written and oral production based on comprehension. As listeners improve their proficiency in the L2, they will use less energy comprehending the message and more processing it further. When they pass the comprehension threshold and move into the realm of utilization, they will be able to focus more attention on salient lexical and other linguistic features of the input.

Just as listening tasks should mirror reality, so should assessment. Although the best overall measure of comprehension of extended discourse is to have listeners restate everything they remember in English, a good argument can be made to have students combine listening with the appropriate logical oral and written tasks. When the task requires use of the L2, assessment should place much more emphasis on correct spelling for an insurance document than a telephone message. When extended L2 writing is part of the assessment, students may be allowed time to think about and revise their work using other sources. Other messages should be summarized and restated orally. In other words, both the task and its assessment should be potentially authentic.

Summary and Conclusions

The discussion opened with the metaphor of a noiseless tree in an unoccupied forest: all listening involves both a sender and a receiver of the message. The interpretation of the message depends on the interaction between the listener and the sender whereby the listener builds a message rather than simply receives it.

Listening strategies do not necessarily transfer from L1 to L2 tasks. To be most effective, practice in strategy awareness and evaluation should be incorporated as part of regular listening activities and assessment. Listeners should begin every task with a plan based on the expectations of the task. They should evaluate and revise their plan in the same manner as they are expected to revise a written assignment. The listener is always the one in control. Thus, the focus is on the process of comprehension as much as it is on the product of comprehension.

Finally, both the listening task and its assessment must be coherent and reasonable. Some tasks require an exact, convergent response; others require a main idea. In the forest, after all, knowing the genus and species of the tree falling in your direction is not necessary in order for you to jump out of the way.

Notes

1. In its purest form, the term *authentic* refers to written or oral text that is produced by and intended for a native speaker of the target language. In listening, this would include radio, television, and other broadcast, recorded, or live sources.

2. Lee (1990) has made the same observation regarding reading.

3. VanPatten (1989) has shown in L2 listening studies that learners can focus on form only at the expense of understanding meaning. Yet in a survey of 980 university students of Spanish, Bacon and Finnemann (1990) found that 47% of the respondents agreed that it was very important to hear verb endings when they listen; 30% stated that they would very likely to listen for verb endings if a native speaker spoke to them. This propensity for hearing verb morphology suggests that the students' previous classroom experience with listening emphasized formal aspects of language over meaning.

4. Each listener brings to the text expectations of what it will contain. These schemata are abstract representations of a generic concept, such as car, football game, or school. When the schemata represent a series of concepts, they are called scripts. "Going shopping" or "getting up in the morning" would bring to mind a typical chain of events that can be associated with the action. See Omaggio (1986) for a more detailed discussion.

5. See Bacon (1989) for sample activities in Spanish.

6. The writing activity may be in L1 or in L2. For purposes of pure comprehension, students should not feel impeded by having to use one or the other.

Works Cited

Anderson, J. R. *Cognitive Psychology and Its Implications*. 2d ed. New York: Freeman, 1985.

Bacon, Susan M. "Listening for Real in the Foreign-Language Classroom." *Foreign Language Annals* 22 (1989): 543-51.

_____ & Michael D. Finnemann. "A Study of the Attitudes, Motives, and Strategies of University-Level Foreign-Language Students and Their Disposition to Authentic Oral and Written Input." *Modern Language Journal* 74 (1990): 459-73.

Bernhardt, Elizabeth B. "Toward an Information Processing Perspective in Foreign Language Reading." *Modern Language Journal* 68 (1984): 322-31.

Breen, Michael P. "Authenticity in the Language Classroom." *Applied Linguistics* 6 (1985): 60-70.

Chamot, Anna Uhl & Lisa Kupper. "Learning Strategies in Foreign Language Instruction." *Foreign Language Annals* 22 (1989): 13-24.

Faerch, Claus & Gabriele Kasper. "The Role of Comprehension in Second-Language Learning." *Applied Linguistics* 7 (1986): 257-74.

Horwitz, Elaine K., M. B. Horwitz & J. A. Cope. "Foreign Language Classroom Anxiety." *Modern Language Journal* 70 (1986): 125-32.

Lee, James. "From Reading Skills to Reading for Content: Contemporary and Complimentary Approaches to Non-native Reading Instruction." Paper presented at the AATSP Annual Meeting, Miami, August 1990.

Markham, Paul. L. "Gender Differences and the Perceived Expertness of the Speaker as Factors in ESL Listening Recall." *TESOL Quarterly* 22 (1988): 397-406.

_____ & Michael Latham. " The Influence of Religion-Specific Background Knowledge on the Listening Comprehension of Adult Second-Language Students." *Language Learning* 37 (1987): 157-70.

Miller, George A. "The Magical Number Seven, Plus or Minus Two: Some Hints on Our Capacity for Processing Information." *Psychological Review* 63 (1956): 81-97.

Omaggio, Alice, C. *Teaching Language in Context*. Boston: Heinle & Heinle Publishers, 1986.

O'Malley, J. Michael & Anna Uhl Chamot. *Learning Strategies in Second Language Acquisition*. Cambridge: Cambridge University Press, 1990.

Oxford, Rebecca L. & David Crookall. "Research on Language Learning Strategies: Methods, Findings, and Instructional Issues." *Modern Language Journal* 73 (1989): 404-19.

VanPatten, Bill. "Can Learners Attend to Form and Content While Processing Input?" *Hispania* 72 (1989): 409-17.

The Oral Task of Picture Description: Similarities and Differences in Native and Nonnative Speakers of Spanish

Terry L. Ballman
California State University at Long Beach

The emphasis on the development of foreign language students' oral abilities has been evident since the 1982 publication of the American Council on the Teaching of Foreign Languages (ACTFL) provisional proficiency guidelines. The revised ACTFL guidelines (1986) use educated, native-speaker-like performance as the ideal on a scale that subsumes the other proficiency levels. In turn, foreign language teachers intuitively hold native or nativelike speech as the model for teaching and learning.

In recent decades, there has been a definite movement away from the teacher-dominated classroom toward a more student-centered or communication-based environment, as evidenced by methods described by Krashen and Terrell (1983), Omaggio (1986), Savignon (1983), and others. The proficiency movement in particular has given many foreign language teachers cause to reflect on the importance of developing oral proficiency and has led to the conclusion that those classroom

221

approaches which require active participation on the part of students are more likely to result in improved performance.

Describing pictures is a common activity in participatory foreign language teaching. Pictures can be used in the classroom as a means to input language, develop vocabulary, and elicit oral production. Pictures can also be used in testing, particularly to examine listening comprehension and oral proficiency skills. Because picture description is a common teaching and testing tool, the present paper examines the type of language produced when describing a picture. Given our profession's obvious concern with native-speaker or native-speaker-like language, it is important to examine native speakers' language and nonnative speakers' language and, specifically, to compare the two as these speakers engage in the same task of picture description.

The Present Study

The general research questions underpinning this study are as follows:

1) What does the monologue discourse of nonnative speakers (NNS) of Spanish look like?
2) How does the monologue discourse of beginning NNS compare with that of advanced NNS?
3) How does the monologue discourse of NNS compare with that of native speakers (NS) of Spanish?

The specific issues examined across the three groups are the following:

1) How is discourse connected? Specifically, what words are used to connect discourse?
2) How do several communication strategies (appeals to interviewer, repeats and self-corrects, borrowing, and circumlocution) vary across the groups?

The study's hypothesis was that since the NS of Spanish and the advanced NNS of Spanish (in that order) possessed a greater linguistic repertoire, they would use more sophisticated syntactic connectors (e.g., *por lo tanto*, "for that reason") and would exhibit fewer communication or repair strategies (e.g., borrowing) than the beginning NNS.

Subjects

Thirty subjects participated in the study: 20 NNS and 10 NS of Spanish. Of the 20 NNS of Spanish, all were NS of English enrolled in Spanish classes: 10 beginners in second-semester classes and 10 advanced students taking classes at the graduate (M.A.) level. All the NS of Spanish had at least the equivalent of a high school education, and all could be classified as being either Spanish-dominant or bilingual. Although currently living in the United States, the NS originally came from Argentina, Chile, Cuba, Mexico, Peru, and Spain.

Procedure and Materials

Students enrolled in an upper-division/graduate-level Spanish course taught by the present investigator were given the assignment of recruiting student volunteers. The NNS and NS were asked to help the interviewers by describing a picture. The NNS volunteers were told that their participation was not part of their evaluation in the classes in which they were enrolled but, rather, was strictly for experimental purposes.

All subjects were shown the same picture of a busy office. The picture was numbered so as to highlight the six scenes shown within the office. After the subjects had the opportunity to read the instructions and to scan and study the picture, the interviewer turned on an audiorecorder. The instructions given to the interviewers were that while they could encourage the subjects by nodding their heads and smiling, they were to refrain from speaking, though they could prompt the subject to elaborate if necessary. Interviews with NS were conducted by the present researcher. NS received the same instructions as NNS. Interviews ranged in length from 9 to 41 minutes.

Evaluation

All picture-description monologues were transcribed by either the researcher herself or the students in the upper-level linguistics course. All utterances were documented, including pauses, vacillating words, self-corrections, and restarts. A pause was defined as a silence of two seconds. All transcriptions done by students were checked over and corrected, when necessary, by the researcher. The researcher identified and counted the communication strategies chosen for analysis. Although distinctions have been made among communication, production, and repair strategies (e.g., see Schwartz, 1980, and Tarone, 1980, 1981), the umbrella phrase "communication strategies" is used to refer to the behaviors examined in this study: appeals to interviewer, repeats and self-corrects, borrowing, and circumlocuting. (Sample transcriptions are provided in the Appendix.)

The data collected are chiefly qualitative.

Results and Discussion

Discourse Features

The first issue for analysis concerns how discourse is connected. Specifically, what words are used to connect discourse? It was predicted that more types of connectors, including more sophisticated ones, would be used by the NS than by the advanced NNS, and more by the advanced NNS than by the beginning NNS.

The first connector examined was *y* ("and"). It was believed that beginning NNS would use *y* more often than advanced speakers and NS because it is a simple way to connect ideas, simpler than embedding, found in examples 1 and 2, respectively:

> 1) *Hay un hombre y trabaja mucho y es simpático.* ("There is a man and he works a lot and he's nice.")
> 2) *Hay un hombre que trabaja mucho y es simpático.* ("There is a man who works a lot and is nice.")

As expected, *y* was used by all three groups, yet it appears that it occurred more in the speech of the advanced NNS and the NS than in the speech of the beginners. What could account for this result is that beginners relied more on pausing, as they needed to think about what they would say next, stopping often after short utterances.

A common connector within sentences in Spanish is *que* ("that" or "who"). It had been predicted that *que* would appear in the discourse of all the speakers, although not with consistency on the part of the beginners. The analysis revealed that of the 10 beginning learners, only 5 used *que* consistently. One beginner used *que* once, 1 beginner twice, and it was not used at all by 3 beginners. Overall, the beginners, especially those who did not use *que*, tended to produce short clauses. One example of short clauses, use of *y*, and no use of the *que* connector is the following: "*Hay un chico. Um.* [pause] *Tiene gafas y un–una corbata. Un chico no quiere estar allí. Quiere estar en la playa y quiere bebe–beber cerveza. Mmm. Y un chico estás working–working very hard. Uh.* [pause] *Hay muchas papeles en la mesa.*"

With regard to the connectors *y* and *que*, *y* was used more by advanced NNS, while *que* was the preferred connector by NS. This finding suggests that NS structure their discourse differently and use more embedding. NS are much more likely to say example 2 than example 1 above, or even example 3, which uses even more embedding:

> 3) *Hay un hombre simpático que trabaja mucho.* ("There is a nice man who works a lot.")

With regard to other connecting structures, NS tended to exhibit a larger number of different connectors. Both NS and advanced NNS used *porque* ("because"), *parece que* ("it seems that"), *por eso* ("for that reason") and *mientras* ("while"), but these were more frequently used by advanced NNS. One advanced NNS and one NS used *sin embargo* ("nevertheless"), and two advanced NNS used *por lo tanto* ("for that reason"). The prediction that NS would use more sophisticated discourse connectors was not supported by these findings. How, then, can it be explained that advanced NNS used sophisticated discourse connectors more often than NS? A possible explanation is that NNS are taught that their language should be coherent and that this quality can be achieved in part if ideas overtly connect well one to the other. This concern could be called "explicit logic." NS, on the other hand, are not concerned with being explicity logical, for they intuitively adhere to the notion of "implicit logic." Sentences 1 and 2, respectively, are examples of explicit and implicit logic:

1) "I'm going to get a glass of water because I'm thirsty."
2) "I'm going to get a glass of water. I'm thirsty."

Clearly, NS of English would utter sentence 2, adhering to implicit logic. This suggests that greater language proficiency (such as that of NS) involves knowing when to be implicity logical, namely, knowing when to *omit* discourse connectors.

Communication Strategies

The communication strategies examined in the study were appeals to interviewers, self-corrects and repeats, borrowing, and circumlocuting. It was predicted that the less advanced the speaker, the more often he or she would appeal to the interviewer. All the subjects, including the NS, made appeals to the interviewer. It appears that beginners sought assistance much more often than the other two groups. For the beginners, a frequent appeal to the interviewer involved asking for vocabulary. Two examples follow:

Beginner 5: "... *¿Cómo se dice 'receptionist'?*" ("... How do you say 'receptionist?' ").

Beginner 3: "... *No quiere trabajar after-after cinco porque quiere ver? to see? [pause] un novia-um* [pause] ..." ("... He doesn't want to work after–after five because he wants to see? to see? [pause] a girlfriend–um [pause] ...").

Another communication strategy is that of repeating, restarting, and correcting. It was expected that the beginning NNS would repeat, restart, and correct more than the advanced NNS, and certainly more than the NS. In general, both groups of NNS frequently repeated and corrected, suggesting that they were very conscious about their language, especially as far as syntax was concerned:

> Beginner 4: *"... él estaba escri–escribando–escribiendo por la máquina ..."* ("... he was wri–writing–writing *with a type-writer ..."*).

> Advanced speaker 1: *". . . ella tiene muchos muchos novios y están–está hablando–está hablando por el teléfono . . ."* ("... she has many many boyfriends and they are–she is talking–she is talking *on the phone . . ."*).

One example of both syntactic repetition and correction from a beginner is the following:

> Beginner 1: *"El hombre te gusta–le gusta–el hombre le gusta la playa . . ."* (*Note:* The correct sentence would be *Al hombre le gusta la playa* ["The man likes the beach"].)

Semantic corrections were more common for the NS than for the NNS. One NS, for example, said *"Hay una vamp, una mujer . . ."* ("There's a vamp, a woman . . .").

The third strategy examined is borrowing. One definition of borrowing is the transfer of a structure or lexical unit from one language to another. Beginning NNS were expected to borrow more than advanced NNS, and no borrowing behaviors were expected on the part of the NS. Indeed, the beginning NNS borrowed more than the advanced NNS, yet two of the NS also borrowed. Two examples of borrowing are these:

> Beginner 6: *"El número uno tiene una hombre que está trabajando a su escritorio–en su escritorio con un–un typewriter cosa . . ."* ("Number one has a man who is working at his desk–at his desk with a–a typewriter thing . . .").

> NS 6: *". . . vemos que están dos personas en su–su–mm 'break' . . ."* (". . . we see that two people are on their–their–mm 'break'. . . .").

In the picture, there was a prominent line graph on the office's wall indicating the business' gains or losses. Interesting to note is that half the NS avoided mentioning the word for "graph" (*gráfico*).

The last communication strategy examined was circumlocution. Circumlocution is used, for example, when the speaker does not know or cannot recall a specific word and so uses other words in the target language to describe it. It was predicted that all three groups would use circumlocution; advanced NNS would exhibit it the most, as they had probably had more experience with the strategy than the beginners, and more linguistic need for it than the NS. Indeed, the advanced NNS exhibited more instances of circumlocution than the NS; however, not one instance of circumlocution by a beginning NNS was produced. Beginners either borrowed from English or employed an avoidance strategy. This latter element is suggested by Schacter (1974), who has found that learners use avoidance, in part out of lack of knowledge and fear of making errors. Here are several examples of advanced NNS and NS circumlocution:

> Advanced speaker 2: *". . . tiene una colección grande de cartas o trabajo o algo . . ."* (". . . she has a large collection of letters or work or something . . ."). (The word described is "pile" of papers.)

> Advanced speaker 3: *". . . están quizás a almuerzo, el tiempo de almuerzo, o algo están, tomando unos momentos libres . . ."* (". . . they are perhaps at lunch, lunchtime or something, taking a few moments . . .") (The concept described is "break.")

> NS 2: *". . . tiene algo en su oficina en la pared – con unas rayas . . ."* (". . . he has something in his office on the wall – with several stripes"). (The concept described is "graph.")

Syntactic Variability

Regarding verb-tense usage, a question that arose was whether the NS would use a wider range of verb tenses than the advanced NNS. In turn, would advanced NNS use a greater variety of verb tenses than beginning NNS? All three groups overwhelmingly used the present indicative and the present progressive. The task of describing a busy office scene logically promoted the present tense. Although the NS and the advanced NNS possessed a greater verb-tense vocabulary than beginning NNS, all subjects used the present tense as appropriate to the task.

The other observation deals with syntactic properties, specifically with object pronouns. Object pronouns were used by the advanced NNS when appropriate, although occasional errors in gender agreement appeared. As would be expected, NS and advanced NNS used object pronouns in their discourse when appropriate. Yet only two of the beginners used object pronouns in their discourse where object pronouns should have been used. Typically, the beginning students would repeat the referent noun instead of replacing it with a pronoun:

> Beginner 8: *"En número dos, dos personas es – beben café, una otra persona oye a – a personas – a otras personas . . ."* ("In number two, two people is – are drinking coffee, another person is listening to people – to [the] other people . . .").

The only other instance in which beginners used object pronouns was in "chunks." A chunk can be defined as a structure that has been learned as a unit but whose underlying syntactic system has not been mastered. For example, the same student who correctly uses *le gusta* ("he or she likes it," or, literally, "to him or her pleases it") may also use *yo gusto* instead of *me gusta*. Four of the beginners used *le gusta* several times.

Pedagogical Implications and Conclusions

This study was undertaken to examine the monologue discourse of beginning (second-semester) and advanced (M.A.-level) students of Spanish and of educated NS of Spanish, all engaged in the common activity of picture description. Based on several of the research findings, the following pedagogical implications are offered.

Regarding discourse features, all speakers used *y* ("and") as a connector. The relative pronoun *que* (usually "that" or "who") – the most frequently used connector by NS because of their tendency toward embedding – was used with consistency by only five of the beginners. As this relative pronoun is so common and useful, early-level learners in particular will benefit from classroom instruction on its use. NNS of various levels may benefit from instruction on how to connect discourse using more sophisticated connectors (e.g., "for that reason," "nevertheless"), as the advanced NNS did in this study. Yet the fact that the NS (not overtly concerned with explicit logic) often omitted connectors suggests that adhering to an implicit logic may be a characteristic of a higher level of proficiency, at least in colloquial speech.

The finding that communication strategies seemed to be used more by NNS than by NS compliments the conclusions of Labarca and Khanji (1986) that the lower the proficiency level, the higher the use of communication strategies. Indeed, the beginners employed more appeals to the interviewer, repetition, restarts, corrections, and borrowing behaviors than the advanced NNS and the NS did. The only strategy not at all present in a particular group was circumlocution among the beginners. The finding that beginners chose either to abandon a topic or to avoid mentioning something altogether because they did not know the word for it suggests that teachers need to encourage paraphrasing in their classes. (An example of a classroom activity that promotes paraphrase is to ask students to give definitions of vocabulary words in the target language.) By encouraging the development of circumlocution, teachers may discourage avoidance and reliance on borrowing.

Another variable involved the use of object pronouns. The total omission of object pronouns by the beginning students and the fact that any consistent use of object pronouns was found only in the form of "chunks" may suggest that teachers can help early-level students by teaching them prefabricated or unanalyzed expressions and structures (Nattinger, 1990).

A major concern is that many of the NNS commented that in their language classes they were rarely given the opportunity to speak, except to answer questions.[1] Even the advanced NNS complained that their teachers did not provide them with opportunities to develop sustained discourse. Despite renewed interest in the development of oral proficiency in their students, teachers must make sure that they provide students with opportunities for language development at the discourse level.

Another large issue involves the task itself. Bacon (1990) has shown that task type and the attitude of the subject toward the task are likely to affect the outcome. In this study, for example, it is probable that the beginning and advanced NNS viewed the task of describing a picture as a chore–not as an opportunity to communicate–similar to an achievement test in that what they said would probably be evaluated for accuracy. In contrast, the NS probably viewed the task as doing the interviewer a favor. Within the confines of describing a picture, it is likely that the NS failed to embellish, digress, or expand as they would otherwise have done in normal conversation. They certainly did not "show off" their linguistic armory, as evidenced by the almost-exclusive use of the present tense and by several instances of borrowing from English.[2] Of note is that the language produced, particulary by the NS, was simple because the task itself was simple. In other words, the language used by the NS was appropriate to the task.

One of the limitations of this study is that the task–picture description–elicits only one kind of monologue discourse, and monologue discourse is only one kind of discourse. A monologue is not a two-way exchange. Consequently, the subjects did not engage in conversational behaviors, such as turn taking (see Allwright, 1980). Managing a conversation with a NS may be the most difficult aspect of acquiring a second language (Brooks, 1988). Monologue discourse like that produced in this study does not elicit many of the characteristics of two-way discourse.

As native or nativelike speech is held to be the model for instruction and evaluation, future research should examine the oral discourse of both NS and NNS speech, particularly in two-way discourse, both qualitatively and quantitatively.

Notes

1. Students taking second-, third-, and even fourth-year level Spanish courses also performed the same task of picture description and made the same comment. (Data from these subjects were not included in the present study).

2. Two NS each used several words borrowed from English, including *break, chart, nerd, freeway,* and *broker.* This suggests that, not surprisingly, living in an English-dominant milieu has begun to influence these subjects' Spanish.

Works Cited

ACTFL. *ACTFL Provisional Proficiency Guidelines*. Hastings-on-Hudson, NY: ACTFL Materials Center, 1982.

_____. *ACTFL Proficiency Guidelines*. Hastings-on-Hudson, NY: ACTFL Materials Center, 1986.

Allwright, R. L. "Turn, Topics, and Tasks: Patterns of Participation in Language Learning and Teaching." *Discourse Analysis in Second Language Research*. Ed. Diane Larsen-Freeman. Rowley, MA: Newbury House, 1980: 165-87.

Bacon, Susan Cameron. "On Topic Choice in Oral Proficiency Assessment." *Second Language Acquisition – Foreign Language Learning*. Ed. Bill Van-Patten & James F. Lee. Clevedon, England: Multilingual Matters Ltd., 1990: 170-80.

Brooks, Frank B. "Learning to *Converse?*" Paper presented at the annual meeting of the American Association of Teachers of Spanish and Portuguese, Denver, 1988.

Krashen, Stephen D. & Tracy D. Terrell. *The Natural Approach*. Hayward, CA: Alemany Press, 1983.

Labarca, Angela & Rajai Khanji. "On Communication Strategies: Focus on Interaction." *Studies in Second Language Acquisition* 8 (1986): 68-79.

Nattinger, James R. "Prefabricated Speech for Language Learning." *Second Language Acquisition – Foreign Language Learning*. Ed. Bill VanPatten & James F. Lee. Clevedon, England: Multilingual Matters Ltd., 1990: 198-206.

Omaggio, Alice. *Teaching Language in Context*. Boston, MA: Heinle & Heinle Publishers, 1986.

Savignon, Sandra. *Communicative Competence: Theory and Classroom Practice*. Reading, MA: Addison-Wesley, 1983.

Schacter, J. "An Error in Error Analysis." *Language Learning* 24 (1974): 205-14.

Schwartz, Joan. "The Negotiation for Meaning: Repair in Conversations between Second Language Learners of English." *Discourse Analysis in Second Language Research*. Ed. Diane Larsen-Freeman. Rowley, MA: Newbury House, 1980: 138-53.

Tarone, Elaine. "Communication Stategies, Foreigner Talk, and Repair in Interlanguage." *Language Learning* 30 (1980): 417-31.

_____. "Some Thoughts on the Notion of Communication Strategy." *TESOL Quarterly* 15 (1981): 285-95.

Appendix
Samples of Transcriptions

Beg. = Beginner (second-semester student of Spanish)
Adv. = Advanced (M.A.-level student of Spanish)
NS = Native speaker

Beg. 8: *"Número uno [pause] este persona es [pause] ub [pause] piensa en la playa y tiene cerveza en su mano, y (pause) no quiero – no quiere – ub [pause] trabajar, y [pause] en pictura número dos este persona mirar los dos personas tomando café . . ."*

Adv. 9: *"En la primera escina-escena, tenemos un hombre que está trabajando en la oficina, sí, um y está usando la máquina de escribir y me parece que él tiene un montón de trabajo. Tiene muchos papeles en una cesta . . ."*

NS 1: *"Este señor en el primer dibujo parece una persona intelec-tual – las gafas, el pelo – parece una persona eh realmente eh metida en el trabajo. Muchos papeles, eh hojeando curiosamente, parece una persona dedicada, ¿no? . . ."*

Contributors

Susan M. Bacon is Assistant Professor of Spanish and director of the undergraduate Spanish program at the University of Cincinnati. In addition to supervising and coordinating the basic Spanish and Italian programs, she teaches courses in methodology for teaching foreign languages at the university, secondary, and elementary levels. Her primary areas of research interest are in foreign language learning, especially aural and spoken Spanish. Her publications appear in *Foreign Language Annals, Modern Language Journal, Hispania, Foreign Language Learning: A Research Perspective*, and *Second Language Acquisition – Foreign Language Learning*.

Terry L. Ballman is Assistant Professor of Spanish at California State University at Long Beach, where she directs the elementary Spanish and German programs, supervises graduate teaching assistants, and teaches courses in language, linguistics, and teacher education. Her research interests include the effects of explicit versus implicit grammar instruction on language acquisition. She is coauthor of the recent introductory, content-based Spanish textbook *¿Sabías que . . . ?*

Elizabeth B. Bernhardt is Associate Professor of Foreign and Second Language Education at Ohio State University. She teaches courses in second-language acquisition, language planning, and second-language literacy. She has published *Reading Development in a Second Language* and has edited the forthcoming volume *Life in Language Immersion Classrooms*.

Craig Deville is a Ph.D. candidate in research and evaluation at Ohio State University. He holds an M.A. in German from the University of Arizona and was a Fulbright recipient. He publishes in the area of writing assessment and teacher candidate evaluation.

Cynthia Ann Druva-Roush currently serves as Assistant Director of the Evaluation and Examination Service for the University of Iowa, and as Assistant Professor in the Department of Psychological and Quantitative Foundations. Her interests include test development, mathematical problem solving, and gender differences in visual-spatial ability.

Ken Fleak is Assistant Professor of Spanish at the University of South Carolina-Columbia, where he coordinates the introductory Spanish courses and supervises the teaching assistant program. He teaches language and methodology courses. His research interests are foreign language pedagogy and testing.

M. Peter Hagiwara is Associate Professor of French at the University of Michigan, where he is the director of a large elementary French program and teaches courses in French language, phonology, morphology, and syntax. His primary research interests are applied linguistics, language teaching methodology, and syntax. His current works involve the preparation of a college-level placement test, the development of computer courseware for the reading proficiency for graduate students, and analyses of modern French phonology and syntax. He has also coauthored several college French textbooks.

Hector Hammerly is Professor of Applied Linguistics at Simon Fraser University. He has taught Spanish and has trained language teachers for many years. His publications include about 30 articles and five books, the latest two of which are *French Immersion: Myths and Reality* and *Fluency and Accuracy*.

L. Kathy Heilenman is Associate Professor of French at the University of Iowa, where she directs language instruction in the first two years. She teaches courses in applied linguistics, second-language acquisition, and research methodology, as well as French-language courses at various levels. Her research interests include testing, the acquisition of French, and writing/composition in foreign languages. She is coauthor of the introductory college textbook *Voilà!* and has published articles in the *Modern Language Journal*, *Language Learning*, *Language Testing*, and *Applied Psycholinguistics*.

Charles J. James is Associate Professor of German at the University of Wisconsin-Madison, where he teaches courses in language and methodology. He edited two ACTFL annual volumes (*Practical Applications of Research in Foreign Language Teaching* and *Foreign Language Proficiency in the Classroom and Beyond*) and has published in the areas of listening comprehension and current German culture. He is a founding member of AAUSC and served as its first treasurer as well as first editor of its newsletter.

James F. Lee is Assistant Professor of Spanish and Director of Basic Language Instruction in the Department of Spanish, Italian, and Portuguese at the University of Illinois at Urbana-Champaign. He publishes extensively in the area of second-language reading research and has coedited several collections of research, including *Foreign Language Learning: A Research Perspective* and *Second Language Acquisition/Foreign Language Learning.* He is the author of *A Manual and Practical Guide to Directing Language Programs and Training Teaching Assistants* and coauthor of the introductory Spanish textbook *¿Sabías que . . . ?*

Sally Sieloff Magnan is Associate Professor of French at the University of Wisconsin-Madison, where she teaches courses in French language and teaching methodology and supervises teaching assistants. Her primary research interests are foreign language teaching methodlogy, error analysis, and proficiency testing. She edited the 1990 volume of this AAUSC series and currently serves as Series Editor. She is also a former president of the organization.

Joyce E. Moore is Acting Director of the Evaluation and Examination Service at the University of Iowa. She specializes in the development of placement, certification, and licensure tests; questionnaire and survey design; and issues related to public policy and standardized testing.

Frank Nuessel is a Professor at the University of Louisville, where he teaches Spanish and Italian in the Department of Classical and Modern Languages and phonetics and syntax in the program in linguistics. He has published essays on language teaching and methodology in *Hispania, Italica, Canadian Modern Language Review*, and *Il Forneri.* Other research areas include Hispanic linguistics and metaphor studies. He currently serves on the editorial and advisory boards of four professional publications and organizations. He has served as associate dean of the College of Arts and Sciences and in other administrative posts.

Richard V. Teschner is Professor of Languages and Linguistics at the University of Texas-El Paso, where he has taught since 1976. He is widely published in such journals as *Hispania, Modern Language Journal, Foreign Language Annals, ADFL Bulletin*, and *Southwestern Journal of Linguistics.* He has served as lower-division Spanish coordinator and undergraduate placement director in his department and is an author of the Spanish-for-native-speakers textbook *Español escrito.* He is past president both of the American Association of Teachers of

Spanish and Portuguese and of the Linguistic Association of the Southwest.

Joel C. Walz is Professor of French in the Department of Romance Languages at the University of Georgia, where he coordinates the elementary-French-language sequence, supervises graduate teaching assistants, and teaches graduate courses in methodology, phonetics, and applied linguistics. He has published books, articles, and reviews in the areas of the French-language and foreign language teaching and is coauthor of the elementary French textbook *Rapports*. He has been French section head for the AAUSC and is editor of the 1992 annual volume.

Irene Wherritt is Associate Professor of Portuguese and Spanish at the University of Iowa and Director of the university's Foreign Language Assessment Project. Her research centers on Portuguese and Spanish applied linguistics and sociolinguistics. Her recent publications address issues in placement testing; Portuguese language maintenance in Goa, India; and Spanish language in the United States.